TRIBALISM AND COSMOPOLITANISM

Hannah Arendt

KARL JASPERS: CITIZEN OF THE WORLD

Nobody can be a citizen of the world as he is the citizen of his country. Jaspers, in his Vom Ursprung und Ziel der Geschichte (1949), discusses extensively the implications of a world-state and a world-empire. No matter which form a world-government with centralized power over the whole globe might assume, the very notion of one sovereign force ruling the whole earth, holding the monopoly of all means of violence, unchecked and uncontrolled by other sovereign powers is not only a forbidding nightmare of tyranny, it would be the end of life all politics as we know it. Political concepts are based on plurality, diversity and mutual limitations. A citizen is by definition a citizen among citizens of a country among countries. His rights and duties must be defined and limited, not only by those of his fellow-citizens, but also by the boundaries of the territory. Philosophy may conceive of the earth as the homeland of mankind and of one unwritten law, eternal and valid for all. Politics deals with men, nationals of many countries and heirs to many pasts; its laws are the positively established boundaries fences which hedge in, protect and limit the space in which freedom is not a concept, but a living, political reality. The establishment of one sovereign world-state, far from being the prerequisite for world-citizenship, would be the end of all citizenship. It would not be the climax of world politics, but quite literally its end.

To say, however, the undesirability of a world-state conceived in the image of sovereign nation-states, as we know them, or of a world-empire conceived in the image of the Roman Empire, (and is dangerous the dominion of the Roman Empire over the civilized world and barbarian parts of the world was bearable only because it stood against the dark and frightening background of the unknown parts of the earth), is no solution for our present political problem. Mankind, which for all preceding generations was no more than a concept or an ideal, has become something of an urgent reality. Europe, as Kant foresaw, has prescribed its laws to all other continents; but the result,

**HANNAH ARENDT'S ANNOTATED MANUSCRIPT PAGE
FOR HER ESSAY "KARL JASPERS: CITIZEN OF THE WORLD"**

Hannah Arendt Papers: Speeches and Writings File, 1923–1975; Essays and lectures; "Karl Jaspers: Citizen of the World," undated. Manuscript/Mixed Material.
https://www.loc.gov/item/mss1105601240/.

HA

Vol. 13/2025

The Yearbook of the Hannah Arendt Center
for Politics and Humanities

TRIBALISM AND COSMOPOLITANISM

How Can We Imagine a Pluralist Politics?

Editor: Roger Berkowitz
Managing Editor: Jana Mader

A Collaboration of Lapham's Quarterly
and the Hannah Arendt Center
for Politics and Humanities at Bard College

DE GRUYTER

HA: The Yearbook of the Hannah Arendt Center for Politics and Humanities at Bard College is a continuation of the *HA Journal* and publishes collections of essays inspired by the annual conferences of the Hannah Arendt Center. Dedicated to urgent political issues of our times, each volume features insightful essays by prominent thinkers alongside an anthology of classical texts related to the actual topic of each volume. Present scholarship and canonical texts are put into conversation to provide an extended sourcebook of ideas for the interested reader.

LAPHAM'S QUARTERLY
AMERICAN AGORA FOUNDATION

ISBN 978-3-11-167468-1
e-ISBN (PDF) 978-3-11-167498-8
e-ISBN (EPUB) 978-3-11-167536-7
ISSN 2168-6572

Library of Congress Control Number: 2025942683

Bibliographic information published by the Deutsche Nationalbibliothek
The Deutsche Nationalbibliothek lists this publication in the Deutsche Nationalbibliografie; detailed bibliographic data are available on the Internet at http://dnb.dnb.de.

© 2025 Walter de Gruyter GmbH, Berlin/Boston, Genthiner Straße 13, 10785 Berlin
Copyediting: Nicholas Dunn
Research assistants: Aleksandar Vitanov, Francis Karagodins, Julia Kiernan
Layout: Claudia Collasch
Cover image: © Fred Stein Archive

www.degruyterbrill.com

Questions about General Product Safety Regulation:
productsafety@degruyterbrill.com

FOREWORD

Roger Berkowitz —— 9

INTRODUCTION

Roger Berkowitz —— 13
Hannah Arendt —— 24

COSMOPOLITANISM

Uday Mehta (with Roger Berkowitz) —— 33
Martha Nussbaum —— 41 / Immanuel Kant —— 43
Anthony Appiah —— 50 / Seyla Benhabib —— 54
Martha Nussbaum —— 66 / Leon Botstein —— 69
Angela Taraborrelli —— 74 / Ifeoma Kiddoe Nwankwo —— 76
King James Bible —— 83 / Epictetus —— 84

TRIBALISM

Sebastian Junger (with Roger Berkowitz) —— 91
Aristotle —— 104 / Lyndsey Stonebridge —— 108
Unknown Author (suaveanddebonair.com) —— 114
Fintan O'Toole (with Joseph O'Neill) —— 117 / Emile Durkheim —— 134
Sigmund Freud —— 139 / King James Bible —— 144
Anna Akhmatova —— 149 / Ibn Khaldûn —— 150

CONVERSATIONS ON TRIBALISM AND COSMOPOLITANISM

Zoë Hitzig and Ann Lauterbach (with Allison Stanger) —— 157
Thomas Chatterton Williams and Ayishat Akanbi (with Roger Berkowitz) —— 176
Shai Lavi and Khaled Furani —— 191
Mandar Apte, Phillip "Rock" Lester, and Gilbert Johnson (with Niobe Way) —— 205

IN MEMORIAM

"In Memoriam: Jerome Kohn" —— 219
Volker März, Thomas Bartscherer, Jack Barth, Roger Berkowitz,
Matthias Bormuth, Wout Cornelissen, Rochelle Gurstein,
Antonia Grunenberg, Wolfgang Heuer, Marie Luise Knott,
Steve Maslow, Elizabeth Minnich, Thomas Wild

CONTRIBUTORS

—— 253

FOREWORD

FOREWORD

ROGER BERKOWITZ

The Make America Great Again (MAGA) movement in the United States gives voice to a rising nationalism and tribalism we see around the world, from Modi's India, to Putin's Russia, Orban's Hungary, and Netanyahu's Israel. Against such a tribalism is the dream of a world citizenship, the cosmopolitan ideal that sees all human beings as part of one large political world. *Tribalism and Cosmopolitanism* is dedicated to exploring the humanity of both tribal affiliation and cosmopolitan dreams.

We are excited to announce significant upgrades to *HA: The Journal of the Hannah Arendt Center*. Now published annually by De Gruyter as the *Hannah Arendt Yearbook*, volume 13 marks a transformative shift from its previous independent, in-house journal format. This edition centers on the compelling theme of Tribalism and Cosmopolitanism and continues to feature edited transcripts from the annual Hannah Arendt Center conference that took place in October, 2024 at Bard College. Readers will find insightful essays by prominent thinkers such as Sebastian Junger, Fintan O'Toole, Seyla Benhabib, Leon Botstein, Lyndsey Stonebridge, Uday Mehta, and more.

A second big change follows from the Hannah Arendt Center's acquisition of the exemplary humanities journal, *Lapham's Quarterly*. We are incorporating Lapham's model of supplementing contemporary essays on a theme with excerpts from classic reflections. As a result, you will find here texts relating to both tribalism and cosmopolitanism from Anthony Appiah, Hannah Arendt, Aristotle, Thomas Aquinas, Amy Chua, Emile Durkheim, Epictetus, Sigmund Freud, Immanuel Kant, Ibn Khaldûn, Martha Nussbaum, and more. The goal is to offer a rich and broad introduction to the inquiry into the human tension between our need to belong to tribes and our aspirations to cosmopolitan humanism. In addition, the mixing of present scholarship with classic texts provides a sourcebook for those who would like to explore these questions with more depth.

What has not changed in our relaunch of the Arendt Center Yearbook is the commitment to provocative, bold, and exciting thinking about the world informed by the humanities and the history of thought. The volume as a whole is inspired by the 2024 Hannah Arendt Center conference, *Tribalism and Cosmopolitanism: How Can We Imagine a Pluralist Politics?* It takes off from Arendt's complicated and nuanced ideas about the humanity and inhumanity of tribalism. Arendt criticized what she calls a mystical tribal consciousness. On the other hand, she called her group of friends a tribe and understood the importance of tribal identifications. But even as she was a cosmopolitan, Arendt believed that the idea of a cosmopolitan world government or unified idea of humanity was dangerous, primarily because she thought that all political entities were susceptible to tyranny or totalitarianism. She believed that plurality is the core of what it means to live a human life. This means that Arendt deeply understands the appeal and human need for tribal identifications even as she sought to live a life that could transcend the prejudices and hatreds such tribalism can provoke.

Finally, this volume of the Arendt Center Yearbook pays tribute to one of the great Arendt scholars who passed away last year, on November 8th, 2024, Jerome Kohn. Jerry was Arendt's friend and research assistant at the New School. Later, he succeeded Mary McCarthy and Lotte Kohler as the trustee for the Hannah Arendt Bluecher Literary Trust. Jerry not only edited numerous volumes of Arendt's posthumous writing, broadening and deepening the reach of her work. He also served as the unofficial Don of the world community of Arendt Scholars. To recognize and remember Jerry, we have asked friends and scholars to write short testaments to his person and work.

INTRODUCTION

"TRIBALISM AND COSMOPOLITANISM"

ROGER BERKOWITZ

I.

I am a cosmopolitan. I am, as Diogenes the Cynic once called himself, a Kosmopolites, a cosmopolitan, a citizen of the world. By cosmopolitan, I mean not only that I have a stamp-filled passport or that I have lived in different countries and regularly share stories with friends in foreign languages across many time zones. My cosmopolitanism means more than the fact that I feel at home in a shul, have attended weddings in churches of multiple denominations, and celebrated Ramadan in a mosque in Jerusalem. Yes, one sense of being cosmopolitan is that we take a meaningful interest in the practices and cultures of people who are different from ourselves. As a cosmopolitan, there is a sense of being at home anywhere – which can also mean, of course, that one is at home nowhere.

I also deeply value my tribal connections. This means that I take seriously my particular identity and citizenship and celebrate certain deeply felt attachments. I am a New Yorker, a Bardian, an Arendtian, and an American. To say I'm an American doesn't mean I'm a nationalist in the sense that George Orwell defines 'nationalism': the "habit of identifying oneself with a single nation or other unit, placing it beyond good and evil and recognizing no other duty than that of advancing its interests" (Orwell 2018). Rather, I'm more closely identified with what Orwell calls a 'patriot': I have a "devotion to a particular place and a particular way of life," one which I believe to be one of the best in the world, but I have no wish to force my way of life on other people (Orwell 2018). Orwell says the patriot believes their people are the best in the world, which on some days is more than I would say.

The word tribe has a bad name in certain progressive and intellectual circles today. For many cosmopolitans, tribalism has the aura of prejudice, nationalism, and even racism. Should I, as an American, prefer Americans to others? As a Jew, should my allegiance be to Jews and to Israel over others? If I were Hindu, should I see India as a Hindu country? If I were German, would I believe that all Germans must embrace a quintessential German *Leitkultur*?

There are, of course, plenty of examples of racist tribalism, what Hannah Arendt calls "pseudomystical" tribal nationalism (Arendt 1976, 226). Tribal nationalism emerged amongst the peoples in the belt of mixed populations after the breakdown of the Austria-Hungarian and Russian Empires. For Arendt, Tribal nationalism is born from the frustrations of peoples who desired a national emancipation but never achieved a state of their own. Without a state or a homeland, peoples like the Jews, Roma, and Slavs, Poles, Germans, and others living outside of Russia, Poland, and Germany, were 'rootless' and 'homeless'. They had no homeland and as such they cultivated an "enlarged tribal consciousness," which means that "members of these peoples had no definite home but felt at home wherever other members of their 'tribe' happened to live" (Arendt 1976, 232). As the Austrian leader of the Pan-German movement Georg Ritter von Schönerer said, "it is our distinction that we do not gravitate toward Vienna but gravitate to whatever place Germans may live in" (Arendt 1976, 232).

The rise of tribal nationalism in the late nineteenth and early twentieth centuries easily bled into racism. The claim for each tribe was that their tribe, based blood and identity, was unique and superior to other tribes. Pseudo mystical nationalism easily transformed into racism that elevates one's own people as divinely superior to others who must be assimilated, expelled, or eliminated to solve social and political problems for which they are imagined to be the cause. Such Tribalism denies the very possibility of the idea of a common humanity of man.

The word 'tribe' comes to us from Latin, where *tribus* with its root of *tri* ('three') names the three tribes – the Latins, Sabines, and Etruscans – that originally joined together in Rome. Under the influence of anthropology and the social sciences, the word came to native ethnic and racial groups organized around clans or families and headed by a chief and connected by ties of blood and descent. Because tribal nationalism speaks the language of friend and enemy based on race and ethnicity, it sits uneasily in our liberal age. The very word 'tribe' sounds a discordant note of racial and ethnic bonds that opposes our ideas of equal dignity and the respect for humanity that underlie much of our system of international law and our ideas of human rights.

There is, however, a positive and redeemable aspect of being part of a tribe that goes beyond the simple fact that we humans all evolved from tribal groups. There is a human need for what Sebastian Junger calls a 'group-founded solidarity'. Members of a tribe, for example, soldiers in a foxhole and coal miners trapped for days in a collapsed mine, share a solidarity born of having suffered together as a distinct group. There is a common bond forged through pain and perseverance. This may be true to a lesser extent for long-suffering Mets fans, but is fundamentally real for Ukrainians, Israelis, and Gazans suffering from harrowing wars.

Tribalism is born not only from suffering together, but also from collective joy. Common rituals from weddings to funerals can cement the loyalties of tribal members. So too can memories of a common past and projections of an imagined future destiny. In both collective pain and common joy, individuals forge bonds of tribal identity that can inspire mutual aid and meaningful sacrifice for fellow tribal members who one barely knows; sometimes even for those one does not like.

One definition of tribalism is the feeling of solidarity with a group of people that would lead you to die for members of your tribe. People come together in a tribe, learn to depend upon and trust one another; they build memories of a past and imaginations of a common future, precisely because solitary life as an individual carries dangers and fears of loneliness that can only be overcome through group solidarity. But the fact that we may prefer a lonely life of peace and plenty to a life of war and poverty doesn't change the fact that having something to sacrifice and die for often makes life more valuable and more satisfying. Tribal solidarity, quite simply, is something we all crave if we are to live rich and purposeful lives.

II.

So, I am a cosmopolitan. And I am a tribalist. For most of my life this tension between my universalist commitments to human dignity and my particularist prejudices for my family, my neighbors, and my various tribes has played itself out as background dissonance. It was something I noticed, at moments, for example, when I read Ralph Waldo Emerson's provocation to the lovers of humanity who want to help the poor and "put all poor men in good situations: Are they my poor!" (Emerson 2000, 135).

Emerson admonishes the philanthropist thusly: "I tell thee, thou foolish philanthropist, that I grudge the dollar, the dime, the cent I give to such men as do not belong to me and to whom I do not belong" (Emerson 2000, 135). Emerson affirms that there are those who are his people, those "to whom by all spiritual affinity I am bought and sold," and those for whom he would "go to prison if need be" (Emerson 2000, 136). He would rather give real solace and help to his poor who belong to his tribe, the poor who are here at home than pursue cosmopolitan philanthropy around the globe. Men do good deeds and give to charities around the world, Emerson saw, as penance for their living badly in their world at home. In a world where refugees across the oceans seem to receive more attention than the homeless on our streets, I've always found such challenges to my cosmopolitan sensibilities bracing.

Over the last year, I have been forced to struggle more directly with the contradictions and inconsistencies in my ambivalent position. Like all good cosmopolitans, I have been angered intensely by the profound suffering of the Chinese Uyghurs in Xinjiang Province, the people of Sudan, Haiti, Ukraine, and many others. And, of course, the people in Gaza. As much as I think that a share of the blame for the suffering in Gaza lies on Hamas and its leadership, who abuse their own people for political gain, the cosmopolitan in me thinks that Israel has defended itself – something it has the right to do – with a tribal ferocity that dehumanizes Palestinian lives.

And yet I am a Jew. As a Jew, I understand that a world without a single Jewish state is very likely a catastrophe for all Jewish people. In living memory, we Jews suffered a genocide that sought to wipe us from the face of the earth. Most of the Jews who came to Israel came not as settlers but as displaced persons and refugees since no other country in the world would take them. Antisemitism is real, it is deadly, and it is very much alive. Since I begin with the belief that a Jewish homeland is a prerequisite for Jewish survival, and since it is clear that Hamas, Hezbollah, and Iran will not rest until Israel is destroyed, it is hard for me to deny Israel the right to defend itself.

I recognize the contradictions inherent in my admittedly tribal position. I see them as deeply human contradictions – a red line running through the fact that cosmopolitanism may be a future ideal, but we humans are tribal creatures. I am a tribal human in spite of my cosmopolitan dreams.

III.

Rightly or wrongly, I take some solace amidst my contradictions in the fact that Hannah Arendt also was inconsistent and contradictory in her attempts to balance cosmopolitan dreams and tribal realities when it came to the question of Israel.

Arendt had, to say the least, a complicated relation to Zionism. In 1933, she was arrested while working for the German Zionists to help collect evidence of Nazi antisemitism. She saw Zionism as the only truly political Jewish movement, a necessary response to the rise of tribal nationalism in European nation states and the failure of Jewish assimilation into European tribal nation states.

By the mid-1940s, however, Arendt had broken with mainstream Zionism. She strongly opposed Theodor Herzl and Vladomir Jabotinsky's aim of creating a Jewish nation-state in Mandate Palestine. She saw that the idea of a Jewish state was grounded in a "Central European ideology of nationalism and tribal thinking" (Arendt 2007, 437). The fundamental problem in the 'Jewish-Arab' question was that all proposed solutions held the "discredited notion that national conflicts can be solved on the basis of guaranteeing minority rights" (Arendt 2007, 194). The attempt to solve what is ultimately a "national conflict" between two peoples demanding national recognition by means of "creating sovereign states and then guaranteeing minority rights within state structures" is destined to fail (Arendt 2007, 194). Arendt had seen how the utter disaster of the Minority Treaties signed in 1918 after the dissolution of Hapsburg Empire had led to an untenable situation in which newly created nation states demanded their minorities to assimilate or leave. The promise of protecting minority rights within a nation-state structure led, she saw, to the exposure of the fundamental paradox of the nation-state system. She thought, and hoped, that the exposure of the failure of nation-states would lead to new ways of organizing peoples.

Specifically, she came to believe that only a true federalist system offered the promise of "the greatest chance for success in solving national conflicts and can thus be the basis for a political life that offers peoples the possibility of reorganizing themselves politically" (Arendt 2007, 195). Fired by her skepticism of the nation-state system, Arendt worried that an exclusively Jewish state amidst an overwhelming Arab population led them to overlook the fate of the native population of the land. Arendt saw fault on both the Arab and Jewish sides. She criticized "Palestinian Arab leaders for insisting on a unitary Arab state as betraying an illusion that the Jewish settlers could be made to leave" (Arendt 2007, 424–25). But as a Jew, Arendt warned her fellow Jews "that Arabs were human beings like themselves and that it might be dangerous not to expect them to act and react in much the same way as Jews" (Arendt 2007, 433).

Unique amongst Zionist writers, Arendt hoped that a humanist Zionism could inspire a new imagination of political organization that would be the beginnings of a new post-nation-state world order. She proposed a federation of homelands in Palestine that might one day spread across the Middle East and into Europe. By speaking of a Jewish homeland instead of a Jewish state, Arendt aimed to allow both Palestinian Arabs and Jews to do justice to their dream of national homelands while leaving the administration to a federated state. "Sovereignty would be dispersed across national communities while governance for the territory at large [would require] mutual action" (Graubart 2023, 65).

In such a Jewish homeland amidst a larger Middle Eastern federation, Arendt hoped that Jews in Palestine could build a "Jewish cultural center [that] would inspire the spiritual development of all Jews in other countries, but would not need ethnic homogeneity and national sovereignty" (Arendt 2007, 442). She was especially happy with the founding of Hebrew University to enrich the study of Jewish thought in collaboration with Palestinians and other peoples. In addition, Arendt embraced a labor Zionism that sought to build a Jewish society on the basis of the kibbutzim to actualize "an age-old Jewish dream of a society based on justice, formed in complete equality [and] indifferent to all profit motives" (Graubart 2023, 58; Arendt 2007, 443). She saw the Zionists who formed kibbutzim and sought to govern themselves independently in small communities as a potential vanguard for a new world order that would abandon the nation-state system.

When Israel was created by the United Nations partition of the Mandate in 1948, and the ensuing war displaced hundreds of thousands of Arabs who were then not allowed to return to their homes, Arendt retreated from Jewish politics, defeated. And yet that does not mean that Arendt denied either the right of Israel to exist or its importance for Jews. Covering the trial of Adolf Eichmann in Jerusalem in 1961, Arendt took great pride in the accomplishments of the Jewish state even as she was intensely critical of the Israeli government. She thought the 1967 war was defensive and reasonable, and wrote to her friend Mary McCarthy, "Any real catastrophe in Israel would affect me more deeply than almost anything else" (Arendt and McCarthy 1995, Dec. 21, 1968). When Egypt and Syria attacked Israel in 1973 on Yom Kippur, Arendt spoke uncritically of Judaism as a national religion and later made a contribution to the United Jewish Appeal (Young-Bruehl 1982, 456).

Critical of the fact that Israel was a nation state and scathing in her attacks on specific Israeli leaders, Arendt nevertheless maintained her absolute support for Israel. She declined an invitation to lecture at the anti-Zionist American Council for Judaism by emphasizing her differences with that group and adding: "I know [...] that should catastrophe overtake the Jewish state, for whatever reason (even reasons of their own foolishness) this would be the final catastrophe for the whole Jewish people" (Young-Bruehl 1982, 361).

IV.
As strongly as Arendt rejects tribal nationalism, she also rejects a liberal cosmopolitan project in which we reject tribal realities and political divisions for a universal idea of world citizenship. After eighteen years as a stateless person, Arendt received United States citizenship in 1950. In a letter to her first husband Günther Anders, Arendt calls her American passport "the most beautiful book" (Taraborrelli 2024, 2). She was as fierce a critic of America as she was of Israel, but she also thought that the United States was the one country in the world that was free from tribal nationalism, an immigrant country in which all people could remain Jewish-American, Black-American, and Mexican-American. She refused to love any people, not the Germans, the Americans, or the Jews. She wrote to Gershom Scholem that while she does not love the Jews and does not believe in the Jews, she does affirm that she belongs to the Jews. It is that belonging to a particularist and tribal group that leads her to affirm in an interview with Günter Gaus: "If one is attacked as a Jew, one must defend oneself as a Jew. Not as a German, not as a world-citizen, not as an upholder of the Rights of Man, or whatever" (Arendt 1994, 12).

The first line of Hannah Arendt's essay for her former teacher and lifelong friend Karl Jaspers reads: "Nobody can be a citizen of the world as he is the citizen of his own country" (Arendt 1968, 81). A citizen, Arendt writes, in her essay "Karl Jaspers: Citizen of the World?", "is by definition a citizen among citizens of a country among countries" (Arendt 1968, 81). We all are members of various nations, so many various political tribes. While philosophers might imagine a world government that is a homeland for all of mankind, "Politics," Arendt writes, "deals with men, nationals of many countries and heirs to many pasts" (Arendt 1968, 81). To dissolve the many countries, peoples, and states in the world into one world state would augur not a world of equality but a centralized world government "holding the monopoly of all means of violence, unchecked and uncontrolled by other sovereign powers" (Arendt 1968, 81). Such a cosmopolitan world government, Arendt argues, "would be the end of all political life as we know it" (Arendt 1968, 81). It would be a forbidding nightmare of tyranny.

V.

At the bleeding heart of tribalism is the conviction that I owe an allegiance to my tribe beyond the care and concern I might have for others. It is precisely this discriminatory distinction between the tribe and outsiders that is, and should be, unsettling to many cosmopolitans. It is easy for me to summon up anger and even hatred for those tribalists who would celebrate the pain and suffering of outsiders.

But here is the problem. Insofar as cosmopolitans see ourselves as superior to those who follow tribal instincts, we too act as a tribe. Cosmopolitans like to think they are free from tribalism, but we are actually a modern-day tribe of racially and religiously and ethnically diverse yet intellectually and economically homogenous global citizens. We may not be willing to die for each other, but that does not mean we are not a tribe; it just means we are a weak tribe, one without a strong sense of solidarity and common purpose. The superficiality of cosmopolitanism is likely one reason for the epidemic of loneliness, depression, and anxiety in cosmopolitan enclaves.

The great divide in modern society is neither racial nor economic; it is, as Ross Douthat writes, between those who, on the one side, "love Afghan restaurants but would never live near an immigrant housing project" – that is, those liberals who "hail the end of whiteness while doing everything possible to keep their kids out of majority-minority schools," and those others who see the cosmopolitan elite as a "a nearly hereditary professional caste of lawyers, journalists, publicists, and intellectuals, an increasingly hereditary caste of politicians, tight coteries of cultural movers-and-shakers richly sponsored by multinational corporations" (Douthat 2016).

We liberal-minded, college-educated, cosmopolitans have faith in reason and technology but are skeptical of folk wisdom. We are at home in the virtual world of the internet or mindfulness retreats but lost in the local pub or NASCAR race. We believe we should listen to qualified experts rather than learn from the experiences of everyday people. We are more at home in libraries and laboratories than on the streets and in factories. Above all, we cosmopolitans look down on those we call tribal, those who value loyalty to their family, their friends, their political party, their region, their ethnicity, their religion, or their race over an uncompromising universalism, and those who prefer local wisdom to tested facts. We can be dismissive of the so-called deplorables who embrace nationalist or ethnic prejudices, as well as those whose opinions we see as backwards and retrograde.

The danger inherent in cosmopolitanism is this belief that as the tribeless tribe we claim to be open to all when, in fact, we act as if we are the highest and most exclusive of tribes. We do not see that without the ability to exclude others who are not members of your community, there is no community.

Arendt rejects cosmopolitan world citizenship as a dangerous intellectualist and rationalist fantasy. The danger of such a gigantic universal state and world citizenship is that "this unity, based on the technical means of communication and violence, destroys all national traditions and buries the authentic origins of all human existence" (Arendt 1968, 87). In a single world state with equal citizens, there is a radical loss of depth that comes from plurality and difference. The result is "shallowness that would transform man, as we have known him in five thousand years of recorded history, beyond recognition. It would be more than mere superficiality; it would be as though the whole dimension of depth, without which human thought, even on the mere level of technical invention, could not exist, would simply disappear" (Arendt 1968, 87). Arendt's suspicion of both cosmopolitanism and world government comes from her insight that "The establishment of one sovereign world state, far from being the prerequisite for world citizenship, would be the end of all citizenship" (Arendt 1968, 82).

VI.
I'd like to end with three speculative thoughts on the subtitle for the conference: 'How Can We Imagine a Pluralist Politics?'

First, plurality is the foundation for Arendt's mantra that there is no truth in politics. And yet, we need truth! In her essay on "Truth and Politics," Arendt writes that the Latin phrase *fiat justitia, et pereat mundus* ('Let Justice be done, even if the world should perish') is simply wrong. The world, she believes, is worth saving even if it is a world that contains injustice. The human world is meaningful even amidst injustice. But when Arendt considers a revision of the phrase that would read *fiat veritas, et pereat mundus* ('Let Truth be done, even if the world perish'), she says that this formulation is actually more defensible. If there is not some truth in the world, there is no human world. The human world is a common world, a world we political creatures share with others. Such a shared world depends on truth. But the importance of truth, she argues, does not mean that truth must be secured by politics. On the contrary, truth is non-political, outside of politics. Truth is, as she metaphorically phrases it, the ground we walk on and the sky above us. We cannot live without a home, a rootedness in the world. We all need a tribe.

Second, in a world of plurality there will be a multitude of overlapping tribes. We need to learn to live amidst strong tribal commitments. This means that we need to hold on to our own traditions and national pasts and also our own collective visions of a common future, and we need to do so even as we also make space for other peoples, other nations, and other tribes to live amidst their own truths, their own traditions. We need, as Arendt says in the essay on Jaspers as a world citizen, to break not with tradition but with the authority of tradition.

Third, a pluralist politics must emerge alongside a new common world without truth, not through the recognition of rationalist ideas, but by the act of talking with those who are members of tribes different from our own. The goal is not one cosmopolitan norm of world citizenship but a federated world of overlapping tribal commitments. One of my favorite of Arendt's insights is: "We become more just and more pious by thinking and talking about justice and piety" (Arendt 2018, 331). In speaking with others, even those we fundamentally disagree with, we build a foundation for a shared conversation, a world in common. Arendt was unusually optimistic on this front when she wrote: "I personally do not doubt that from the turmoil of being confronted with reality without the help of precedent, that is, of tradition and authority, there will finally arise some new code of conduct" (Arendt 2018, 330). The potential rebirth of a new common ethical world is not only possible, but likely. It depends on the courage to speak honestly and openly absent ideological rigidity.

Arendt's biographer, Elizabeth Young-Bruehl, wrote of how Arendt spoke of her friends as her tribe. Young-Bruehl describes Hannah Arendt's tribe as a little island of cosmopolitanism and pariah consciousness. The word for tribe in German is *Stamm* – literally, the truth of a tree. It is our tribe that places us in the world and gives us a refuge and a home. But our tribe also grows. It can support us as we branch out on adventures and take risks, but it is the world we come home to. As a circle of friends – both personal and political – our tribe is much more than an '-ism'. It need not reject plurality. On the contrary, only with a strong tribe are we able to take the risks to build a world of true plurality and true cosmopolitanism, a world that aims not at world citizenship, but at the venturing forth in the uncertainty of the public world of tribes.

REFERENCES

Arendt, Hannah. 2018. "The Crisis Character of Modern Society." In *Thinking Without a Bannister*, edited by Jerome Kohn, 328–31. Penguin Random House.
Arendt, Hannah. 2007. *The Jewish Writings*, edited by Jerome Kohn and Ron H. Feldman. Schocken Books.
Arendt, Hannah. 2006. "Truth and Politics." In *Between Past and Future*, 223–59. Penguin Books.
Arendt, Hannah. 1994. "What Remains? The Language Remains." In *Essays in Understanding, 1930–1954: Formation, Exile, and Totalitarianism*, edited by Jerome Kohn, 1–23. Schocken Books.
Arendt, Hannah. 1976. *The Origins of Totalitarianism*. A Harvest Book.
Arendt, Hannah. 1968. *Men in Dark Times*. Harcourt Brace Jovanovich.
Arendt, Hannah, and Mary McCarthy. 1995. *Between Friends: The Correspondence of Hannah Arendt and Mary McCarthy, 1949–1975*, edited by Carol Brightman. Harcourt Brace.
Douthat, Ross. "The Myth of Cosmopolitanism." *The New York Times*. July 2, 2016. https://www.nytimes.com/2016/07/03/opinion/sunday/the-myth-of-cosmopolitanism.html.
Emerson, Ralph Waldo. 2000. *The Essential Writings of Ralph Waldo Emerson*. Modern Library Paperback Edition.
Graubart, Jonathan. 2023. *Jewish Self Determination Beyond Zionism: Lessons from Hannah Arendt and Other Pariahs*. Temple University Press.
Orwell, George. 2018. *Notes on Nationalism* [1945]. Penguin.
Taraborrelli, Angela. 2024. *Hannah Arendt and Cosmopolitanism*. Bloomsbury.
Young-Bruehl, Elisabeth. 1982. *Hannah Arendt: For the Love of the World*. Yale University Press.

"KARL JASPERS: CITIZEN OF THE WORLD?"

HANNAH ARENDT

HANNAH ARENDT. Born in 1906 in Hanover, Germany, Arendt was a German-Jewish political theorist who explored themes of exile, identity, and responsibility. She fled Nazi Germany in 1933 and later became an influential thinker in the United States. In "Karl Jaspers: World Citizen?", originally published in 1957, she reflects on her mentor's vision of global citizenship grounded in dialogue and moral independence. Having lived through the rise of totalitarianism, Arendt was deeply suspicious of what she calls "mystical tribal nationalism." At the same time, Arendt was wary of the abstract universalist ideals of cosmopolitanism. Arendt's work emphasizes the need for individuals to belong to strong and meaningful communities even as they also engage with diverse perspectives to foster understanding and resist totalitarianism.

Nobody can be a citizen of the world as he is the citizen of his country. Jaspers, in his *Origin and Goal of History* (1953), discusses extensively the implications of a world state and a world empire.[1] No matter what form a world government with centralized power over the whole globe might assume, the very notion of one sovereign force ruling the whole earth, holding the monopoly of all means of violence, unchecked and uncontrolled by other sovereign powers, is not only a forbidding nightmare of tyranny, it would be the end of all political life as we know it. Political concepts are based on plurality, diversity, and mutual limitations. A citizen is by definition a citizen among citizens of a country among countries. His rights and duties must be defined and limited, not only by those of his fellow citizens, but also by the boundaries of a territory. Philosophy may conceive of the earth as the homeland of mankind and of one unwritten law, eternal and valid for all. Politics deals with men, nationals of many countries and heirs to many pasts; its laws are the positively established

---

Excerpted from: Arendt, Hannah. 1968. *Men in Dark Times*. Harcourt Brace & Company, 81–84.

fences which hedge in, protect, and limit the space in which freedom is not a concept, but a living, political reality. The establishment of one sovereign world state, far from being the prerequisite for world citizenship, would be the end of all citizenship. It would not be the climax of world politics, but quite literally its end.

To say, however, that a world state conceived in the image of sovereign nation states or of a world empire in the image of the Roman Empire is dangerous (and the dominion of the Roman Empire over the civilized and barbarian parts of the world was bearable only because it stood against the dark and frightening background of unknown parts of the earth) is no solution for our present political problem. Mankind, which for all preceding generations was no more than a concept or an ideal, has become something of an urgent reality. Europe, as Kant foresaw, has prescribed its laws to all other continents; but the result, the emergence of mankind out of and side by side with the continued existence of many nations, has assumed an altogether different aspect from the one which Kant envisaged when he saw the unification of mankind "in a far distant future."[2] Mankind owes its existence not to the dreams of the humanists nor to the reasoning of the philosophers and not even, at least not primarily, to political events, but almost exclusively to the technical development of the Western world. When Europe in all earnest began to prescribe its "laws" to all other continents, it so happened that she herself had already lost her belief in them. No less manifest than the fact that technology united the world is the other fact that Europe exported to the four corners of the earth its processes of disintegration which had started in the Western world with the decline of the traditionally accepted metaphysical and religious beliefs and had accompanied the grandiose development of the natural sciences and the victory of the nation state over all other forms of government. The same forces which took centuries to undermine the ancient beliefs and political ways of life, and which have their place in the continuous development of the West alone, took only a few decades to break down, by working from without, beliefs and ways of life in all other parts of the world.

It is true, for the first time in history all peoples on earth have a common present: no event of any importance in the history of one country can remain a marginal accident in the history of any other. Every country has become the almost immediate neighbor of every other country, and every man feels the shock of events which take place at the other side of the globe. But this common factual present is not based on a common past and does not in the least guarantee a common future. Technology, having provided the unity of the world, can just as easily destroy it and the means of global communication were designed side by side with means of possible global destruction. It is difficult to deny that at this moment the most potent symbol of the unity of mankind is the remote possibility that atomic weapons used by one country according to the political wisdom of a few might ultimately come to be the end of all human life on earth. The solidarity of mankind in this respect is entirely negative; it rests, not only on a common interest in an agreement which prohibits the use of atomic weapons, but, perhaps also – since such agreements share with all other agreements the uncertain fate of being based on good faith – on a common desire for a world that is a little less unified.

This negative solidarity, based on the fear of global destruction, has its correspondence in a less articulate, but no less potent, apprehension that the solidarity of mankind can be meaningful in a positive sense only if it is coupled with political responsibility. Our political concepts, according to which we have to assume responsibility for all public affairs within our reach regardless of personal "guilt," because we are held responsible as citizens for everything that our government does in the name of the country, may lead us into an intolerable situation of global responsibility. The solidarity of mankind may well turn out to be an unbearable burden, and it is not surprising that the common reactions to it are political apathy, isolationist nationalism, or desperate rebellion against all powers that be rather than enthusiasm or a desire for a revival of humanism. The idealism of the humanist tradition of enlightenment and its concept of mankind look like reckless optimism in the light of present realities. These, on the other hand, insofar as they have brought us a global present without a common past, threaten to render irrelevant all traditions and all particular past histories.

It is against this background of political and spiritual realities, of which Jaspers is more aware than probably any other philosopher of our time, that one must understand his new concept of mankind and the propositions of his philosophy. Kant once called upon the historians of his time to write a history "with cosmopolitan intent." One could easily "prove" that Jaspers's whole philosophical work, from its beginnings in the *Psychology of World Views* (1919) to the world history of philosophy,[3] was conceived with "intent toward world citizenship." If the solidarity of mankind is to be based on something more solid than the justified fear of man's demonic capabilities, if the new universal neighborship of all countries is to result in something more promising than a tremendous increase in mutual hatred and a somewhat universal irritability of everybody against everybody else, then a process of mutual understanding and progressing self-clarification on a gigantic scale must take place. And just as the prerequisite for world government in Jaspers's opinion is the renunciation of sovereignty for the sake of a world-wide federated political structure, so the prerequisite for this mutual understanding would be the renunciation, not of one's own tradition and national past, but of the binding authority and universal validity which tradition and past have always claimed. It is by such a break, not with tradition but with the authority of tradition, that Jaspers entered philosophy. His *Psychology of World Views* denies the absolute character of any doctrine and puts in its stead a universal relativity, in which each specific philosophical content becomes means for individual philosophizing. The shell of traditional authority is forced open and the great contents of the past are freely and "playfully" placed in communication with each other in the test of communicating with a present living philosophizing.

In this universal communication, held together by the existential experience of the present philosopher, all dogmatic metaphysical contents are dissolved into processes, trains of thought, which, because of their relevance to my present existing and philosophizing, leave their fixed historical place in the chain of chronology and enter a realm of the spirit where all are contemporaries. Whatever I think must remain in constant communication with everything that has been thought. Not only because, "in philosophy, novelty is an argument against truth," but because present philosophy cannot be more than "the natural and necessary conclusion of Western thought up to now, the candid synthesis brought about by a principle large enough to comprehend everything that in a sense is true." The principle itself is communication; truth, which can never be grasped as dogmatic content, emerges as "existential" substance clarified and articulated by reason, communicating itself and appealing to the reasonable existing of the other, comprehensible and capable of comprehending everything else. "*Existenz* only becomes clear through reason; reason only has content through *Existenz*."[4]

The pertinence of these considerations for a philosophical foundation of the unity of mankind is manifest: "limitless communication,"[5] which at the same time signifies the faith in the comprehensibility of all truths and the good will to reveal and to listen as the primary condition for all human intercourse, is one, if not the central, idea of Jaspers's philosophy. The point is that here for the first time communication is not conceived as "expressing" thoughts and therefore being secondary to thought itself. Truth itself is communicative, it disappears and cannot be conceived outside communication; within the "existential" realm, truth and communication are the same. "Truth is what binds us together."[6] Only in communication-between contemporaries as well as between the living and the dead-does truth reveal itself.

A philosophy that conceives of truth and communication as one and the same has left the proverbial ivory tower of mere contemplation. Thinking becomes practical, though not pragmatic; it is a kind of practice between men, not a performance of one individual in his self-chosen solitude. Jaspers is, as far as I know, the first and the only philosopher who has ever protested against solitude, to whom solitude has appeared "pernicious" and who has dared to question "all thoughts, all experiences, all contents" under this one aspect: "What do they signify for communication? Are they such that they may help or such that they will prevent communication? Do they seduce to solitude or arouse to communication?"[7] Philosophy has lost both its humility before theology and its arrogance toward the common life of man. It has become *ancilla vitae*.[8]

This attitude is of special relevance within the German philosophical tradition. Kant seems to have been the last great philosopher who was still quite confident of being understood and of being able to dispel misunderstandings. Hegel's remark on his deathbed – *se non è vero, è bene trovato* – has become famous, "Nobody has understood me except one; and he misunderstood me." Since then, the growing loneliness of philosophers in a world that does not care about philosophy because it has become entirely fascinated by science has resulted in the well-known and often denounced ambiguity and obscurity which to many appear to be typical of German philosophy and which certainly are the hallmark of all strictly solitary, uncommunicative thought. On the level of common opinion, this means that clarity and greatness are seen as opposites. Jaspers's numerous utterances after the war, his articles, lectures, radio broadcasts, have all been guided by a deliberate attempt at popularization, at talking philosophy without using technical terminology, that is, by the conviction that one can appeal to reason and to the "existential" concern in all men. Philosophically this has been possible only because truth and communication are conceived to be the same.

From a philosophical viewpoint, the danger inherent in the new reality of mankind seems to be that this unity, based on the technical means of communication and violence, destroys all national traditions and buries the authentic origins of all human existence. This destructive process can even be considered a necessary prerequisite for ultimate understanding between men of all cultures, civilizations, races, and nations. Its result would be a shallowness that would transform man, as we have known him in five thousand years of recorded history, beyond recognition. It would be more than mere superficiality; it would be as though the whole dimension of depth, without which human thought, even on the mere level of technical invention, could not exist, would simply disappear. This leveling down would be much more radical than the leveling to the lowest common denominator; it would ultimately arrive at a denominator of which we have hardly any notion today.

Notes
1 *Origin*, pp. *193ff.*
2 "Idea for a Universal History with Cosmopolitan Intent" (1784).
3 See now *The Great Philosophers*, vol. I, 1962, vol. II, 1966.
4 *Reason and Existence*, New York, 1955, p. 67.
5 "Grenzlose Kommunikation" is a term which appears in almost all of Jaspers's works.
6 Cf. "Vom lebendigen Geist der Universität" (1946) in: *Rechenschaft und Ausblick* (Munich, 1951), p. 185.
7 Cf. *"Uber meine Philosophie"* (1941) in Ope cit., pp. 350, 352.
8 Jaspers does not use this term. He mentions often that philosophizing is "inner action," practice, etc. The relationship between thinking and living cannot be discussed here. But the following sentence may show in which sense my interpretative use of *ancilla vitae* could be justified: "*Was* im *denkenden Leben getan werden muss, dem soll ein Philosophieren dienen, das erinnernd und vorausgreifend die Wahrheit offenbar mach!.*" *Ibid.*, p. 356.

COSMOPOLITANISM

"THE EQUIVOCATIONS OF TRIBALISM"

UDAY MEHTA
(WITH ROGER BERKOWITZ)

Tribalism and cosmopolitanism operate in distinct ways, though they overlap in important respects. They offer different kinds of solace and challenges. At its core, tribalism is about belonging and identity, while cosmopolitanism is structured around contracts and agreements. Tribalism asks: Do human beings have souls? Where does my identity come from? Which tribe was I born into? What is my standing within it? How does my tribe relate to others?

Tribes often exist in close proximity, asking the same fundamental questions but arriving at different answers. That tension – different answers to shared questions – often breeds suspicion and conflict, sometimes leading to war. As Harold Laski observed, nationalism, perhaps the most pervasive modern form of tribalism (along with family and religion), has stiff joints. Tribal identities are embedded in grand narratives, much like national identities. Nations construct founding myths to define themselves.

For example, Cotton Mather's famous sermon on the *Arabella* spoke of a "shining city on a hill," shaping America's founding self-conception. Other nations root their identity in divine authority, ethnicity, or royal lineage. These narratives carry a metaphysical dimension – not in the way pragmatist philosophers dismiss metaphysics as a game without rules, but in a stricter sense, prescribing origin stories within rigid structures. These rules and structures are often intricate, which is why generations of anthropologists have studied them.

At the root of tribal formation is the covenant – a kind of passport, a ritual that reenacts the larger metaphysical story. Tribal identity is often marked by specific dress, names, and symbols – whether a hijab, a yarmulke, a MAGA hat, or even a Nazi salute. Membership must be recognizable. Yet, some tribes are defined by their invisibility – secrecy is their distinguishing feature, with only insiders aware of who belongs. Intelligence agencies, for instance, evaluate recruits based on whether they can blend in; standing out can be a liability.

Tribes also control access to specific spaces. In this way, they function like passports – you cannot enter without the proper credentials. Consider temples, synagogues, or even nations – each has rules for entry.

Covenants are often linked to rites of passage: baptism, communion, bar and bat mitzvahs, the Hindu thread ceremony, circumcision, tattoos. These rituals signify transformation. They are, in effect, stigmata – markers of identity that distinguish members from outsiders.

More than anything, tribes are about identity. They answer the question: Who are you? What makes you different from others? Because identity is paramount, fairness becomes secondary. Justice applies only once membership has been established. Tribal identity is the foundation – everything else follows from that.

Tribes establish ontological markers. They foreclose certain questions, replacing them with declarations of belonging. While other frameworks ask, 'Is this good for me?' – essentially a utilitarian question – tribal thinking asks, 'Are you one of us?' That question displaces all others. The covenant is, above all, a marker of identity, the process by which you and I become a 'we'.

In contrast, cosmopolitanism – rooted in the social contract tradition – takes people as they are. It does not demand transformation, only adherence to agreed-upon rules. Contracts are based on interests, which are negotiable. Each contract outlines conditions, and if parties accept them, they proceed. If not, they walk away. Ideally, contracts are voluntary in a way that tribal belonging is not – you inherit a tribal identity before you even have a choice.

Contracts assume that individuals, groups, and nations are sovereign. They enter agreements freely, without prior obligations imposed by identity. This flexibility allows for diverse associations – groups of doctors, museumgoers, single women who love cats. These groups can be local, national, or international. Nothing about them is predetermined.

Unlike tribes, these associations do not rely on grand metaphysical stories. You don't need to believe in immaculate conception, the resurrection of Christ, or that the Prophet Muhammad received divine revelation despite being illiterate. You don't need to accept Hinduism's caste system. Cosmopolitanism avoids these mysteries altogether; its glue is shared interest.

Associations form when interests align, and they dissolve when interests change. Some simply disappear. When I was young, the Organization of African States mattered. So did the Non-Aligned Movement – important to India at the time. Now, they barely register. Voluntary associations emerge and fade based on shifting priorities.

There are also associations with lower entry barriers, like human rights organizations. Unlike becoming a doctor, which requires education and certification, being human is the only prerequisite for membership in groups like Amnesty International or the Association Against Torture. Members of these organizations may have strong metaphysical beliefs, but those beliefs are optional. You could be a devout Christian without believing in six-day creationism.

One analogy that comes to mind is Wittgenstein's view of language. Some believe language must be taken in one big gulp, as an inseparable whole. Others – particularly those skilled in multiple languages – see language as a set of adaptable rules. In a similar way, cosmopolitans can hold the same beliefs as tribalists, but with a crucial difference: they recognize their beliefs as chosen, not inherited.

A world where choice defines everything can feel lonely and unstable. It may be like living in a house where you can decorate the walls as you wish – but without foundations, the next storm could wipe it away.

Some embrace that risk. But living without a fixed foundation does not mean life is shallow or meaningless. Depth can be chosen. It doesn't require a foundation – only richness, like a broad vocabulary.

For example, I love Chopin's nocturnes. They give me a sense of the infinite. He is possibly my favorite composer – though that may not be true; I also love Bach's *Suites for Unaccompanied Cello*, especially when played by Pablo Casals. That music gives me a sense of depth. My point is that the richness of life is substantially shaped by choice.

Yesterday at lunch, Roger asked me: if I couldn't live in America, where would I go? I said, possibly India or England. He replied, 'Oh, so you feel patriotic about India? Would I be willing to die for India?' I said no.

I would go to India because of familiarity – the smells, the streets, the sounds. They mean something to me, but that is not patriotism. Khaled made a similar point yesterday about tradition. The contrast between tribalism and cosmopolitanism misses this intervening term: tradition. It also misses familiarity, which can be cultivated and invested in. It, too, can have depth.

So let me return to what I said at the beginning. Tribalism and cosmopolitanism offer different solace and challenges. The challenge of tribalism is that too much is given to you; the solace is that it provides security. Cosmopolitanism, on the other hand, can feel cold and rootless.

I grew up in a family where my mother did not want us to feel rootless. But she grounded us in our own values, not in Hinduism or any religious doctrine. I also have a deep attachment to my ancestral home – not out of tribal loyalty, but because I feel at home there. That is where I'd like to end. To return to my ongoing conversation with Roger, I don't think we truly disagree – we just place emphasis on different aspects of the debate.

ROGER BERKOWITZ [RB]: I love the clarity with which you describe tribalism as a covenant – something exclusive, something that requires transformation. You gave examples like the thread ceremony, bar and bat mitzvahs, baptism, confirmation. It's worth noting that most tribes have rituals for becoming an adult, while cosmopolitanism may not. I wonder if it does. Sebastian Junger also mentioned yesterday that being asked to become an adult is part of what gives life depth and meaning.

You contrast that with cosmopolitanism, which is based on contract. It takes people as they are; they don't need to transform into it. It's voluntary. But, as you point out, that can make it feel cold and rootless. And here's what I find particularly challenging in your argument: you insist that cosmopolitanism is not shallow – that it, too, can have depth. So, I want to ask you about that. What does the depth of cosmopolitanism look like?

I'll frame my question in two ways. First, you said you might return to India because it's familiar – the smells, the tastes, the food. But we all know the stereotype of the cosmopolitan who enjoys eating at Indian, Afghan, Jewish, and Palestinian restaurants without actually knowing anything about those cultures. Familiarity alone doesn't seem to be enough for depth. I can't speak to your experience of India, but surely it's more than just how it smells. You described it as a home, but home isn't just a sensory experience – it has to be more than that.

Here's the harder part of my question, because I'm asking about something you know more about than I do. Your second book, *Liberalism and Empire*, which has won too many awards to mention, argues that liberalism is imperialistic because it only grants liberal freedoms to those who have been educated into becoming good liberal citizens. You reveal the tribalism within liberalism.

It seems to me that for cosmopolitanism to have depth, it must function as a kind of tribe. It needs its own narrative, its own education, its own sense of belonging. And this is something I've asked you before: What's the flag of cosmopolitanism? What gives it depth? What allows someone to become a cosmopolitan? You seem to argue that cosmopolitanism doesn't require transformation – it simply takes people as they are. But if that's the case, then where does its depth come from?

UM: I was recently reading an article by the late Richard Rorty, the great philosopher. In it, he describes having lunch with his son and nephew after being diagnosed with inoperable pancreatic cancer. His nephew, a Baptist, asked if this diagnosis had led him to read about religion or God. His son asked if it had led him to read more philosophy. Rorty replied: 'Neither'. So they asked, 'What are you reading?' He answered, 'Poetry'. And he added, 'I wish I remembered more poetry. As I leave this world, my regret is that I remember less poetry'.

That, to me, is a form of depth. And it doesn't require a flag. Let me say this: not everything in my life is equal. My family clearly matters more to me. But I don't think of that as tribal. They matter because I've known them all my life, because they've been there for me in critical moments. The same goes for my ancestral home. The comfort it gives me has nothing to do with belonging to a tribe. It's a place I've lived, a place I have strong associations with.

RB: I love the poetry question. It makes me wonder, do we write poetry as members of a tribe or as cosmopolitans? To read a poem, to seek out the past, to engage with a story: poetry comes from a tradition, from a history. It isn't written by AI, at least not yet. It emerges from something larger. Chopin isn't just music; he's Western classical music.

UM: But what if he weren't? I don't know much about the tradition Chopin comes from. I just listen to his music. I find it moving. It stirs something in me.

RB: What comes to mind is the difference between someone who eats at a Middle Eastern restaurant and someone like Lawrence of Arabia – or Richard Burton, the first Westerner to go on the Hajj. Anthony Appiah writes about Burton and calls him a true cosmopolitan – someone who didn't just sample cultures but immersed himself in them so deeply that it became unclear where his loyalties lay. I suppose my question is: to truly love Indian poetry, don't you have to learn something about India?

UM: Now you're talking about something I know very little about. I don't know Indian poetry. All I know is Western poetry, Western music – specifically classical, to the great embarrassment of my daughter, who wishes I'd broaden my taste. But in any case, I don't believe depth comes from being tribal.

Q1: I found your distinction between tribe, tradition, and familiarity really thought-provoking – especially how you described growing up with Indian traditions but not feeling that they were something you would die for. It's something you were born into, but not something you see as your tribe. My family are Liberian immigrants. I know Liberian flavors, smells, and traditions, and I know a little of its history. But I wouldn't say I'd die for Liberia. I would, however, die for my family – or rather, I'd live for them. I think of my connection to Liberia as familiarity, as tradition, but not as a tribal belonging where the group itself is what matters to me. Instead, it's the people in my life who matter. So, I wanted to ask: How do you distinguish between a tribe, a tradition, and a familiarity?

UM: Each of these can produce depth. You can have a deep investment in tribal identity, just as you can have a deep investment in familiarity or tradition. The point is to cultivate a rich life. I believe cosmopolitanism gives people a kind of richness – it requires it. But that doesn't mean it necessitates travel. Villagers can have deeply cosmopolitan lives without ever leaving their village. Illiterate people can live cosmopolitan lives without stepping beyond their small community. That's the kind of world I want to live in – a world where richness doesn't depend on geography.

Q2: Your discussion of covenants and contracts reminded me of your late colleague Charles Mills and *The Racial Contract*. Listening to you, I wondered if Mills was inviting people who see their racial identity as a covenant to instead think of it as a contract – something they might divest from. At the same time, as W.E.B. Du Bois wrote, whiteness comes with a "public and psychological wage." Some people might find that their investment in racial identity serves their interests. How do you think about the problem of identities that start as covenants but become contractual in nature? And do you see this as fundamentally anti-liberal or anti-cosmopolitan?

UM: Although I deeply admire Charles Mills – his office was right next to mine – I think his argument was that the liberal contract is, in reality, a racial contract. My argument is a little different. Mills believed that liberalism claims to be universal but is, in fact, built for white people. And I think he was probably right – just as Carole Pateman made an important point in *The Sexual Contract* about how Locke's work implicitly justifies gender inequality. Pateman comes close to saying that Locke accepted rape, simply because he never challenges the structural inequality between men and women. But that's a specific critique of liberalism. I'm talking about contract as a concept – not any one articulation of it.

Q3: I've been thinking about poetry in light of our discussion, and it reminded me of Thomas Chatterton Williams' comment yesterday about reading Dostoevsky. He described it as a transformative experience – something that connected him to the deep, universal questions of the human condition. That also made me think of Azar Nafisi's *Reading Lolita in Tehran* – how literature can have transformative power, even in oppressive settings. I work for a Jewish cultural organization called The Workers Circle [*Der Arbeter Ring*]. We have a phrase: 'Jewish culture for a just world'. It bridges the divide between particularism and cosmopolitanism – one doesn't have to be Jewish to appreciate its values. Could you speak about how art and culture can serve as invitations to cosmopolitanism?

UM: I can't say it better than Thomas did yesterday. He talked about reading a 19th-century Russian novel and how it transformed him – that it helped unmake his tribalism. I found that to be a deeply moving example. But it's not exceptional. Certain novels and poems have also transformed my life. I used to be obsessed with World War I poetry. I remember reading a Thomas Hardy poem. I wish I could remember which one! But I was in school, and when I read it, it meant something to me. It would be an exaggeration to say it changed my life, but it definitely shaped my intellectual orientation. It made my life richer.

"CITIZENS OF THE KOSMOS"

MARTHA NUSSBAUM

MARTHA NUSSBAUM. Born in 1947 in New York City, Nussbaum is a prominent philosopher known for her work in ethics, political philosophy, and human rights. She has taught at Harvard, Brown, and the University of Chicago. In *The Cosmopolitan Tradition*, Nussbaum explores the Stoic roots of cosmopolitanism and proposes a framework for global justice rooted in empathy, dignity, and shared humanity. Nussbaum's concept of the "cosmic city" highlights a commitment to universal justice that transcends human-centered perspectives and champions the well-being of all sentient life.

Asked where he came from, Diogenes the Cynic answered with a single word: *kosmopolitês*, meaning, "a citizen of the world" (Diog. Laert. VI.63). This moment, however fictive, might be said to inaugurate a long tradition of cosmopolitan political thought in the Western tradition. A Greek male refuses the invitation to define himself by lineage, city, social class, even free birth, even gender. He insists on defining himself in terms of a characteristic that he shares with all other human beings, male and female, Greek and non-Greek, slave and free. And by calling himself not simply a dweller in the world but a citizen of the world, Diogenes suggests, as well, the possibility of a politics, or a moral approach to politics, that focuses on the humanity we share rather than the marks of local origin, status, class, and gender that divide us. It is a first step on the road that leads to Kant's resonant idea of the "kingdom of ends," a virtual polity of moral aspiration that unites all rational beings (although Diogenes, more inclusive, does not limit the community to the "rational"), and to Kant's vision of a cosmopolitan politics that will join all humanity under laws given not by convention and class but by free moral choice. Diogenes, they say, "used to make fun of good birth and distinctions of rank and all that

---

Excerpted from: Nussbaum, Martha. 2021. *The Cosmopolitan Tradition: A Noble but Flawed Ideal.* Harvard University Press, 1–3.

sort of thing, calling them decorations of vice. The only correct political order was, he said, that in the world (*kosmos*) as a whole" (VI.72).

Cynic/Stoic cosmopolitanism urges us to recognize the equal, and unconditional, worth of all human beings, a worth grounded in moral choice- capacity (or perhaps even this is too restrictive?), rather than on traits that depend on fortuitous natural or social arrangements. The insight that politics ought to treat human beings both as equal and as having a worth beyond price is one of the deepest and most influential insights of Western thought; it is responsible for much that is fine in the modern Western political imagination. One day, Alexander the Great came and stood over Diogenes, as he was sunning himself in the marketplace. "Ask me for anything you want," Alexander said. He said, "Get out of my light" (VI.38). This image of the dignity of humanity, which can shine forth in its nakedness unless shadowed by the false claims of rank and kingship, a dignity that needs only the removal of that shadow to be vigorous and free, is one endpoint of a line that leads to the modern human rights movement.

In the tradition I shall describe, dignity is non-hierarchical. It belongs – and in equal measure – to all who have some basic threshold level of capacity for moral learning and choice. The tradition explicitly and pointedly excludes non-human animals, and I shall return to this problem in Chapter 7, rejecting that judgment; in some versions, though not that of Diogenes, it Also excludes, though less explicitly, humans with severe cognitive disabilities.

These shortcomings must be addressed in any contemporary version of the idea. The idea of dignity is not, however, inherently hierarchical or based on the idea of a rank-ordered society. In the medieval and early modern era, versions of the idea of dignity did crop up that were hierarchical and suited to a feudal society. I do not study these ideas here, or the traditions they ground. It is important to emphasize the egalitarian heart of this Stoic type of cosmopolitanism, since some scholars writing about dignity recently have supposed that the entire history of that concept derives from ideas of rank and status in hierarchical societies.

Notes
[1] See Martha C. Nussbaum, "Human Dignity and Political Entitlements." In *Human Dignity and Bioethics: Essays Commissioned by the President's Council on Bioethics*, 351–380. Washington, D.C.: U.S. Government Printing Office, 2008.
[2] See Jeremy Waldron, *Dignity, Rank, and Rights*. New York: Oxford University Press, 2012.

"IDEA FOR A UNIVERSAL HISTORY FROM A COSMOPOLITAN POINT OF VIEW"[1]

IMMANUEL KANT

IMMANUEL KANT. Born in 1724 in Königsberg (now Kaliningrad, Russia), Kant was a central figure in modern philosophy. His influential works on metaphysics, ethics, and political theory shaped Enlightenment thought. In this essay, Kant envisions human history as progressing toward a cosmopolitan future, where individual freedom and collective moral development align. Kant's essay was originally published in *Berlinische Monatsschrift* in 1784. While it is often overshadowed by his "Perpetual Peace" essay, which is more detailed in its political policy proposals, the "Idea for a Universal History" essay develops Kant's teleological rationalist ideas to argue that the 'crooked timber of humanity' must be made straight by a universal reason – the problem that occupies much of Kant's Critical and also political thinking.

INTRODUCTION

Whatever concept one may hold, from a metaphysical point of view, concerning the freedom of the will, certainly its appearances, which are human actions, like every other natural event are determined by universal laws. However obscure their causes, history, which is concerned with narrating these appearances, permits us to hope that if we attend to the play of freedom of the human will in the large, we may be able to discern a regular movement in it, and that what seems complex and chaotic in the single individual may be seen from the standpoint of the human race as a whole to be a steady and progressive though slow evolution of its original endowment. Since the free will of man has obvious influence upon marriages, births, and deaths, they seem to be subject to no rule by which the number of them could be reckoned in advance. Yet the annual tables of them in the major countries prove that they occur according

---

Excerpted from: Kant, Immanuel. 1963. *On History*. Edited and translated by Lewis White Beck. The Bobbs-Merrill Co.

to laws as stable as [those of] the unstable weather, which we likewise cannot determine in advance, but which, in the large, maintain the growth of plants the flow of rivers, and other natural events in an unbroken uniform course. Individuals and even whole peoples think little on this. Each, according to his own inclination, follows his own purpose, often in opposition to others; yet each individual and people, as if following some guiding thread, go toward a natural but to each of them unknown goal; all work toward furthering it, even if they would set little store by it if they did know it.

Since men in their endeavors behave, on the whole, not just instinctively, like the brutes, nor yet like rational citizens of the world according to some agreed-on plan, no history of man conceived according to a plan seems to be possible, as it might be possible to have such a history of bees or beavers. One cannot suppress a certain indignation when one sees men's actions on the great world-stage and finds, beside the wisdom that appears here and there among individuals, everything in the large woven together from folly, childish vanity, even from childish malice and destructiveness. In the end, one does not know what to think of the human race, so conceited in its gifts. Since the philosopher cannot presuppose any [conscious] individual purpose among men in their great drama, there is no other expedient for him except to try to see if he can discover a natural purpose in this idiotic course of things human. In keeping with this purpose, it might be possible to have a history with a definite natural plan for creatures who have no plan of their own.

We wish to see if we can succeed in finding a clue to such a history; we leave it to Nature to produce the man capable of composing it. Thus Nature produced Kepler, who subjected, in an unexpected way, the eccentric paths of the planets to definite laws; and she produced Newton, who explained these laws by a universal natural cause.

FIRST THESIS
All natural capacities of a creature are destined to evolve completely to their natural end.

Observation of both the outward form and inward structure of all animals confirms this of them. An organ that is of no use, an arrangement that does not achieve its purpose, are contradictions in the teleological theory of nature. If we give up this fundamental principle, we no longer have a lawful but an aimless course of nature, and blind chance takes the place of the guiding thread of reason.

SECOND THESIS
In man (as the only rational creature on earth) those natural capacities which are directed to the use of his reason are to be fully developed only in the race, not in the individual.

Reason in a creature is a faculty of widening the rules and purposes of the use of all its powers far beyond natural instinct; it acknowledges no limits to its projects. Reason itself does not work instinctively, but requires trial, practice, and instruction in order gradually to progress from one level of insight to another. Therefore a single man would have to live excessively long in order to learn to make full use of all his natural capacities. Since Nature has set only a short period for his life, she needs a perhaps unreckonable series of generations, each of which passes its own enlightenment to its successor in order finally to bring the seeds of enlightenment to that degree of development in our race which is completely suitable to Nature's purpose. This point of time must be, at least as an ideal, the goal of man's efforts, for otherwise his natural capacities would have to be counted as for the most part vain and aimless. This would destroy all practical principles, and Nature, whose wisdom must serve as the fundamental principle in judging all her other offspring, would thereby make man alone a contemptible plaything.

THIRD THESIS
Nature has willed that man should, by himself, produce everything that goes beyond the mechanical ordering of his animal existence, and that he should partake of no other happiness or perfection than that which he himself, independently of instinct, has created by his own reason.

Nature does nothing in vain, and in the use of means to her goals she is not prodigal. Her giving to man reason and the freedom of the will which depends upon it is clear indication of her purpose. Man accordingly was not to be guided by instinct, not nurtured and instructed with ready-made knowledge; rather, he should bring forth everything out of his own resources. Securing his own food, shelter, safety and defense (for which Nature gave him neither the horns of the bull, nor the claws of the lion, nor the fangs of the dog, but hands only), all amusement which can make life pleasant, insight and intelligence, finally even goodness of heart-all this should be wholly his own work. In this, Nature seems to have moved with the strictest parsimony, and to have measured her animal gifts precisely to the most stringent needs of a beginning existence, just as if she had willed that, if man ever did advance from the lowest barbarity to the highest skill and mental perfection and thereby worked himself up to happiness (so far as it is possible on earth), he alone should have the credit and should have only himself to thank-exactly as if she aimed more at his rational self-esteem than at his well-being. For along this march of human affairs, there was a host of troubles awaiting him. But it seems not to have concerned Nature that he should live well, but only that he should work himself upward so as to make himself, through his own actions, worthy of life and of well-being.

It remains strange that the earlier generations appear to carry through their toilsome labor only for the sake of the later, to prepare for them a foundation on which the later generations could erect the higher edifice which was Nature's goal, and yet that only the latest of the generations should have the good fortune to inhabit the building on which a long line of their ancestors had (unintentionally) labored without being permitted to partake of the fortune they had prepared. However puzzling this may be, it is necessary if one assumes that a species of animals should have reason, and, as a class of rational beings each of whom dies while the species is immortal, should develop their capacities to perfection.

FOURTH THESIS
The means employed by Nature to bring about the development of all the capacities of men is their antagonism in society, so far as this is, in the end, the cause of a lawful order among men.

By "antagonism" I mean the unsocial sociability of men, i.e., their propensity to enter into society, bound together with a mutual opposition which constantly threatens to break up the society. Man has an inclination to associate with others, because in society he feels himself to be more than man, i.e., as more than the developed form of his natural capacities. But he also has a strong propensity to isolate himself from others, because he finds in himself at the same time the unsocial characteristic of wishing to have everything go according to his own wish. Thus he expects opposition on all sides because, in knowing himself, he knows that he, on his own part, is inclined to oppose others. This opposition it is which awakens all his powers, brings him to conquer his inclination to laziness and, propelled by vainglory, lust for power, and avarice, to achieve a rank among his fellows whom he cannot tolerate but from whom he cannot withdraw. Thus are taken the first true steps from barbarism to culture, which consists in the social worth of man; thence gradually develop all talents, and taste is refined; through continued enlightenment the beginnings are laid for a way of thought which can in time convert the coarse, natural disposition for moral discrimination into definite practical principles, and thereby change a society of men driven together by their natural feelings into a moral whole. Without those in themselves unamiable characteristics of unsociability from whence opposition springs-characteristics each man must find in his own selfish pretensions-all talents would remain hidden, unborn in an Arcadian shepherd's life, with all its concord, contentment, and mutual affection. Men, good-natured as the sheep they herd, would hardly reach a higher worth than their beasts; they would not fill the empty place in creation by achieving their end, which is rational nature. Thanks be to Nature, then, for the incompatibility, for heartless competitive vanity, for the insatiable desire to possess and to rule! Without them, all the excellent natural capacities of humanity would forever sleep, undeveloped. Man wishes concord; but Nature knows better what is good for the race; she wills discord. He wishes to live comfortably and pleasantly; Nature wills that he should be plunged from sloth and passive contentment into labor and trouble, in order that he may find means of extricating himself from them. The natural urges to this, the sources of unsociableness and mutual opposition from which so many evils arise, drive men to new exertions of their forces and thus to the manifold development of their capacities. They thereby perhaps show the ordering of a wise Creator and not the hand of an evil spirit, who bungled in his great work or spoiled it out of envy.

FIFTH THESIS
The greatest problem for the human race, to the solution of which Nature drives man, is the achievement of a universal civic society which administers law among men.

The highest purpose of Nature, which is the development of all the capacities which can be achieved by mankind, is attainable only in society, and more specifically in the society with the greatest freedom. Such a society is one in which there is mutual opposition among the members, together with the most exact definition of freedom and fixing of its limits so that it may be consistent with the freedom of others. Nature demands that humankind should itself achieve this goal like all its other destined goals. Thus a society in which freedom under external laws is associated in the highest degree with irresistible power, i.e., a perfectly just civic constitution, is the highest problem Nature assigns to the human race; for Nature can achieve her other purposes for mankind only upon the solution and completion of this assignment. Need forces men, so enamored otherwise of their boundless freedom, into this state of constraint. They are forced to it by the greatest of all needs, a need they themselves occasion inasmuch as their passions keep them from living long together in wild freedom. Once in such a preserve as a civic union, these same passions subsequently do the most good. It is just the same with trees in a forest: each needs the others, since each in seeking to take the air and sunlight from others must strive upward, and thereby each realizes a beautiful, straight stature, while those that live in isolated freedom put out branches at random and grow stunted, crooked, and twisted. All culture, art which adorns mankind, and the finest social order are fruits of unsociableness, which forces itself to discipline itself and so, by a contrived art, to develop the natural seeds to perfection.

SIXTH THESIS
This problem is the most difficult and the last to be solved by mankind.

The difficulty which the mere thought of this problem puts before our eyes is this. Man is an animal which, if it lives among others of its kind, requires a master. For he certainly abuses his freedom with respect to other men, and although as, a reasonable being he wishes to have a law which limits the freedom of all, his selfish animal impulses tempt him, where possible, to exempt himself from them. He thus requires a master, who will break his will and force him to obey a will that is universally valid, under which each can be free. But whence does he get this master? Only from the human race. But then the master is himself an animal, and needs a master. Let him begin it as he will, it is not to be seen how he can procure a magistracy which can maintain public justice and which is itself just, whether it be a single person or a group of several elected persons. For each of them will always abuse his freedom if he has none above him to exercise force in accord with the laws. The highest master should be just in himself, and yet a man. This task is therefore the hardest of all; indeed, its complete solution is impossible, for from such crooked wood as man is made of, nothing perfectly straight can be built.[2] That it is the last problem to be solved follows also from this: it requires that there be a correct conception of a possible constitution, great experience gained in many paths of life, and – far beyond these-a good will ready to accept such a constitution. Three such things are very hard, and if they are ever to be found together, it will be very late and after many vain attempts.

Notes
[1] A statement in the "Short Notices" or the twelfth number of the Gothaische Gelehrte Zeitung of this year [1784], which no doubt was based on my conversation with a scholar who was traveling through, occasions this essay, without which that statement could not be understood. [The notice said: "A favorite idea of Professor Kant's is that the ultimate purpose of the human race is to achieve the most perfect civic constitution, and he wishes that a philosophical historian might undertake to give us a history of humanity from this point of view, and to show to what extent humanity in various ages has approached or drawn away from this final purpose and what remains to be done in order to reach it."]
[2] The role of man is very artificial. How it may be with the dwellers on other planets and their nature we do not know. If, however, we carry out well the mandate given us by Nature, we can perhaps flatter ourselves that we may claim among our neighbors in the cosmos no mean rank. Maybe among them each individual can perfectly attain his destiny in his own life. Among us, it is different; only the race can hope to attain it.

"A TRAVELER'S TALE"

ANTHONY APPIAH

KWAME ANTHONY APPIAH. Born in 1954 in London to a Ghanaian father and British mother, Appiah is a philosopher, cultural theorist, and novelist. He has taught at Princeton University and NYU. In "A Traveler's Tale," Appiah blends personal narrative with philosophical reflection, advocating for a cosmopolitan ethic that values cultural difference while recognizing our shared moral responsibilities.

We shall be meeting many cosmopolitans and anti-cosmopolitans in this book, but none, I think, who so starkly combines elements of both as the character who will be the first companion on our journey. Sir Richard Francis Burton was a Victorian adventurer whose life lent credence to that dubious adage about truth being stranger than fiction. Born in 1821, he traveled, as a child, with his family in Europe, and spent time getting to know the Romany people; his English contemporaries liked to say that he had acquired some of the Gypsy's wandering ways. He learned modern Greek in Marseilles and French and Italian, including the Neapolitan dialect, as his family moved between the British expatriate communities of France and Italy; and he arrived at Oxford knowing Béarnais – a language intermediate between French and Spanish – and (like every other student in those days) classical Greek and Latin as well.

Burton was not just an extraordinary linguist. He was one of the greatest European swordsmen of his day. Before being expelled from Oxford (for ignoring a college ban on going to the races), he challenged a fellow student to a duel because that young man had mocked his walrus mustache. When this fellow didn't grasp that he had been challenged, Burton concluded that he was not among gentlemen but among "grocers."

Excerpted from: Appiah, Anthony. 2007. *Cosmopolitanism: Ethics in a World of Strangers*. W. W. Norton & Company.

It is just possible, of course, that his adversary was a gentleman who had heard of Burton's prowess with the saber.

At the age of twenty-one, Richard Burton went to work for the East India Company in Sindh, where he added Gujarati, Marathi, Afghan, and Persian to his knowledge of modern and classical European languages, while deepening his mastery of Arabic and Hindi, which he had begun to study in England. Despite being (at least nominally) a Christian, he managed, in 1853, to be admitted to Mecca and Medina as a pilgrim, posing as a Pathan from India's Northwest Frontier Province. He traveled widely in Africa, as well. In 1858, he and John Hanning Speke were the first Europeans to see Lake Tanganyika, and he visited, among other places, Somalia (where he passed as an Arab merchant) as well as Sierra Leone, Cape Coast and Accra (in what is now Ghana), and Lagos. He knew large swaths of Asia and of Latin America; and he translated the Kama Sutra from Sanskrit and the Perfumed Garden and the Thousand and One Nights from Arabic (the latter in sixteen volumes, with a notorious "terminal essay" that included one of the first cross-cultural surveys of homosexuality). Aptly enough, he also translated Luiz Vaz de Camões' Lusiads – a celebration of that earlier global explorer Vasco da Gama – from the Portuguese. His translations made him famous (notorious even, when it came to the Oriental erotica); he also wrote grammars of two Indian languages and a vast number of the most extraordinary travel accounts of a century in which there was a good deal of competition in that genre. And, in 1880 he published a long poem that was, he said, a translation of "the Kasidah of Haji Abdu El-Yezdi," a native of the desert city of Yazd, in central Persia (one of the few substantial centers of Zoroastrianism remaining in Iran).

A qasida (as we would now write it) is a pre-Islamic classical Arab poetic form, with strict metrical rules, that begins, by tradition, with an evocation of a desert encampment. Although the form was highly respected before the rise of Islam, it saw its heyday in Islam's early days, before the eighth century AD, when it was regarded by some as the highest form of poetic art. But qasida have been written over the centuries through much of the Islamic world, in Turkish and Urdu and Persian as well as in Arabic. Burton's Haji Abdu of Yazd was devoted to "an Eastern Version of Humanitarianism blended with the sceptical or, as we now say, the scientific habit of mind." He was also, as one might guess from reading the poem, a fiction. For though the Kasidah is infused with the spirit of

Sufism – Islam's mystical tradition – it also alludes to Darwin's evolutionary theory and to other ideas from the Victorian West. Burton, the "translator," offered to explain this by writing, in his notes, that Haji Abdu added to a natural facility, a knack of language learning,....a store of desultory various reading; scraps of Chinese and old Egyptian; of Hebrew and Syriac; of Sanskrit and Prakrit; of Slav, especially Lithuanian; of Latin and Greek, including Romaic; of Berber, the Nubian dialect, and of Zend and Akkadian, besides Persian, his mother-tongue, and Arabic, the classic of the schools. Nor was he ignorant of "the—ologies" and the triumphs of modern scientific discovery.

If the linguistic gifts of this imaginary Sufi read a little too like Burton's own, Burton's conceit was not designed to deceive. At the start of the note, we're told that Abdu "preferred to style himself El-Hichmakâni... meaning 'Of No-hall, Nowhere.'" And though Burton's point is, in part, that Haji Abdu is, like himself, a man with no strong sense of national or local identity (dare I say it, a rootless cosmopolitan), it is also, surely, to give us the broadest of hints that El-Yezdi is his own invention.

Certainly the author of the Kasidah expressed views that, for a traditional Muslim, are more than mildly heretical. In one stanza he announces,

There is no Heav'en, there is no Hell;
these be the dreams of baby minds...
In another he says,
There is no Good, there is no Bad;
these be the whims of mortal will...

In short, he can sound – appropriately enough, perhaps, for a native of Zoroastrian Yazd – less like a Persian Sufi and more like Nietzsche's Zarathustra. One thing, though, about the author is not a fiction: since Burton had, in fact, made his pilgrimage to Mecca, the Kasidah's author certainly was a hajji – one who has made the hajj.

Of course, one characteristic of European cosmopolitanism, especially since the Enlightenment, has been a receptiveness to art and literature from other places, and a wider interest in lives elsewhere. This is a reflection of what I called, in the introduction, the second strand of cosmopolitanism: the recognition that human beings are different and that we can learn from each other's differences. There is Goethe, in Germany, whose career as a poet runs by way of a collection of Roman Elegies, written at the end of the 1780s, to the West-Eastern Divan of 1819, his last great cycle of poems, inspired by the oeuvre of the fourteenth-century Persian poet Hafiz (author, as Sir Richard Burton would certainly have pointed out, of extremely popular qasida). There is David Hume, in eighteenth-century Edinburgh, scouring traveler's tales, to examine the ways of China, Persia, Turkey, and Egypt. A little earlier still, across the English Channel in Bordeaux, there is Montesquieu, whose monumental Spirit of the Laws, published anonymously in Geneva in 1748, is crammed with anecdotes from Indonesia to Lapland, from Brazil to India, from Egypt to Japan; and whose earlier witty satire of his own country, the Persian Letters, ventriloquizes a Muslim. Burton's poet, too, seems mostly to speak for Burton: himself an agnostic of a scientific bent, with a vast store of knowledge of the world's religions and an evenhanded assessment of them all.

All Faith is false, all Faith is true:
Truth is the shattered mirror strown
In myriad bits; while each believes
His little bit the whole to own.

Burton's voracious assimilation of religions, literatures, and customs from around the world marks him as someone who was fascinated by the range of human invention, the variety of our ways of life and thought. And though he never pretended to anything like dispassion, that knowledge brought him to a point where he could see the world from perspectives remote from the outlook in which he had been brought up. A cosmopolitan openness to the world is perfectly consistent with picking and choosing among the options you find in your search. Burton's English contemporaries sometimes thought he displayed more respect for Islam than for the Christianity in which he was raised: though his wife was convinced that he had converted to Catholicism, I think it would be truer to say that he was, as W. H. Wilkins wrote in The Romance of Isabel Lady Burton, "a Mohammedan among Mohammedans, a Mormon among Mormons, a Sufi among the Shazlis, and a Catholic among the Catholics."[1]

Notes
[1] The Romance of Isabel Lady Burton, ed. by W. H. Wilkins, vol. 2 (New York: Dodd Mead, 1897), p. 712.

"TRIBALISM AND COSMOPOLITANISM: ARE THEY REAL OPPOSITES?"

SEYLA BENHABIB

I. VARIETIES OF COSMOPOLITANISM

The intense interest in cosmopolitanism in the social and political sciences, cultural and legal studies dates back to the last two decades of the twentieth century. With the Fall of the Berlin Wall in 1989, the unification of Germany, and the extension of the European Union to east and central European Countries, the Kantian cosmopolitan ideal of uniting diverse countries under the rule of law, respect for human rights, and the free movement of peoples, goods and services across borders – the mission of the European Union Common Market – seemed to come alive.[1]

Today, it is tempting to see such universalism and cosmopolitanism as wholly passé and grossly inadequate. Many postcolonial and decolonial thinkers have argued that a provincialized European identity must require an awareness that its universalism derives not from an unchangeable normative core but stands in need of constant renewal from the margins. However, instead of engaging in exercises of postcolonial and decolonial criticisms of this European legacy, we can transform this "hermeneutics of suspicion," in Paul Ricoeur's famous words (1965) and reconstruct its insights in order to transform Eurocentric cosmopolitanism into a more universal cosmopolitanism. This has been my goal in a number of works of the last two decades, a project which I have called "another cosmopolitanism" (Benhabib 2006).[2]

In addition to the post-colonial critiques of cosmopolitanism, there are two lines of argument which are based on a misunderstanding of this concept, and in particular, of the Kantian tradition from which it stems. The first line of critique confuses globalist free market neo-liberalism with cosmopolitanism. Both right and left-wing populists find comfort in attacking global cosmopolitan elites, and take pleasure in reducing cosmopolitanism to the ideology of "frequent flying" jet setters.[3] Theirs is a polemical rejection of the Kantian cosmopolitan tradition, which, as I will argue below, can nonetheless deliver us criteria for a critique of neo-liberal capitalism, as well.

The second strand of criticism is being voiced by many in this conference. I find that the term "tribalism" is not helpful for distilling the kernel of truth in the reservations and misgivings many have about cosmopolitanism. I will restate these legitimate objections in the following terms: Does cosmopolitanism deny the importance of ethical bonds and affinities or associational obligations which result from our being embedded and situated in communities of language, ethnicity, religion, and history? My own answer is, "no, of course not." It is a matter of assessing the value of these affiliations and the obligations they place upon us in the light of more universalist principles – and weighing them properly in relation to each other.

Historically, some ancient Greek and Roman cosmopolitans such as Diogenes the Cynic denied the claim of all such special obligations upon us. In view of the realities of the ancient world, in which not to be a member of a polis and to accept its ethos, was the equivalent of being "a God or a beast," as Aristotle famously formulated it (Book 1, ch. 2), it is understandable that those who wished to distance themselves from the practice of slavery in the polis would assume such extreme attitudes. Ancient cosmopolitan ethics rejected slavery in the ancient world and asserted the equal and unconditional worth of all human beings, and this critical attitude was often expressed polemically as denying the value of all particularistic association and affiliations in the ancient city. As Martha Nussbaum expresses in her excellent study of this tradition, "Just as we can defend the intrinsic and motivational importance of ties to family and friends without denying that we owe something to all our fellow citizens [...] [we can also defend] a type of patriotism that [...] builds ties of recognition and concerns with people outside our national borders" (Nussbaum 2021, 13).[4] I am less sanguine than Nussbaum about patriotism and how exactly it can be reconciled with ties of recognition and concern beyond our borders unless nation-states are embedded in cosmopolitan international and multinational institutions. But Nussbaum's insights about developing a moral psychology reconciling particularistic attachments with universalizing 'circles of sympathy' is one I share.

In contemporary post-modern societies, that is, capitalist societies that still pay lip service to the autonomy of the individual and the sanctity of individual choice, the question is whether any ethical bonds and obligations resulting from non-elective affinities and affiliations, can survive the dissolving acid forces of the market and of consumer culture. I believe this a legitimate anxiety lurking behind the term 'tribalism'. It is an anxiety with which I empathize, but which has little to do with the Kantian cosmopolitan tradition which I defend. Identifying Kantian cosmopolitanism with a defense of neo-liberal globalization *tout court* is based on a mistake. There have been different interpretations of the implications of Kantian cosmopolitanism for global distributive justice. While John Rawls (2001), following Kantian premises, defends a liberal nationalism in the international domain, Thomas Pogge (2023), a Kantian cosmopolitan, has proposed a more redistributionist approach to global justice. It is thus not correct to dismiss Kantian cosmopolitanism as being equivalent to a defense of neo-liberal globalization.

After a brief excursus into Kant's work, I want to turn to Hannah Arendt's essay on Karl Jaspers, called "Karl Jaspers: Citizen of the World." Arendt had delivered a *Laudatio* for Jaspers when he received the Peace Prize of the German book trade in 1958, after the publication of his *The Atom Bomb and the Future of Mankind* (1963).[5] Arendt embraces much in the Kantian cosmopolitan tradition, as well as voicing some skepticism about its claims, but this by no means leads her to endorse tribalism and to reject universalism. She remains true to the Kantian tradition.

2. REVISITING "PERPETUAL PEACE"

The seminal work in the tradition of Kantian cosmopolitanism is the 1795 essay on "Towards Perpetual Peace: A Philosophical Sketch" [PP] which Kant wrote after the conclusion of the revolutionary wars between France and Prussia. The essay begins with a well-known joke. Kant writes: "We can leave open the question whether this satirical caption (meant is the German phrase: *Zum ewigen Frieden*, eternal peace) to the picture of a graveyard, which was painted on the sign of a Dutch innkeeper, applies to human beings in general, or specifically to the heads of state, who can never get enough of war, or even just to philosophers who dream the sweet dream of perpetual peace" (Kant, PP, 67). Whether it is humanity at large, leaders of states, or maybe even philosophers, who dream the sweet dream of 'eternal' or 'perpetual' peace is moot, says Kant. The point is that one can enjoy 'this sweet dream' not in life but only in death. Of course, Kant, who proceeds to propose preliminary and definitive articles of peace among states, is himself aware of the irony that accompanies his philosophical proposal, which he therefore calls an *Entwurf* – a proposal or a sketch. Yet he is not deterred from trying to make perpetual peace among nations possible.

The first definitive article of "Perpetual Peace" states, "The Civil Constitution of Every State shall be Republican" (Kant, PP, 74). In such a republic, the principles of *freedom* for all members of society, dependence upon a common legislation as *subjects* and legal equality for everyone as *citizens*, should be guaranteed. Such a *republican constitution*, Kant claims, would serve peace, because if the consent of the citizens were consulted, it is unlikely that they would "call upon themselves all the miseries of war" (Kant, PP, 74). This claim subsequently has become known in political science as the theorem of 'democratic peace', namely that "democracies do not make war against each other" (Hook 2011; Doyle 2011).

For Kant, respect for the autonomous person within a republican constitutional order requires peace among nations. This is why the second definitive article of "Perpetual Peace" states "International Right (*Völkerrecht*) shall be based on the *Federalism* of Free States" (Kant, PP, 78). The distinctiveness of this kind of federalism is that it is a "a pacific federation (*foedus pacificum*) which is different from a *peace treaty* (*pactum pacis*) because a pacific federation seeks to end not merely *one* war, as does the latter, but rather to end all wars forever" (Kant, PP, 80). There has been a wide-ranging discussion as to whether such a federation of free states means a world-state (*Weltstaat*) or a world-republic (*Weltrepublik*) and how the latter is to be understood (Bohman and Lutz-Bachman 1997). Kant definitely rejects the idea of a world-state as a form of "soulless despotism" (Kant, PP, 95). Postcolonial critics have also pointed out that it is unclear whether Kant thought that *all peoples* of the world would be capable of forming a republican constitution (Valdez 2019; Kleingeld 2014). Left unanswered by Kant's multiple formulations is whether polities such as the Ottoman Empire of Kant's time would be considered a party to such a pacific federation.[6] In other words, does international law in Kant's formulation presuppose a specific state form alone? And can this state form be universalized to polities with different religious, ethical, and cultural traditions? Must all states subject to Kantian international law be republican in form?

Historical developments have shown that the republican form of self-government, based on the principle of the equality of all under the jurisdiction of a common law, is universalizable. Through anti-colonial struggles of the 1960's, this ideal has even transcended the narrow boundaries of a Westphalian state-model; projecting instead the elimination of racial and imperial hierarchies among nations and even envisaging an egalitarian and non-hierarchical international order. Kant's last proposal in this essay is "a cosmopolitan right" (*ein kosmopolitischer Recht*). The third definitive article of "Perpetual Peace" reads, "Cosmopolitan Right shall be limited to the conditions of universal hospitality" (Kant PP, 82). Kant emphasizes that this is not a matter of philanthropy but of right and adds: "[I]t means the right of a stranger not to be treated in a hostile manner by another upon his arrival on the other's territory. If it can be done without causing his death (Untergang) the stranger can be turned away [...]" (Kant, PP, 82).

Kant reformulates cosmopolitanism as a form of world-citizenship which would apply to persons insofar as they meet and interact with one another at the borders of their polities and in a global sphere of commerce and trade, science and exploration, and more problematically, religious evangelizing. He is clear that cosmopolitan right is distinct from state law (*Staatsrecht*) as well as international law (*Völkerrecht*) (Kant 2003, 121). But what is it then? Since there is no world-state, can cosmopolitan right really be a source of law and right, as the ambiguities of the German term "Recht," which in English can mean both right and law suggest? While we can see in the third article of "Perpetual Peace" a kernel of a "right to asylum," Kant is clear that this is a right of visitation alone (*Gastrecht*) and not a right to residency, for which one needs a "charitable contract" (*einen wohlwollender Vertrag*), which the host has to accept as well. Still Kant insists that "in virtue of the right to *common possession of the surface of the earth*," every human being can present himself to the land of another and seek "access" (*Zugang*) but is not entitled to "access" (*Einlass*) (Kant, PP, 82–83).

3. CRITIQUES OF LIBERAL COSMOPOLITANISM

In the last decades, every aspect of this Kantian project has been subject to criticism. It has been objected that Kant's critique of European imperialism was quite equivocal, permitting access (*Zugang*) to foreign territories but not entry (*Einlass*). Access, however, would suffice to establish the kind of trading colonies which western empires such as the British and the Dutch wanted to establish in China and Japan in particular. James Tully is critical of Kant's idea of hospitality, seeing in it not only a thinly veiled attempt at the imperialist domination of other lands and cultures by establishing trading colonies but also an excuse for Christian proselytizing and converting the natives to Christianity. He writes: "Kant combined two very powerful imperial stories: a presumptively universal and Eurocentric narrative of historical development or modernization and a presumptively universal theory of global justice" (Tully 2008, 148).

While we must heed these objections and formulate a self-reflective cosmopolitanism, freed from unquestioned assumptions regarding the superiority of European norms and patterns of development, Kantian cosmopolitanism is not about jet-setting elites; rather, it provides the foundations for a model of international relations based upon respect for the equality of sovereign polities and the human rights of their citizens. With his concept of cosmopolitan right, Kant goes even further and envisages a world-wide civil society which would be governed by certain laws and norms. Kant gives us the essence of what has become known as 'liberal internationalism'. This is a term that refers to the views of an influential group of theorists, including Hans Kelsen, Ronald Dworkin, Harold Koh, Anne-Marie Slaughter, and Samantha Power.[8]

Liberal Internationalists argue that it is wrong to think of sovereignty as a unilateral prerogative to be wielded against other sovereigns. Rather, states exist within *regimes of sovereignty* that change over time (Cohen 2012). The Westphalian model of the absolute jurisdiction of a central authority over all that is living and dead on its territory, is a myth of the past (if it was ever a historical reality is doubtful). For liberal internationalists, sovereignty can only be exercised within a system of international law and is regulated by institutions such as the United Nations Charter, the UDHR, and regimes of human rights that have been created in the aftermath of World War II. Among the best known of such multilateral human rights treaties are the International Covenant of Civil and Political Rights; the International Covenant of Social, Economic and Cultural Rights; CEDAW- Convention on the Elimination of all Discrimination Against Women; Convention of the Elimination of All Racial Discrimination, and the 1951 Convention of the Status of Refugees. In protecting their borders, states must balance self-interest and international obligations. Such balancing is beneficial economically as well because international prosperity requires respecting the rules of the game, be it of trade or of diplomacy. According to this position, while respecting their obligations under international law, states have the prerogative to define their labor market policies as they choose. Migration policies that privilege meritocracy or those that give first priority to family affiliations are both acceptable. The rights of strangers among us ought to be determined in accordance with national and regional, as well as international, norms.

Today this model of international relations is in a shambles, threatened by conflicts extending from the Ukraine to Palestine, from the Sudan to Venezuela. Debunking this tradition in the name of a realism of power relations is quite different than reconstructing it, and it is the latter route which I follow. The ideal of a world of polities based upon mutual respect for the rule of law and for supra-national international institutions, such as the International Court of Justice and the International Criminal Court, is being challenged in the name of renewed super-power competition each jostling for their sphere of influence. Carl Schmitt's concept of the *Lebensraum* has found new fans in Putin's Russia as well as in China. In the United States, as well, liberal internationalism is in a battle for the soul of the nation against an unprincipled transactional autocracy, represented by the Trump administration, which in its first weeks in power has shown how close it is to fascist ideals. In order to help us get gain a clear view on what we would lose by the demise of liberal internationalism let me turn to Hannah Arendt and Karl Jaspers.

4. ARENDT ON WORLD CITIZENSHIP

In "Karl Jaspers: Citizen of the World," Arendt begins by rejecting world government and world citizenship, but concedes to Kant's cosmopolitanism the insight that, "Mankind, which for all preceding generations was no more than a concept or an ideal, has become something of an urgent reality" (Arendt 1958 [1970], 82). She continues:

> [F]or the first time in history, all peoples on earth have a common present: no event of any importance in the history of one country can remain a marginal accident in the history of any other. Every country has become

the almost immediate neighbor of every other country, and every man feels the shock of events which take place at the other side of the globe" (Arendt 1958, 82).

This common present does not emerge from a common past, nor does it guarantee a common future. It is technology which has united the world, and it can just easily destroy it. Whereas the technology of communication has enabled the unity of mankind, the technology of mastering the forces of the universe through the splitting of the atom presages a destructive force which can end human life on earth. "This negative solidarity, based on the fear of global destruction, has its correspondence in a less articulate, no less potent, apprehension that the solidarity of mankind can be meaningful in a positive sense only if it is coupled with political responsibility" (Arendt 1958 [1970], 83). How can such negative solidarity become a sense of shared political responsibility "beyond political apathy, isolationist nationalism, or desperate rebellion" (Arendt 1958, 83)? Neither a world-state nor world-citizenship can be solutions to this predicament. Kant had named such a world state "a soulless despotism," but was not willing to give up the ideal of world-citizenship, which for him meant precisely a sense of shared responsibility in that the injustice done in one part of the world would be seen to affect all others as well (Kant, PP, 95).

For Arendt, as for Jaspers, the emergence of mankind as a "tangible political reality" is a new epoch in the history of mankind. But this mankind (*Menschheit*) which emerges is not a "species being" (*Gattungswesen*), as Feuerbach or Marx may have said. The philosophy of Mankind must not envisage Man, as a singular subject, "talking to himself," but rather "men talking and communicating with each other." The human condition is one of plurality, not of singularity. The human condition on earth does not yet coincide with the dignity of all human beings; it is not a sociological reality and will probably never become one. It is, rather, the striving towards in ideal of humanity in all its plurality and diversity that paves the path towards genuine solidarity.

Arendt concludes: "Politically, the new fragile unity brought about by technical mastery over the earth can be guaranteed only within a framework of universal mutual agreements, which eventually *would lead into a world-wide federated structure*" (Arendt 1958 [1970], p. 93). There are interesting tensions as well as complementarities between Arendt's civic republicanism, her ideals of active and engaged citizenship, and her federationalism. It is important that, already in mid-twentieth century, both Arendt and Jaspers deeply reflected on the solidarity and interdependence which the new technologies of communication, as well as the realities of the atomic age, seemed to require. In our age of the world-wide internet, the ever-rapid movement of new, germs, and fashions across borders, the enormous netting of state economies into a world-system of finance such interdependence has magnified in unimaginable ways. Arendt, in particular, emphasized human plurality and insisted that a negative solidarity must be transformed into some kind of worldly politics, in which "universal mutual agreements would lead to a world-wide federated structure." She was less sanguine than Jaspers that such a federation could in fact emerge; for her, the destruction of European Jewry, whom she called "the weakest link in the chain of Europe's nations," proved how difficult it was to construct a common world of institutions and practices, promises and commitments (Arendt 1943, 66). Nonetheless, she admired such political new beginnings, and, in her clairvoyant essays on Zionism, even advocated a "Mediterranean unity of peoples" as the solution to the Israel-Palestine quandary (Arendt 1945, 163).

One of the most striking insights of her essay on Karl Jaspers is that she very appropriately observes that the burdens of global political responsibility may not lead to a new form of solidarity, "beyond political apathy, isolationist nationalism, or desperate rebellion" (Arendt 1958 [1970], p. 83). And these are all the issues we still face today: apathy, nationalism, and desperate rebellion, which can assume the form of widespread political nihilism. Arendt is not advocating the rejection of global responsibility but raising serious questions about the ethical and political forms it may or could take.

Such global responsibility cannot be achieved by dismantling the institutions of liberal internationalism even further. If this were to happen, the future would be dominated by tyrants and autocrats, who, emboldened by the disappearance of multilateral institutions and the drying up of international law, would see no limits to the exercise of their powers. The only difference between 'another cosmopolitanism', which I advocate, and 'liberal internationalism', which defends the achievement of cosmopolitan institutions established in the wake of World War II, is that I insist on broadening and deepening international law in our world such as to take the perspective of scholars into account who call their views 'Third World

Approaches to International Law'. Incorporating such a perspective means challenging principles of international law which disempower countries of the global south from having full access to their own natural resources (among many other issues). Such cosmopolitanism leads to a critique of global inequalities and cannot be reduced to neo-liberal globalization.

5. AFTER THE ISRAEL-GAZA WAR OF 2023-2024

In view of world events, since the brutal Hamas attack on Isreal of October 7, 2023, and the unfolding genocidal war against the people of Gaza, which has gone beyond any moral or political reasons of Israel's right of self-defense,[10] I have often found myself conversing with Hannah Arendt. What would she have thought? Would she have said, "I warned you so?" Hard to know. But of one point I am certain: she would have been surprised by (but would not have rejected) the case brought by South Africa and supported by Ireland against the State of Israel in front of the International Criminal Court. Perhaps she would have been sad, and may have even shed a tear, as I did, that it had come to this for Israel and for the Jewish people. It is the legacy of the cosmopolitan tradition that such institutions as the International Criminal Court exist – not virtually, as a court of world opinion alone, but actually. We can all watch those impressive proceedings and educate and enlighten ourselves about the laws of war among nations, and learn how, even under such conditions, human dignity and rights must be respected. Perpetual peace it is not, but why give up hope for it?

Notes

1 See, e.g., Held (1994); Held (2010); Archibugi, Held, and Kohler (1998); Habermas (2001); Habermas (2006); Delanty (2009).

2 See also Benhabib (2025), where this argument is developed at greater length in the light of recent world-events.

3 One of the earliest critiques of cosmopolitans as heartless globalists was voiced by Huntington (2004). For an early statement by a progressive thinker, see Calhoun (2002). I discuss these positions in Benhabib (2011, 1–20).

4 I have disagreements with Nussbaum's views of international law, see Benhabib (forthcoming).

5 See Young-Bruehl (1982) for the details of Arendt's *Laudatio*, 300–301.

6 The Congress of Berlin (June 13 – July 13, 1878), concluding the Russo-Turkish War of 1877–1878, was one of the first muti-national diplomatic meetings to reorganize the Balkan states which had been freed by Russia from the control of the Ottoman Empire. In addition to Russia, Great Britain, France, Austria-Hungary, Italy, Germany, the Ottoman Empire, and four Balkan states – Greece, Serbia, Romania and Montenegro – were represented in the meeting.

Chancellor Bismarck wanted to weaken the Ottoman Empire's influence in the Balkans but also avoid the domination of the Balkans by Russia. His politics of balancing the interests of "great powers," left small Bakan countries such as Rumania and Bulgaria dissatisfied, and prefigured the development of the Mandate System which emerged after WWI and supposedly intended to ameliorate the inequality and domination of smaller nations by European great powers: https://en.wikipedia.org/wiki/Congress_of_Berlin. Accessed 2/29/2024.

7 Whether Kant's formulation of "hospitality" lead to the imperialist right of Europeans to expand into other territories and colonize them has been debated. I have argued that Kant, in fact, criticizes imperialism. See Benhabib (2004, 26–43) and Muthu (2004). For a more critical view, see McCarthy (2009).

8 I deal with these authors and their work in great detail in Benhabib (2025, 89–91).

9 See the illuminating article by Brang (2024).

10 South Africa charged that Israel was committing genocide in Rafah, brought in front of the ICJ on December 29, 2023. See https://en.wikipedia.org/wiki/South_Africa%27s_genocide_case_against_Israel.

REFERENCES

Archibugi, Daniel, David Held, and Martin Kohler. 1998. *Re-Imagining Political Community. Studies in Cosmopolitan Democracy*. Stanford: Stanford University Press.

Arendt, Hannah. 1943. "We Refugees." *Menorah Journal*, reprinted in *The Jew as Pariah: Jewish Identity and Politics in the Modern Age*, edited and with an Introduction by Ron H. Feldman, 55–67. New York: Grove Press, 1986.

Arendt, Hannah. 1945. "Zionism Reconsidered." Reprinted in *The Jew as Pariah: Jewish Identity and Politics in the Modern Age*, edited and with an Introduction by Ron H. Feldman, 163–200. New York: Grove Press, 1986.

Arendt, Hannah. 1958. "Karl Jaspers: Citizen of the World." In *Men in Dark Times*. New York and London: Harcourt, Brace & Company.

Arendt, Hannah. 2007. *The Jewish Writings*. Edited by Jerome Kohn and Ron H. Feldman. New York: Schocken Books.

Arendt, Hannah. *Men in Dark Times*. Harcourt Brace Jovanovich, 1968.

Arendt, Hannah. 1967. "Truth and Politics." The New Yorker, February 25. Later included in *Between Past and Future*. Penguin Books, 2006.

Arendt, Hannah, and Mary McCarthy. 1995. *Between Friends: The Correspondence of Hannah Arendt and Mary McCarthy, 1949–1975*. Edited by Carol Brightman. Harcourt Brace.

Aristotle. 1984. *The Politics*, translated and with an Introduction, Notes, and Glossary by Carnes Lord. Chicago: The University of Chicago Press.

Benhabib, Seyla. 2004. *The Rights of Others: Aliens, Citizens, and Residents*. Cambridge, UK: Cambridge University Press.

Benhabib, Seyla. 2006. *Another Cosmopolitanism: The Berkeley Tanner Lectures*, with Jeremy Waldron, Bonnie Honig, and Will Kymlicka. Edited by Robert Post. Oxford: Oxford University Press.

Benhabib, Seyla. 2011. *Dignity in Adversity: Human Rights in Troubled Times*. Cambridge, UK, and Malden, MA: Polity Press.

Benhabib, Seyla. 2025. *At the Margins of the Modern State: Critical Theory and Law*. Cambridge, UK: Polity Press.

Benhabib, Seyla. Forthcoming. "Cosmopolitanism." In *The Oxford Handbook of Cosmopolitanism*, edited by Prathama Banerjee, Dipesh Chakrabarty, Sanjay Seth, and Lisa Wedeen. New York: Oxford University Press.

Bohman, James, and Matthias Lutz-Bachman, eds. 1997. *Essays on Kant's Cosmopolitan Ideal.* Boston, MA: MIT Press.
Brang, Lucas. "Von Carl Schmitt über Dugin bis Trump: Die neue Rechte in China." *Blaetter fuer deutsche und internationale Politik* 6: 101–110.
Calhoun, Craig. 2002. "The Class-Consciousness of Frequent Travelers: Toward a Critique of Actually Existing Cosmopolitanism." *South Atlantic Quarterly* 101, no. 4: 869–97.
Cohen, J. L. 2012. Globalization and Sovereignty: Rethinking Legality, Legitimacy and Constitutionalism. Cambridge: Cambridge University Press.
Delanty, Gerard. 2009. *The Cosmopolitan Imagination: The Renewal of Critical Social Theory.* Cambridge: Cambridge University Press.
Doyle, Michael. 2011. *Liberal Peace: Selected Essays.* Oxfordshire, UK: Routledge.
Habermas, Jürgen. 2001. *The Postnational Constellation: Political Essays.* Edited and translated by Max Pensky. Cambridge, MA: MIT Press.
Habermas, Jürgen. 2006. *The Divided West.* Translated by Ciaran Cronin. Cambridge, UK, and Malden, Mass.: Polity Press.
Held, David. 1994. *Democracy and the Global Order.* Stanford: Stanford University Press.
Held, David. 2010. *Cosmopolitanism: Ideas and Realities.* Cambridge, UK: Polity Press.
Hook, S. W., ed. 2011. *Democratic Peace in Theory and Practice.* Ohio: Kent State University Press.
Huntington, Samuel. 2004. "Dead Souls: The Denationalization of the American Elite." *The National Interest*: 5-18.
Jaspers, Karl. 1963. *The Atom Bomb and the Future of Man.* Chicago: University of Chicago Press.
Kant, Immanuel. 2003. "Public Right" [1797]. In *The Metaphysical Elements of Justice*, edited and translated by Mary J. Gregor. Cambridge, UK: Cambridge University Press.
Kant, Immanuel. 2006. "Perpetual Peace" [1795]. In *Toward Perpetual Peace and Other Writings on Politics, Peace, and History*, edited by M.W. Doyle and A. Wood, translated by D. L. Colclasure. New Haven, CT: Yale University Press.
Kant, Immanuel. 1968. *Die Metaphysik der Sitten* [1797]. In Immanuel Kant Werkausgabe, Bd. viii, edited by Wilhelm Weischedel. Frankfurt: Suhrkamp, 1968.
Kleingeld, Pauline. 2014. "Kant's Second Thoughts on Colonialism." In *Kant and Colonialism*, edited by Katrin Flickschuh and Lea Ypi. Oxford: Oxford University Press, 43–68.
McCarthy, T. A. 2009. *Race, Empire, and the Idea of Human Development.* Cambridge, UK: Cambridge University Press.
Muthu, Sankar. 2003. *Enlightenment and Empire.* Princeton, NJ: Princeton University Press.
Nussbaum, Martha. 2021. *The Cosmopolitan Tradition: A Noble but Flawed Ideal.* Cambridge, Mass.: Harvard University Press.
Orwell, George. [Provide specific work title for citation.]
Pogge, Thomas. 2023. *World Poverty and Human Rights.* 2nd ed. Cambridge, UK: Polity Press.
Rawls, John. 2001. *The Law of Peoples: With "The Idea of Public Reason Revisited."* Cambridge, Mass.: Harvard University Press.
Ricoeur, Paul. 1965. *De l'interprétation: Essai sur Freud.* Paris: Seuil. [Translated as *Freud and Philosophy: An Essay on Interpretation*, by Denis Savage. New Haven: Yale University Press, 1970.]
Tully, James. 2008. Public Philosophy in a New Key, Volume II: Imperialism and Civic Freedom. Cambridge: Cambridge University Press.
Valdez, Inés. 2019. *Transnational Cosmopolitanism: Kant, Du Bois, and Justice as a Political Craft.* Cambridge: Cambridge University Press.
Young-Bruehl, Elisabeth. 1982. *Hannah Arendt: For Love of the World.* 2nd ed. New Haven, Conn. and London: Yale University Press.

"THE STATESMEN'S BIBLE"

MARTHA NUSSBAUM

MARTHA NUSSBAUM examines the contributions of thinkers like Cicero, Hugo Grotius, and Adam Smith, exploring how their ideas have shaped contemporary understandings of cosmopolitanism and the role of the state. In this excerpt, Nussbaum revisits the intersection of politics and ethics, critiquing traditional models of statecraft that neglect individual dignity. She highlights the role of compassion and moral reasoning in fostering inclusive governance and social justice.

For many years the international community has been working with an account of some transnational duties that commands a wide consensus. These include duties of nations and their agents in time of war and duties of all nations to uphold (some) human rights, those that are standardly called "civil and political." While there is much debate about when and how nations are permitted to interfere in the affairs of other nations (a topic I shall take up in Chapter 4), there is general agreement that the community of nations must work to secure and protect (some) human rights for all the world's people. Theories of the proper conduct of war, and of proper conduct toward the enemy during war; theories about torture and cruelty to persons; theories even about the rape of women and other transnational atrocities; theories about aggressive acts of various other sorts toward foreign nationals, whether on our soil or abroad; even theories about our duties to support other first-generation human rights, such as the freedom of speech and association – all these things nations have seen fit to work out in some detail, and our theories of international justice have been dealing with them at least from the first century BCE,

---

Excerpted from: Nussbaum, Martha. 2021. *The Cosmopolitan Tradition: A Noble but Flawed Ideal.* Harvard University Press, 18–21.

when Cicero described the "duties of justice" in his work *De Officiis* ('On duties'), perhaps the most influential book in the Western tradition of political philosophy. Cicero's ideas were further developed in the Middle Ages by thinkers such as Aquinas, Suarez, and Gentili; they were the basis for Grotius's account of just and unjust war, for many aspects of the thought of Wolff and Pufendorf, and for Kant's thinking about cosmopolitan obligation in Perpetual Peace. By now we understand many nuances of this topic and have a rich array of subtly different views – for example, on such questions as whether it is permissible to lie to the enemy in war time, a subject concerning which Cicero and Kant are the rigorists, and Grotius takes a more indulgent line.

The rights that are standardly called "social and economic rights," however, have as yet received no clear transnational analysis. Material inequalities across national boundaries are a glaring fact of twenty-first century life. But our philosophical theories of international law and morality have relatively little to say about what obligations, if any, flow from these inequalities. We have quite a few accounts of personal duties of aid at a distance, and in recent years theorists of global justice have begun to work out the foundations for a theory of material transfers between nations, but we have virtually no consensus on this question, and some of our major theories of justice are virtually silent about it, simply starting from the nation-state as their basic unit. Nor has international law progressed far in this direction. Although many international documents by now do concern themselves with what are known as second-generation rights (economic and social rights) in addition to the standard political and civil rights, they typically do so in a nation-state-based way, portraying certain material entitlements as what all citizens have a right to demand from the state in which they live.

This is an uneasy position, to put it mildly. It is obvious that human lives are deformed by poverty and by the lack of social and economic goods, such as health care and education, just as much as they are deformed by the absence of political liberties, and that these deprivations are in multiple ways interconnected. Moreover, it is pretty obvious that the so-called first-generation rights cannot be protected without money, so the distinction between the two types cannot plausibly be that the former are free of cost. Most of us, if pressed, would admit that we are members of a larger world community and bear some type of obligation to give material aid to poorer members of that community. But we have no clear picture of what those obligations are, of what entity (the person, the state) is the bearer of them, and of how they ought to be fulfilled.

I shall argue here that not only our insights into the "duties of justice," but also our primitive thinking about the duties of material aid – and about the material component involved in fulfilling duties of justice – can be laid at the door of Cicero. In *De Officiis* he elaborates a distinction between these two types of duties that, like everything he wrote in that book, has had enormous influence on the course of political thought since. The general line he takes is that duties of justice are very strict and require high moral standards of all actors in their conduct across national boundaries. Duties of material aid, however, allow much elasticity, and give us a lot of room to prefer the near and dear. Indeed, Cicero thinks that we positively ought to prefer the near and dear, giving material aid to those outside our borders only when that can be done without any sacrifice to ourselves. In *De Officiis*, he cites a famous poem of Ennius to make this point:

> *A man who graciously shows the way to a someone who is lost*
> *kindles, so to speak, a light from his own light.*
> *For his own shines no less because he has lit another's* (I.51).

That is how Cicero wants us to think about duties of material aid across national boundaries: we undertake them only when it really is like giving directions on the road or lighting someone's torch from your own: that is, when no significant material loss ensues. And, as we all know, that is how many of us have come to think of such duties.

"HANNAH ARENDT AND COSMOPOLITANISM"

LEON BOTSTEIN

The word 'cosmopolitan' (or 'cosmopolitanism') comes from Greek and has a myriad of established uses in English. When thinking about Hannah Arendt, I considered how she might have understood the word 'cosmopolitan'. In German, the word *Weltbürger* – which translates roughly to 'world citizen' – carries a particular meaning within eighteenth- and nineteenth-century German thought. A few years after Arendt was born, the historian Friedrich Meinecke wrote a significant book, *Weltbürgertum und Nationalstaat*, a study of the ideas of cosmopolitanism and the nation-state. It was an influential work; Meinecke trained generations of German historians.

The term *Weltbürger* first gained traction in the German language in the eighteenth century. You find it in Wieland, Schiller, Goethe, and even Herder. It describes a person whose ethics are universal and rational, and whose outlook derives from the assumption of a shared civic, moral, or ethical status shared by all human beings. This in turn frames a cross-cultural empathy and sensibility. The allegiance to the cosmopolitan was often contrasted with patriotism and, at times, with a more restrictive notion of group solidarity and of nationhood and a presumed historical homogeneity, or *Vaterland*. The idea of the cosmopolitan is rather more distinctly urban. But it seems rather detached from the practical dynamics and realities of existence (e.g., place and family). This dispassionate distance from seemingly more "organic" and less abstract human loyalties suggests a certain predilection, ethically speaking, towards tolerance and human equality in the face of wide differences within the human species.

This talk was given as Bard President Leon Botstein's welcoming speech to the second day of the conference on Tribalism and Cosmopolitanism.

Politically speaking, the cosmopolitan came to be understood as being in tension with the national. In 1953, the German press reported an incident outside Buckingham Palace in which a 31-year-old American publicly renounced his U.S. citizenship in order to declare himself a cosmopolitan. The German media framed it as an attempt to become a *Weltbürger* in the way that term had been understood in the late eighteenth century.

By the nineteenth century, however, the concept of the cosmopolitanism had shifted away from its apparent idealism. A lesser-known but important German political critic, Wilhelm Riehl, transformed the term from its positive eighteenth-century roots in Weimar classicism into something negative – a self-image and identity that was detached from the real lives of people. This critique fed into one of the most well-known fin de siècle sociological distinctions: the contrast between *Gemeinschaft* (community) and *Gesellschaft* (society).

Hannah Arendt had an ambivalent relationship with the idea of cosmopolitanism. The most striking example of this appears in her review of Stefan Zweig's *The World of Yesterday*, where she sharply criticizes Zweig for idealizing a purely international world of cosmopolitan elites as a sufficient political and social construct. She saw this vision of one's place in the world as detached from reality, self-indulgent, and, ultimately, a form of snobbery.

What's significant about her critique is that it underscores her belief in the indispensable political character of membership in a community – the necessity of a framework of law, constitutionalism, and citizenship. Especially after coming to America, she saw citizenship as something that should be capable of being rationally and deliberately acquired rather than something one is simply born into. In principle, citizenship does not entail privilege or inherited status; it is a legal and political foundation of human equivalence, individual self-realization and freedom. Arendt recognizes that there is something hollow about the ideal of cosmopolitanism – something lacking in its concrete sense of belonging, a deficiency not present in the categories of nationality, race and ethnicity.

From a historical perspective, cosmopolitanism has taken on different connotations. One of its prominent negative associations has been its use to characterize European Jewry, whose members existed within communities defined, overwhelmingly by populations that shared a nativist national homogeneity. Over time, the term became an instrument of criticism and racial discrimination, and tied to a negative sense of influence of an elite defined by learning, cultural refinement, and aesthetic judgment. It suggested a kind of intellectual superiority that was politically unwelcome and an irritant. It's difficult, after all, to imagine an illiterate cosmopolitan.

I want to turn briefly to the idea of tribalism. This is a word I also struggle to understand.

In the American context, the term is familiar because of how we recount the history of indigenous populations. But if we consider the German language – thinking again of Arendt – the closest equivalent to tribe would probably be *Stamm*. Where would Arendt have encountered the idea of tribe? Likely through Roman sources – Tacitus, for instance, and his discussions of Germanic tribes. Another term related to tribe is clan, which, unlike a tribe, can be joined by oath rather than by birth – a key distinction.

There is also the biblical source: the twelve tribes of Israel, a notion Arendt would have been quite familiar with. In the eighteenth and nineteenth centuries, *Stamm* was commonly used in this sense – referring to the twelve tribes and also the ten lost tribes. But *Stamm* is a complex word. It also means trunk; it has biological connotations, which tribe in English does not. *Stamm* implies organic origins, like the trunk of a tree, and has multiple, layered meanings.

It also has religious significance. The term was used to describe the wood of the cross on which Christ was crucified. And if we look at the argument by the teacher of Karl Jaspers (Arendt's mentor), Max Weber, we encounter one of his key sociological distinctions. Judaism, unlike Christianity and Islam, is a tribal religion, not a universal one. It does not aspire to universal membership; conversion is possible but extremely difficult and often impermanent – unlike, for example, baptism, which some argue is indelible.

A tribe can also be defined by descent from a common origin, fitting neatly with the story of Abraham and his descendants. The Covenant is a tribal pact with loyalty to a single tribe, which then divides into many. Conveniently, ten of them are lost, but the fundamental idea in Judaism is that of a closed, religious community with an exclusive contract with the divine.

Cosmopolitanism, on the other hand, is rooted in a secular vision of an open universal social and political organization. What distinguishes cosmopolitanism – whatever it may mean – is that it allows for a politics that does not require prior religious allegiance or a biological basis for membership. In contrast, tribal identity depends more on a distinct social lineage. In German, the word *Stamm* serves as the foundation for later pseudo-scientific theories of race, shifting the focus from ancestry to blood purity. This transformation played a key role in nineteenth-century German racial thought.

Bettina Stangneth's *Eichmann Before Jerusalem* is a book published about ten years ago and presents a persuasive challenge to Arendt's characterization of Adolf Eichmann. Stangneth's argument is that Arendt had the right theory but the wrong person. The *Stassen Papers*, which surfaced from Argentina, revealed that Eichmann was in fact an ideologue and fanatic. Within the émigré Nazi community in Argentina, he was known as one of the most ideologically extreme. He believed in the purity of the Aryan race and the toxic nature of Jews. After the failed 1956 invasion of the Suez Canal by Israel, France, and Britain, he and his circle believed that the Arab world would finish the job they had failed to complete: the extermination of the Jewish people.

The Nazis justified the extermination by racial theory, as codified in the Nuremberg Laws, themselves based on primitive and scientifically false notions of blood purity. This was an invented science. Cosmopolitanism, as a political principle, demands no such biological foundation. Instead, it operates on the assumption that every human being is equal – an idea rooted more in Newtonian reasoning about our common biological structure as a species.

Tribal identity evolved from a historical concept of shared parentage, which might allow for racial mixing. Membership in a tribe did not necessarily rest on claims of purity, that, for example, both parents be of the same lineage or share the same physical traits. Tribal identity, then, is more complex than it might initially seem.

Personally, I am not sure we live in an age of tribes. I've never considered myself a member of one. This is, vis a vis Jewish identity, certainly a legacy of the nineteenth-century Reform movement in Judaism, which, among other things, liberalized conversion for those who were religiously inclined.

I'm not convinced we live in a world of tribes. One of the interesting things about tribal identity is its murky flexibility; it is often entirely invented. Many symbols and traditions we associate with apparently authentic tribalism, such as Scottish clan identities, were actually nineteenth-century creations. There is something conveniently archaic about the idea of a tribe, but at the same time it possesses something that cosmopolitanism lacks: an emotional, irrational but easy basis for attachment to others. This is what makes cosmopolitanism seem overly abstract. It lacks the immediate emotional plausibility that tribal membership offers. Tribal identity, even more than racial purity, is something one can feel intuitively through repetition and the use of markers and symbols.

In German, for example, a *Stammgast* is a regular at a restaurant or pub; the notion draws on the idea of belonging to a group, merely through habitual presence. This kind of communal dynamic does not emerge easily from the cosmopolitan ideal.

I want to sincerely thank the Hannah Arendt Center for forcing me to think about something I otherwise never would have. Reflecting on these differences has made me realize that the word 'tribe' in English may have different connotations and usages than *Stamm* in German. In German, *Stamm* has multiple uses and seems to have less of an archaic character than 'tribe' has in English.

I remain an advocate for the political implications of cosmopolitanism: the ability to acquire equal citizenship without reference to history, or origins of heritage. I also share its aspirations to empathetic understanding and to the cultivation of judgment, the life of the mind, the love of learning and the admiration of excellence. The hope that the values of cosmopolitanism can be integrated into a functioning politics explains Arendt's profound attachment to the potential, though not the reality, of American democratic politics.

"THE MANIFESTO OF ARENDTIAN COSMOPOLITANISM"

ANGELA TARABORRELLI

ANGELA TARABORRELLI is an Italian philosopher and scholar of political theory at Cagliari University, Italy. Her work focuses on cosmopolitanism, global ethics, and the ideas of Hannah Arendt. In this essay, Taraborrelli examines Arendt's belief in active citizenship, pluralism, and human dignity, advocating for a cosmopolitan ethic that balances cultural diversity with shared values and human rights. Taraborrelli aims to enlist Arendt for a cosmopolitan project, albeit one that sits uneasily with Arendt's suspicion of universalism.

As we saw, Arendt was criticized for having failed to explain the core meaning of the status of the right to have rights, as well as the practical value that such status should have, absent any specific institutional agency vested with acknowledged authority and a power to enforce it. Her silence on these matters allegedly exposed her to the very objections she leveled at both the French Declaration of the Rights of Man and of the Citizen (1789) and the contemporary attempts to outline a declaration of human rights. Actually, as we shall see, Arendt provides answers to both issues, from the meaning of the status to the effective protection of the right to have rights. Importantly, her answers are revealing of the extent to which cosmopolitanism is rooted in her thought.

The "Preface" to the first edition of *The Origins of Totalitarianism* ends with the following words:

> Antisemitism (not merely the hatred of Jews), imperialism (not merely conquest), totalitarianism (not merely dictatorship)-one after the other,

---

Excerpted from: Taraborrelli, Angela. 2024. *Hannah Arendt and Cosmopolitanism: State, Community, Worlds in Common*. Bloomsbury, 17–18.

one more brutally than the other, have demonstrated that human dignity needs a new guarantee which can be found only in a new political principle, in a new law on earth, whose validity this time must comprehend the whole of humanity while its power must remain strictly limited, rooted in and controlled by newly defined territorial entities.

I believe that these words should be read as a manifesto of Arendtian cosmopolitanism. In light of such manifesto – which is simultaneously a program-it is possible to engage in a reinterpretation and reconstruction of Arendt's thought as committed to protecting the dignity of humanity, rather than of the sole Jewish people. To this end, Arendt undertakes the search of a new political principle and a new law, valid for the whole of humanity, the power of which should be exercised and controlled by humanity itself by means of a new legal and political way of organizing the individuals and the peoples on Earth. This new organization should be structured upon a plurality of territorial units conceived of as alternative to the sovereign nation-state.

"BLACK COSMOPOLITANISM: MODERNITY, COSMOPOLITANISM, AND THE BLACK SUBJECT"

IFEOMA KIDDOE NWANKWO

IFEOMA KIDDOE NWANKWO is a scholar of African American and Caribbean literature and culture and Dean of the College of Liberal & Creative Arts at San Francisco State University. Her work highlights the global networks of Black intellectuals and cultural figures, revealing how they engaged with cosmopolitan ideals while navigating issues of race, identity, and colonialism. Nwankwo founded Voices from Our America, "an international digital & public humanities project integrating research, curriculum development, and community engagement.

Implicit in the Atlantic power structures' fear of violent uprising and designation of people of African descent as less than a whole (hu)man was the notion that they were primitive savages, that is to say, premodern barbarians. The perception of people of African descent as less than human and not worthy of being seen as equal to those of European descent operated in tandem with the construction of people of African descent as an antithesis of the modern. People of African descent's desire to be seen as equal was always already bound up with their desire to be seen as modern, so statements made in the public sphere were grasped firmly as opportunities to prove the individual's or the community's modernity. Cosmopolitanism, the definition of oneself through the world beyond one's own origins, was a crucial element of modernity (and the Enlightenment). Imperialism and Orientalism were in fact forms of European cosmopolitanism, and more specifically of the ways Europeans constructed their definitions of self and community in relation to and through their relationship to the broader world. Orientalism, as Edward Said explicated

---

Excerpted from: Nwankwo, Ifeoma Kiddoe. 2005. *Black Cosmopolitanism.* University of Pennsylvania Press, 9–14.

it, "is [...] a certain will or intention to understand, in some cases to control, manipulate, even to incorporate, what is a manifestly different (or alternative and novel) world." It should come as no surprise, then, that responses and resistance to these totalizing and hegemonic cosmopolitanisms also often employ cosmopolitanism as a conceptual frame. Immanuel Kant, for example, had a vision "of cosmopolitical culture as the promise of humanity's freedom from, or control over "the finitude of human existence." Karl Marx also posited a utopian cosmopolitanism, through which the proletariat would cast off loyalty to the nation and its economy in favor of the creation of "a universal class transcending boundaries." As part of this historical and ideological context, people of African descent in the nineteenth century evaluated the usefulness of cosmopolitanism for their struggle to be recognized as human and equal.

People of African descent's approaches to public self-representation were born, in significant part, of the Atlantic power structure's attempts to deny them access to cosmopolitan subjectivity. The White fear that arose in the wake of the Haitian Revolution was not only a fear of violence, but also a fear of people of African descent's embrace of cosmopolitanism – of their defining themselves through a Black world that included the Haitians. This denial of access for people of African descent to cosmopolitan subjectivity coexisted with a denial of access for that same population to both national subjectivity and human subjectivity, and, perhaps most significantly, with an emphasis (from above) on their race, effectively determining the possible parameters of identity for people of African descent. The result was a uniquely tenuous situation. Race, nation, and humanity were three major referents through which individuals defined themselves and others in their world (the Atlantic world), but only one of the three referents was allowed people of African descent: race. Consequently, this population essentially had to prioritize, and choose which of the parameters denied them they most wished to challenge, and by extension which referent they most wanted to have the right to claim.

The modes of self-definition I describe collectively as "Black cosmopolitanism" were, consequently, born in this period. The term is not meant to indicate that people who were already "Black" became cosmopolitan, or that cosmopolitanism was a corrective alternative to Blackness, but rather that Blackness and cosmopolitanism became two pivotal axes of identity in relation to which public people of African descent defined themselves.

The Blackness of Black cosmopolitanism inheres not in the race of the individuals who express it (as illustrated by the fact that analyses of Cuban government documents and White abolitionist writings are key subjects in this study)," but rather in the ways individuals and entities seek to define people of African descent and articulate the relationship among them and between them and the world at large. Faced with dehumanization and the Atlantic power structures' obsession with preventing the blossoming of their cosmopolitanism, people of African descent decided to stake their claim to personhood by defining themselves in relation to the new notions of "Black community" and ubiquitous manifestations of cosmopolitanism that the Revolution produced. The fear created by the Haitian Revolution forced these individuals to take a position on both Blackness and cosmopolitanism whether or not they wished to do so. At the same time, they were forced to work through and with the three aforementioned referents: race, nation, and humanity.

In both its emphasis on engagements with an Enlightenment approach to self-definition (cosmopolitanism) and its allowing for the possibility of racial disidentification, this notion differs significantly from Pan-Africanism. Central to Pan-Africanism as understood by Pan-Africanist leaders and scholars then and now is political action that seeks to ameliorate the lives of all people of African descent everywhere. Consequently, I do not use the term to describe the writing or ideology of most of the writers I engage. I call attention instead to the complexity of their perceptions of and relation-ships with people of African descent from other places. Instead of taking pan-Africanism as a given or as a broad spectrum term that can be applied to all texts that treat the experiences of people of African descent in different locations, I choose to move more methodically by analyzing the method, ideology, and implications of those treatments.

The term transnationalism is also inadequate for indexing the complicated approaches to defining self, community, and other I uncover here. Although useful for referring to general physical or ideological movements across national boundaries its usefulness for describing how and why such movements drive or constitute arguments with dominant nineteenth-century discourses about civilization versus barbarism (and, in particular, people of African descent's barbarism) as well as about appropriate bases for identity is limited. In addition, it foregrounds geographical-national boundaries and presumes them to be salient, which is not a viewpoint put forth by a number of the individuals and ideologies engaged in this study. The term cosmopolitanism allows for attentiveness to a range of modes of defining oneself and one's community in relation to the world.

Cosmopolitanism is not posited here, however, as a race-less panacea that serves as a counterpoint to an essential or essentializing notion of Blackness, but rather as one of the master's tools (Blackness being another) that people of African descent tested for its possible usefulness in attempting to at least get into the master's house, if not to destroy it. The goal is to explicate the stance toward cosmopolitanism and Blackness taken by individuals occupying a range of geographical and identificatory positions, rather than to attach a particular value judgment to any of them. Because of the Haitian Revolution, the constitution and articulation of "Blackness" at this moment was always already bound up with a decision about whether or not to espouse cosmopolitanism. In investigating the ways in which a range of thinkers of African descent negotiated between the two and came to vastly different conclusions about how to best locate themselves, this study simultaneously interrogates the notion that cosmopolitanism was an unproblematic and always desirable alternative and reveals the mechanisms by which Black identity and community were imagined.

Black cosmopolitanism therefore does not simply complicate, but also often undercuts traditional understandings of cosmopolitanism. The cosmopolite is typically understood as a "citizen of the world," whose relationship to a specific nation is distant if it exists at all. In Mihai Grunfeld's discussion of cosmopolitanism, for example, he describes the cosmopolite as "un ciudadano universal, una persona que considera el universo como patria suya" ("a citizen of the universe, a person who considers the universe as his nation"). Grunfeld presents cosmopolitanism in opposition to national identification-a conceptualization frequently replicated throughout the scholarly discourse on cosmopolitanism This binary is insufficient for interpreting the relationship between cosmopolitan subjectivity and national affinity for people of African descent in the nineteenth century. It cannot take into account the power dynamics that produce or prevent the production of the cosmopolite, and more specifically the ways in which the Atlantic power structures' denial of humanity, cosmopolitanism, and national citizenship to people of African descent, their obsessive fear of their cosmopolitanism, and their obsessive focus on defining them racially, and people of African descent's own desire to be recognized as equal interacted to produce distinctively configured approaches to engaging the world and representing the self.

The person of African descent's citizenship in his or her specific nation of residence has been denied, negated, and generally troubled. Positing national identity and cosmopolitan subjectivity as polar opposites presumes that national identity is available to all individuals. Our understanding of cosmopolitanism must consider that, for some (people of African descent in this case) national identity may be desired but inaccessible, and consequently that cosmopolitanism, while not necessarily the object of desire, may be conceptualized as a means to the end of gaining access to national identity (as it is for Frederick Douglass) and/or as the basis of a substitute national identity in itself (as it is for Martin Delany). In addition, that substitute national identity may include people in places they have never visited, and with whom they have never had contact, because the connection they imagine is based on the common experiences of slavery and dis-crimination and African heritage, rather than shared terrain or face to face encounters.

As a result, the questions whether the person of African descent in the Americas conceptualizes him-or herself as a citizen of a specific nation or of the Black world, or how she or he claims citizenship in both, demand answers that go beyond positing cosmopolitanism and national affinity as two sides of a neat binary. The dynamic interaction between the two, and the push/pull forces that have pushed the person away from cosmopolitanism, national identity, and humanity and toward race have produced his or her approach to self-representation. Black cosmopolitanism is born of the interstices and intersections between two mutually constitutive cosmopolitanisms: a hegemonic cosmopolitanism, exemplified by the material and psychological violence of imperialism and slavery (including dehumanization), and a cosmopolitanism that is rooted in a common knowledge and memory of that violence. The violence may remain unacknowledged, but is nevertheless the basis of the desire exhibited by public figures of African descent to imagine or reject a connection with people of African descent in other sites or with the world at large. The desire to be recognized as an agent is interwoven with the desire to be a citizen, and both desires determine both individual identity and textual and ideological engagements with people of African descent in other sites.

Contemporary and historical definitions of the cosmopolite characterize (and gender) him or her as one who loves to travel. As scholars such as Melvin Dixon have pointed out, Black people's relationship to travel and movement is inherently fraught because of the way in which they were brought to the Americas. People of African descent did not "travel" to the Americas, inasmuch as travel implies leisure and volition. They were forcibly brought as commodities. Given this history, one of the pivotal questions of this study is whether a slave can "travel," define himself/herself through the places to which s/he travels, and by extension be considered cosmopolitan. Slavery sought to control the movements of people of African descent (both free and slave). This effort was quite often in vain. People of African descent found ways to move between physical and/or geographical sites. They also, as is evident in the texts interpreted here, moved conceptually between sites as they constructed their ideologies and identities. Those conceptual movements, whether manifested through an explicit bonding with people of African descent in other sites as in Martin Delany's Blake; Or, the Huts of America (1861–62) or through the dedication of a Romantic poem to Poland as in Plácido's poem "A Polonia" took place in the service of eking out a space for subjectivity--a space wherein an individual or a community could be recognized as human and as equal to those at the top of the Atlantic world.

Traditional understandings of the cosmopolite assume that the person has the means to travel, reflecting the inherently classed nature of cosmopolitanism as most often articulated. Inderpal Grewal has hinted at this issue in her discussion of the classed nature of the terms immigrant and exile. Those with education and means are exiles. Everyone else is denigrated and designated an immigrant. Similarly cosmopolitan is reserved for those at the top, and everyone else is viewed as comfortably provincial. Black Cosmopolitanism traces the dialectics of a cosmopolitanism from below. It is one that came of age at the same time that the forces of hegemonic cosmopolitanism in the Atlantic world (cosmopolitanism from above) were forced to reconfigure themselves to deal with the new threats posed by the uprising in Haiti.

It is worth noting, however, that the drive to be acknowledged as equal ensures that not all those who display Black cosmopolitanism have a desire to travel, whether materially or conceptually, in terms of the definition of self or community. In fact, even the individuals who seem to travel the most simultaneously exhibit a certain resistance to doing so. This irony inheres both in hegemonic forms of cosmopolitanism (as Said's aforementioned comment on Orientalism suggests) and in "cosmopolitanism from below" because the latter, although resistant, is fundamentally concerned with proving a group or individual an equal member of the societies that produced the hegemonic forms. In fact, in people of African descent's published demands for citizenship, cosmopolitanism is often viewed both as an obstacle to the achievement of that goal and as the quality that proves that the individual or group is worthy of citizenship. The case of ex-slave Frederick Douglass who became U.S. consul to Haiti shows this conundrum especially clearly. Douglass and other U.S. Black writers are one part of a continent-wide discourse inspired by the revolution in Haiti on the question of how people of African descent should locate their own subjectivities in relation to each other and the broader Atlantic world.

1 CORINTHIANS 1:10–17: 'A CHURCH UNDIVIDED'

KING JAMES BIBLE

THE KING JAMES BIBLE was commissioned by King James I of England in 1604 and published in 1611. This passage speaks to the tension between unity and division within the Christian community, where the Apostle Paul calls believers to rise above factionalism and find common ground in their shared faith. He urges them to look beyond human leaders, reminding them that their true unity is rooted in Christ, who binds the community together across social and cultural divides.

---

10 I appeal to you, brothers and sisters, in the name of our Lord Jesus Christ, that all of you agree with one another in what you say and that there be no divisions among you, but that you be perfectly united in mind and thought. **11** My brothers and sisters, some from Chloe's household have informed me that there are quarrels among you.

12 What I mean is this: One of you says, "I follow Paul"; another, "I follow Apollos"; another, "I follow Cephas"; still another, "I follow Christ." **13** Is Christ divided? Was Paul crucified for you? Were you baptized in the name of Paul? **14** I thank God that I did not baptize any of you except Crispus and Gaius, **15** so no one can say that you were baptized in my name. **16** (Yes, I also baptized the household of Stephanas; beyond that, I don't remember if I baptized anyone else.)

17 For Christ did not send me to baptize, but to preach the gospel – not with wisdom and eloquence, lest the cross of Christ be emptied of its power.

"WHAT ARE THE CONSEQUENCES FOR US OF BEING RELATED TO GOD?"

EPICTETUS

EPICTETUS was born in 50 AD in Hierapolis (modern-day Turkey). Epictetus was a Roman Stoic philosopher who emphasized self-discipline, rational thought, and moral responsibility as the foundation for ethical living in a cosmopolitan world.

---

[1] If what philosophers say about the kinship of God and man is true, then the only logical step is to do as Socrates did, never replying to the question of where he was from with, 'I am Athenian,' or 'I am from Corinth,' but always, 'I am a citizen of the world.' **[2]** After all, why say, 'I am Athenian'? Why not just identify yourself with the exact spot your sorry body was dropped at birth? **[3]** Clearly, you prefer the higher designation because it not only includes that insignificant spot, it also includes your parents and all your ancestors before you; and it's on these grounds that you characterize yourself as Athenian or Corinthian.

[4] But anyone who knows how the whole universe is administered knows that the first, all-inclusive state is the government composed of God and man. He appreciates it as the source of the seeds of being, descending upon his father, his father's father – to every creature born and bred on earth, in fact, but to rational beings in particular, **[5]** since they alone are entitled by nature to govern alongside God, by virtue of being connected with him through reason. **[6]** So why not call ourselves citizens of the world and children of God? And why should we fear any human contingency?

Excerpted from: Epictetus. 2008. *Discourses* and Selected Writings. Edited by Robert Dobbin. Penguin Classics, book 1, chapter 9.

[7] If being related to the emperor or any of the other great ones at Rome is enough to live without fear, in privilege and security, shouldn't having God as our creator, father and defender protect us even more from trouble and anxiety?

[8] 'But how am I supposed to eat, if I am destitute?' someone says.

Well, what about slaves, what about runaways – what do they depend on when they flee their masters? On their lands, their servants and their silver plate? Hardly; they rely on themselves, and still manage to survive. **[9]** So is our philosopher citizen-of-the-world going to rest his confidence in others wherever he lives or travels, rather than depend on himself? Is he going to be even lower and more servile than irrational wild beasts, all of whom are self-sufficient, provided with food and a mode of survival adapted to and in harmony with their nature?

[10] Personally I think that, as I am older than you, I shouldn't have to sit here trying my best to keep you from thinking small, or having mean and humble thoughts about you. **[11]** On the contrary, if there are young men among you who know of their kinship with the gods, and know that we have these chains fastened upon us – the body, possessions and whatever is required for our biological support and sustenance – I should be discouraging them from the wish to shed all these things as so many chains and return to their kind.

[12] That's the effort that should absorb your teacher and mentor, if he really were one. And you for your part would come to him saying, 'Epictetus, we can no longer stand being tied to this hateful body, giving it food and drink, resting it and cleaning it, and having to associate with all manner of uncongenial people for its sake. **[13]** Such things are indifferent, are they not, and as nothing to us; and death no evil thing? Aren't we akin to God, having come from him? **[14]** Let us go home, then, to be free, finally, from the shackles that restrain us and weigh us down. **[15]** Here we find robbers and thieves, and law-courts, and so-called despots who imagine that they wield some power over us precisely because of our body and its possessions. Allow us to show them that they have power over precisely no one.'

[16] Then it would be my turn to say, 'Friends, wait upon God. Whenever he gives the sign and releases you from service, then you are free to return. But for now agree to remain in the place where you've been stationed. **[17]** Your time here is short enough, and easy to endure for people of your convictions. No despot, thief or court of law can intimidate people who set little store by the body and its appurtenances. So stay, don't depart without good reason.'

[18] That is the kind of advice that should pass between a teacher and an idealistic youth. **[19]** But what's the reality? You – and your teacher – are no better than carcasses. No sooner have you eaten your fill today than you sit and start worrying about where tomorrow's food will come from. **[20]** Look, if you get it, then you will have it; if not, you will depart this life: the door is open. Why complain? What place is there left for tears? What occasion for flattery? Why should one man envy another? Why should he admire those who have many possessions, or those who are strong in power and quick to anger? **[21]** What can they do to us, or for us, after all? The things they have power to do are of no interest to us; and as for the things we do care about, these they are powerless to affect. No one with convictions of this kind can be made to act against their will.

[22] So how did Socrates stand in this regard? Exactly how one would expect of someone who perceived keenly his kinship with the gods. **[23]** 'If you were to say to me now, "We will release you on these conditions, that you no longer engage in these dialogues that you have been engaging in up to now, and won't give any more trouble to anyone young or old," **[24]** I will answer that it is absurd to suppose that, if a general of yours stationed me at a post, I would have to maintain and defend it, choosing to die a thousand times rather than quit, but if God has assigned us a post with a set of duties, we might decide to abandon that.'

[25] There you have a man who was a genuine kinsman of the gods. **[26]** But we, on the other hand, identify with our stomachs, guts and genitals. Because we are still vulnerable to fear and desire, we flatter and creep before anyone with the power to hurt us where any of those things are concerned.

[27] A man once asked me to write to Rome for him because he had met with what most people consider misfortune. He had once been rich and famous but later lost everything, and was living here in Nicopolis. So I wrote a letter on his behalf in a deferential tone.
[28] When he had read the letter he handed it back to me, saying, 'I wanted your help, not your pity; nothing really bad has happened to me.'

[29] Similarly, Musonius used to test me by saying, 'Your master is going to afflict you with some hardship or other.' **[30]** And when I would answer, 'Such is life,' he would say, 'Should I still intercede with him when I can get the same things from you?' **[31]** For in fact it is silly and pointless to try to get from another person what one can get for oneself. **[32]** Since I can get greatness of soul and nobility from myself, why should I look to get a farm, or money, or some office, from you? I will not be so insensible of what I already own.

[33] For men who are meek and cowardly, though, there is no option but to write letters for them as if they were already dead. 'Please grant us the body of so-and-so together with his meagre ration of blood.' **[34]** For, really, such a person amounts to no more than a carcass and a little blood. If he were anything more, he would realize that no one is ever unhappy because of someone else.

TRIBALISM

"TRIBALISM AND THE HUMAN CONDITION"

SEBASTIAN JUNGER
(WITH ROGER BERKOWITZ)

Let me say this upfront: I'm an unabashed lifelong liberal, and I hope to offer a critique of how liberals attempt to combat negative tribalism. I believe the issue of negative tribalism – while there are, of course, positive aspects to tribalism – is, if you want to be blunt, just another name for fascism. It is the defining struggle of our generation and, quite possibly, of human history for as long as we exist. It will always be a battle.

My father was a refugee three times over, born in Dresden in 1923. His father was Jewish. They fled in 1933 to Spain, only to leave three years later when the Fascists, under Franco, took power. They went to France – where history took its well-known turn – then moved to Portugal, a neutral country, and eventually to the United States. He stayed here because, as he put it, 'fascism would never follow him to these shores'. I still believe that to be true.

I often say that because of the fascists, my father spoke five languages fluently – they chased him across Europe for his entire youth. He knew firsthand what negative tribalism looked like.

My own experience as an American was entirely different. I was lucky to see the positive aspects of tribalism. As a war reporter, I found myself in Sierra Leone in 1998, during the civil war. I was in the small town of Kenema, which was about to be attacked by the RUF, a brutal rebel group known for committing unspeakable atrocities. They had just overrun a UN base and were advancing toward Kenema. I remember the terrifying hours and days leading up to it – people gathering in the streets in a panic, women shouting at the men: 'Go out and defend us! That's your job. Fight. Stop the RUF from taking the town'. And they did. The men grabbed whatever weapons they could – cutlasses, shotguns, old hunting rifles, a couple of rusty AK-47s – and managed to hold Kenema.

Years later, during Hurricane Sandy in New York City, the power went out from 34th Street down. A powerless New York at night is a frightening place. My wife, Barbara, and I lived in the Lower East Side at the time, where we now live with our daughters, in a tenement building in a mixed-race, mixed-language, mostly Spanish-speaking neighborhood. When the lights stayed out for a week, people in the building – many of them poor – were afraid of break-ins. It's a rough area. So what happened? One of the mothers found a machete and organized a rotating guard of young men she knew. They took turns standing watch at the front door with the machete until the power returned.

One striking thing about this, beyond the deep loyalty people have to their own, is that we need to acknowledge something: women are absolutely capable of violence when circumstances demand it. Let's not pretend that one sex is violent and the other is not. Women are far too practical to ignore that reality. Often, they delegate violence to men, but they are fully capable of considering it when necessary.

Finally, I spent time embedded with an American airborne unit in eastern Afghanistan, in an area of heavy combat and high casualties. I was with a platoon – upwards of fifty men, all male because it was a combat infantry unit – at a small outpost called Restrepo. One of the soldiers said something to me I'll never forget: 'You know what's amazing? There are guys in the platoon who straight-up hate each other, but we would all die for each other'.

That is positive tribalism. It's the transcendent feeling that I do not matter – my group matters, and I will do anything for it. Understand that we are the only species that thinks this way. Our closest mammalian relatives, chimpanzees, do not. We are the only species where a young male will willingly die for a same-sex peer he's not related to, simply because they are part of the same group. It is a profound form of love. It helped me understand something.

I wrote a book called *Tribe*, and it took me years to define the word. Then, not too long ago, it came to me. A tribe is this idea: What happens to you, happens to me. If you're hungry, I'm hungry with you. If you're in danger, I'm in danger with you. We will get through this together, or we will perish together.

That's the positive side of tribalism. One of the most intoxicating experiences a human being can have is that feeling of deep belonging.

It's on par with romantic love in its intensity and sense of transcendence – except instead of being with just one person, it's with an entire group.

No society can survive if it cannot defend itself. Just ask the people of Ukraine. What sustains them right now in their fight against – let's be clear – fascism, in Putin's military incursion into their country, is a sense of unity. We are Ukrainian. We are defending our families, our homes, our land, our traditions, our history, our values.

Reason alone cannot do that. Reason is an incredible tool for understanding how the world works. But emotions – fear, anger, love, envy – are what actually move us to act. Reason will never carry the day against emotion. If you doubt that, think back to a time when you tried using calm, dispassionate logic with an upset lover, sibling, or child. It doesn't work. Emotion wins.

So, what I want to explore is: How do we tap into the positive emotions of tribal responsibility? Can we elevate the idea that what happens to you, happens to me? Can we scale that up – from small human groups, which have defined our history as a species, to a town, a nation, even to all of humanity?

That remains to be seen. But make no mistake: if it scales, it will scale through emotion, not reason. Reason is for things.

I'm going to speak briefly about our human origins. I'm an anthropologist by training. The hard sciences and social sciences are infamous for challenging political pieties and cherished cultural ideals, but this issue – fascism, equality, and fairness in society – is too important for anything but an honest and clear discussion. That's what I intend to do. If it makes anyone uncomfortable or even offends them, that might just be part of the process of confronting these issues.

For most of human history, we lived in groups of 30 to 50 people, intensely loyal to one another. These groups were survival units. Humans were largely patrilocal, meaning that women moved into the man's community and family. This had a major advantage: it kept blood kin together as a fighting group, which was crucial for survival. You would almost certainly die for your brother or sister, but maybe not for your brother-in-law from another community. Keeping male kin together helped ensure the physical safety of the group.

These early human societies, much like present-day hunter-gatherer communities, were remarkably egalitarian. The Hadza, one of the last hunter-gathering societies in the world, have been well studied. Their Gini coefficient – a measure of income inequality – is about 0.25. A score of zero means everyone has exactly the same, which isn't ideal. A score of one means one person has everything while no one else has anything, which is obviously catastrophic. A coefficient of 0.25 is often considered a sweet spot for human society. By comparison, the US has a post-tax Gini coefficient of 0.4 – roughly equivalent to the Roman Empire. Before taxes, it rises to 0.6, on par with highly corrupt countries like Haiti and Botswana. This will be important in a moment.

And finally, these kinds of early human societies, hunter-gatherer societies, are enormously appealing when they exist alongside the modern world, as they occasionally have throughout history. Typically, the struggle for 'civilized' societies has been to keep individuals from fleeing – fleeing – into tribal communities. The closeness and cohesion of those societies have been incredibly compelling. Many historians believe that the Great Wall of China was built as much to keep Chinese peasants in as it was to keep the Mongols out. Likewise, along the American frontier, colonists and farmers were frequently absconding into the wilderness to join tribal societies. According to contemporaries of that era, it never happened in reverse.

So, here's a final point about early human societies, which is fascinating: all human societies are divided almost exactly fifty/fifty between conservative and liberal political beliefs. Conservatism is typified by skepticism, distrust, or even animosity toward strangers, an extreme protectiveness, and a strong investment in hierarchy, sanctity, and purity. Liberals, by contrast, are less concerned with external threats and more focused on internal threats – issues like injustice, unfairness, and income disparities. If the gap between rich and poor becomes too great, it destabilizes the group. And if the group fractures, everyone is at risk.

Studies of identical versus fraternal twins raised separately have found that forty to sixty percent of the variation in political belief – whether someone leans conservative or liberal – is genetically determined. Think about that. Our political beliefs are partially derived from our genetics.

That makes perfect sense. A society without at least some people focused on external threats won't last long – it will be overrun. At the same time, a society that neglects internal ideals of fairness and justice will fracture and fail. The idea that these two basic survival strategies have a genetic component suggests they were adaptive, encoded in our chromosomes over time. We are the product of earlier humans who evolved these strategies to protect themselves – not just from external enemies but also from their own worst impulses within their communities. If you're skeptical, I highly recommend Our Political Nature by Avi Tuschman, which explores this fascinating phenomenon in depth.

Now, what does this mean for our current political climate? If a conservative says to liberals, 'You're wrong, you're immoral, and you don't deserve to exist', they are mistaken – at least in evolutionary and Darwinian terms. The same goes for liberals who say the same about conservatives. We are wrong. And I say we because I am liberal myself, and I assume most people in this room are as well.

Here's the grim reality: in evolutionary, biological, and genetic terms, it is the liberals of any society – the genetic and cultural liberals – who are responsible for advocating and ensuring fairness and justice within the community, rather than focusing on defense. You can see this in the military, where conservatives tend to dominate. I've spent time with the military, and even among the younger recruits, they lean conservative; it's simply an unavoidable truth. Likewise, those involved in social justice movements trend liberal. That's how evolution has shaped us. It's how the human race is designed to function, and, when allowed to work as intended, it functions quite well.

But here's the problem for us in America right now: The left is charged with advocating fairness and justice and preventing this country from fracturing along tribal lines. Culturally and even genetically, that responsibility falls on us. And we are failing – not just in results but by our own standards.

In my lifetime, the political left in this country has become more and more of an elite institution. We have completely lost the blue-collar working-class vote – not just among white workers but among people of color as well. We have given that voting bloc up to conservatives, who, of course, were more than happy to take them in.

The conversation we refuse to have is about class. Liberals will talk about gender – great, incredibly important. Race – absolutely, crucial to running a fair society. Diversity in many forms – again, essential. But class? We won't touch it. And that is a tragedy.

A high Gini coefficient – a measure of income inequality – is a well-documented predictor of civil unrest, violence, and the erosion of democratic ideals. It has preceded these outcomes time and again. So when we refuse to have a real conversation about class, we are dooming this country to a catastrophic split.

And I'm going to say something uncomfortable, but I think – and I hope – we all recognize it as true. I completely understand the concept of white privilege and white male privilege. I get it. Probably everyone in this room does. But let's be honest: A young white man in Kentucky, working a blue-collar job, maybe in the coal mines – does he, in any real sense, have the political clout, the economic resources, or the cultural influence of a person of color earning a law degree from Princeton? He just doesn't.

Is that the only conversation we should be having? Of course not. But it's one of the conversations we must have. Because if we don't, we lose that young man in Kentucky. And most recently, we lost him to someone named Donald Trump.

We need to have that conversation.

Another way we have abdicated our responsibility is by completely abandoning the idea of patriotism and love of country. We have surrendered those noble words, those noble ideals, to conservatives – who have twisted them beyond recognition. We walked away.

I am fully aware of this country's flaws, its tragedies, and the crimes in its history. As a journalist, I've spent part of my career writing about them. I don't need to be schooled on that, and I doubt anyone in this room does. But let's not forget that we fought our bloodiest war – a civil war – to end slavery. Hundreds of thousands of young white men died to bring slavery to an end in this country. And we did it again in World War II to stop fascism, as my father never let me forget.

I remember the day I received my Selective Service card in the mail. I grew up during Vietnam, the draft, all of it. And my reaction was: 'What the hell is this? The government wants to know where I live so they can draft me if they need me? I'm not signing this'. But my father – an implacable pacifist – insisted. 'No', he said, 'you are signing that'. He told me, 'If a war is immoral, it's your moral duty to protest it, to go to jail if necessary. But you don't know what the future holds. You may have to fight fascism again. And if that happens, you may owe your country your life. I hope not – but you do owe your country something. So you're signing that card'. And suddenly, I felt an enormous sense of pride in doing so.

This country was among the first to establish suffrage, women's rights, labor rights, civil rights. If you think we owe our country nothing, ask the Ukrainians how they feel about that idea. See what they say.

When we, as a political force, walk away from these powerful ideas – when we leave them to people who use them irresponsibly – we send a message: 'We want unity, but we can't actually offer you a compelling, emotional reason to believe in this place'. And when you fail to provide people with positive reasons to believe in their country, you leave them vulnerable to the negative tribalism that has taken hold of this nation in the last decade. That is the cost of our abdication.

Now, my final point is about the liberal love affair with technology, particularly with smartphones. Smartphones go against everything we stand for. They are a known addiction. The data are clear. They threaten the mental and physical well-being of our young people. Anxiety, depression, suicide, suicide attempts – these have all skyrocketed since the rise of these infernal devices. And, of course, their algorithms fuel partisan hate and division, feeding us only the truths we prefer to believe.

One of the saddest things I've ever seen was during Barack Obama's final speech as president. I believe it was New Year's Eve in Chicago, a massive auditorium packed with thousands of adoring supporters. Near the end of his speech, he said, 'And may we all, in the new year, spend less time on our phones'. The crowd erupted in cheers – while holding up their phones to record the moment.

That is the irony. That is the hypocrisy. That is the tragedy of the state of liberal thought in this country today. But if we can confront those three things – our abandonment of class, of patriotism, and of our addiction to technology – I believe we can begin to heal this country.

ROGER BERKOWITZ [RB]: Thank you, Sebastian; that was fantastic and inspiring. I want to start with some of the points you made at the end, as they are deeply meaningful. You mentioned that, as a liberal, we have walked away from an emotional reason to believe in this country and in tribes. I'd like to understand what you mean by liberal and what an emotional reason is that liberals can embrace to believe in this country.

SJ: I'm inspired by Dr. Martin Luther King, which is why I love this country and what it's capable of at its best. I'm willing to serve this country, even if it means sacrificing my life to preserve it. That's a positive emotional appeal, not an abstract intellectual one.

I'm not saying everything needs to be emotional, but the decision to stop focusing on working-class voters has led to the demographic collapse of the Democratic Party. We're in a tight race against someone who, frankly, is a fascist. I understand his appeal to some, but it shouldn't be this close. If we had the support of working-class people across the country, if we truly listened to them and respected them from our elite institutions, it wouldn't even be close. But it is. And that's on us. We can demonize the GOP all we want, but ultimately, it's our responsibility that we've reached this terrible impasse.

RB: One of the things that struck me when I read your book, *Tribe*, was how you connected the mental health epidemic to a liberal civilization that doesn't embrace the concept of tribe. You cite Benjamin Franklin and other contemporary observers who noted how it was the colonists who joined Native American tribes, not the other way around. On college campuses today, there's a clear epidemic of depression and anxiety, especially among young people. There's a missing sense of tribalism in our lives. How do you address this in your life and the lives of your friends? How can we make our lives more tribal in a way that won't harm us?

SJ: First, I must reiterate that the alienating effects of excessive phone use are devastating to our sense of belonging. It's particularly harmful for young women, especially teenage girls. As a father of two girls, I'm deeply concerned about this. We don't allow our daughters any devices any more than we would buy them cigarettes. The average teenage girl spends forty hours a week on her phone – there's no way they'll experience tribe in any positive sense with so much time spent on something as ephemeral as looking at pixels on a screen.

To heal society, we need a few things: first, sensible safeguards against the toxic effects of cell phone technology, especially on young people. We need to protect them. I also think mandatory national service could be an enormous blessing. It could break down class, race, education, and political divides. The military is great at putting people together from all backgrounds. Whether you like it or not, you get to know your brothers and sisters across the country, and that leads to a sense of unity. These two measures could do a lot of good.

On the individual level, I'll send it back to you: How can we, as individuals, feel part of something greater than ourselves? This is a vast, mechanized country, and we are small individuals. How can we feel connected? There are three ways:

I almost died from blood loss four years ago. I needed ten units of blood to survive. I came within minutes of dying, but I survived because ten strangers donated their blood. Now my daughters still have a father. Donate blood – it will save someone who's loved by many people, and it may one day save you or your child. You'll feel part of something greater than yourself, which is one of the most powerful human experiences.

Serve on a jury. Don't come up with excuses for why you're too busy. Jury duty protects us against tyranny. It ensures that no one person, whether a sheriff, a judge, or a president, can decide the fate of another. If you've never served, you won't deserve a jury, but you'll get one anyway.

And finally, vote. It's wonderful to vote on policy, but we're not in that place anymore. Vote for the person who will unite this country rather than tear it apart. For the foreseeable future, that will be the deciding factor for me, not their policies, but their character. Are they approaching their role with love, courage, and benevolence, or with selfishness, callousness, and nihilism?

RB: I love what you said about jury duty. I've never been able to get on a jury, especially when I tell them I study jury nullification; they don't seem to like that. But one of my favorite thinkers, Alexis de Tocqueville, said that the most important institution in American democracy is the jury. He argued that the jury teaches a small group of people to set aside their personal ideas of justice, elevate their opinions, and decide what is right or wrong. It trains them to think from the public perspective rather than the private one.

Many of us who can avoid jury duty because we think we're too important or too busy don't realize how critical it is. At the Arendt Center, we're involved in a movement called citizen assemblies, or civic juries, where we bring randomly selected groups together to discuss issues for days or weeks to elevate the conversation. It's about creating a sense of belonging and restoring tribal nature. Civic virtue, the idea of Americans gathering in town hall meetings to participate, has really declined. I think that ties into your point about jury duty. We need to figure out how to bring that back into our daily lives.

SJ: You can still find these things in surprising places. I read a great column by David French, a columnist for the New York Times, who started out as a Republican but became a fierce critic of Donald Trump and the Republican apologists for him. As a result, he started receiving death threats. At one point, the police sent a cruiser to guard his family, and he spoke with a young officer. The officer said, 'What did you do to deserve this?' David explained that he had criticized Trump in an article. The officer replied, 'I vote Republican, and I'll keep voting that way, but how about this? You keep writing those articles, and I'll keep protecting you.' That's the kind of spirit we need – finding common ground despite differences. What about cultural exchange programs for young people between red states and blue states, or between red and blue communities? Imagine teenagers spending a summer living with a family from the opposite political side. That could make a real difference. This is a generational issue; it's not going to change overnight or even in a few years. It might take a generation, but if we don't start now, it will never change.

RB: I want to ask one last question before we open it up. I really loved your new definition of tribe today – 'What happens to you happens to me. If you're in danger, I'm in danger'. You mentioned it as an intoxicating experience. Where have you felt that kind of experience?

SJ: The first time I experienced that feeling was, of course, with my family. If you have children, it arises naturally, almost uncontrollably, if you're psychologically healthy. But I first experienced it with same-sex peers, which is different. Evolutionarily, it makes sense to risk your life to protect your offspring because you're protecting your genetic investment in the next generation. It even makes sense to protect your mate. But it makes no sense, at least in Darwinian terms, to die protecting a same-sex peer who won't pass on your genes. Yet, we do it – humans are the only species that does. Even chimpanzees don't do that. It's one of the things that makes us extraordinary and capable of thriving in a threatening world.

I first experienced it in combat with American forces. I wasn't carrying a rifle; I was carrying a video camera. I spent about a year with them, and over time, I became part of the platoon, emotionally and psychologically. There was zero objectivity about what they were doing, but I wasn't looking for objectivity about the war. I was seeking to understand the subjective experience of being a soldier.

That feeling of loyalty to the group, once you feel it, is almost like a riptide pulling you away from the familiar shore into unknown waters – and you realize, 'This is okay. I'm fine out here'. It happens very quickly, and it was reciprocated by the platoon members toward me and my colleague, Tim Hetherington.

There are downsides to this loyalty. If something happens to any of your brothers or sisters, you immediately and forever feel responsible, no matter the circumstances. Tim was killed in Libya, during the civil war, on an assignment I was supposed to be on. He was hit by shrapnel from a mortar fired by Gaddafi's forces outside Misrata. He bled out 6,000 miles from New York. I had nothing to do with it, but when I found out, I felt overwhelming guilt and shame – it should have been me, I wasn't there to protect him. That's a reaction I don't think I'll ever fully recover from. This is the downside of this profound love – there's no other word for it – this profound love that can be felt within a group.

Q1: I want to repeat your argument and ask a question. Please feel free to correct me if I'm wrong or answer the question directly. As I understand it, you're saying that liberals are responsible for maintaining internal coherence in society, while conservatives are tasked with protecting against external threats. One of the problems with liberals in the US is that they've failed to activate the tribal energies needed to hold the society together. My question is: if liberals did activate these energies and became a stronger tribe, why wouldn't that just turn against conservatives? Wouldn't it lead to further fragmentation instead of helping to hold society together?

SJ: That's a great question, and maybe I wasn't clear earlier. When I talk about activating tribal loyalty, I don't mean loyalty to liberals; I mean loyalty to the country. One way that liberals could do this is by embracing the concerns of working-class conservatives. They could say, 'You're an

American too. What happens to you happens to me, and we'll address your economic concerns, even though you vote against us. We will, because we believe in this country'. That's what I mean by applying a tribal ethos to the whole nation.

When I say 'job', I'm referring to the typical concerns of conservatives and liberals in terms of our human evolution. Conservatives focus on external threats to keep us safe, while liberals focus on internal threats – unfairness, injustice, inequality – to ensure our safety within. Those are the typical concerns of each group.

If liberals fail to address the things that are fracturing the group, like ignoring real issues or failing to sound the alarm when there's a fire, then we're falling short in our role. If we don't do it, the conservatives won't either, and they'll say, 'If we don't protect the country, the left won't do it, so we'll step up'. In some ways, they're right, and we're right. It worked well when both sides respected each other and the country was fifty/fifty.

Q2: I'm a teacher at Bard DC, and I have a question about education. A bit of background: I'm from China, where only one voice is allowed. When I came to this country, I was amazed by how people could argue and present opposing views. This is a precious aspect of American democracy. However, I've noticed something troubling when teaching students. For example, I teach a seminar called 'Justice, Democracy, and Immigration'. Most of my students are so liberal that when I present another perspective, such as discussing America as a sovereign country with immigration policies, they accuse me of being unpatriotic or racist. They're so liberal that they almost can't accept a different viewpoint. My question is: what's your suggestion for balancing these two ideologies in education?

SJ: Extremism, in all its forms, is abhorrent and destroys the moral and social fabric of a community. The left can be particularly extreme, especially in terms of language enforcement. They often demand you speak a certain way – 'Repeat after me'.

The right wing – trust me, I don't have much affection for them right now – but they don't enforce language as aggressively as we do. This happens in universities, and it's appalling. It's essentially an embryonic form of a fascist state on the left. How do we handle it? I'm not sure. If professors stand up to this kind of nonsense and get penalized with furloughs or firings, nothing will change. Universities need to back their professors, and the political left should support universities when we insist on respectful norms for dialogue – where virtually all ideas are considered and discussed, except those that are clear insults to human dignity. Those have no place in our discussions. But that's not what we're talking about.

RB: You've covered a lot of wars, and you likely know many people involved in or covering the war in Ukraine. There are also a lot of people who left Ukraine. I've spoken to some of them, and they've said, 'This is a stupid war. I don't care who runs Ukraine. I'd rather not have war'. How does that fit in? It seems to me like they're saying they'd prefer peace without the suffering, regardless of whether they're Ukrainian or Russian. It doesn't seem intellectual; it seems emotional. They just want peace and no war.

SJ: Look, the Jews of Europe in the mid-twentieth century would have preferred to live in peace rather than face war, but that wasn't an option, was it? What those people are really saying is, 'I'd rather be a refugee or find another place to belong than stay Ukrainian and fight'. That's fine; I don't have a problem with that. But at this moment, being Ukrainian means staying and defending Ukraine. If it's not important to you to defend Ukraine, then you're no longer Ukrainian in any moral sense.

If you're not committed to what happens to your country, it's fine to move somewhere else – France, the US, wherever. Welcome. But no army, no group of people wants members who aren't committed to the cause. If you're not committed, you're just a drain on resources. Go somewhere else, and that's fine.

I don't know what I would do if I were Ukrainian. I'd like to think I'd stay and fight, but I can't say for sure. If rebels were heading toward this town, would I grab a weapon and try to defend it? Who would fight to defend Bard College right now, risking their life?

"AGAINST THE UNITY OF THE POLIS"

ARISTOTLE

ARISTOTLE. Born in 384 BC in Stagira, Greece, Aristotle was a philosopher whose works spanned politics, ethics, and metaphysics. In this text, Aristotle critiques the notion of an excessively unified state, arguing that true political stability does not require a full unity as Plato argued in *The Republic*. Instead, a polis is a fundamental plurality of persons who must share a common world but not be fully unified.

PART I

Our purpose is to consider what form of political community is best of all for those who are most able to realize their ideal of life. We must therefore examine not only this but other constitutions, both such as actually exist in well-governed states, and any theoretical forms which are held in esteem; that what is good and useful may be brought to light. And let no one suppose that in seeking for something beyond them we are anxious to make a sophistical display at any cost; we only undertake this inquiry because all the constitutions with which we are acquainted are faulty.

We will begin with the natural beginning of the subject. Three alternatives are conceivable: The members of a state must either have (1) all things or (2) nothing in common, or (3) some things in common and some not. That they should have nothing in common is clearly impossible, for the constitution is a community, and must at any rate have a common place – one city will be in one place, and the citizens are those who share in that one city. But should a well ordered state have all things, as far

---

Excerpted from: Aristotle. 1996. *The Politics* and *The Constitution of Athens*. Edited and translated by Stephen Everson. Cambridge University Press, 22–25.

as may be, in common, or some only and not others? For the citizens might conceivably have wives and children and property in common, as Socrates proposes in the Republic of Plato. Which is better, our present condition, or the proposed new order of society.

PART II
There are many difficulties in the community of women. And the principle on which Socrates rests the necessity of such an institution evidently is not established by his arguments. Further, as a means to the end which he ascribes to the state, the scheme, taken literally is impracticable, and how we are to interpret it is nowhere precisely stated. I am speaking of the premise from which the argument of Socrates proceeds, 'that the greater the unity of the state the better.' Is it not obvious that a state may at length attain such a degree of unity as to be no longer a state? since the nature of a state is to be a plurality, and in tending to greater unity, from being a state, it becomes a family, and from being a family, an individual; for the family may be said to be more than the state, and the individual than the family. So that we ought not to attain this greatest unity even if we could, for it would be the destruction of the state. Again, a state is not made up only of so many men, but of different kinds of men; for similars do not constitute a state. It is not like a military alliance The usefulness of the latter depends upon its quantity even where there is no difference in quality (for mutual protection is the end aimed at), just as a greater weight of anything is more useful than a less (in like manner, a state differs from a nation, when the nation has not its population organized in villages, but lives an Arcadian sort of life); but the elements out of which a unity is to be formed differ in kind. Wherefore the principle of compensation, as I have already remarked in the Ethics, is the salvation of states. Even among freemen and equals this is a principle which must be maintained, for they cannot an rule together, but must change at the end of a year or some other period of time or in some order of succession. The result is that upon this plan they all govern; just as if shoemakers and carpenters were to exchange their occupations, and the same persons did not always continue shoemakers and carpenters. And since it is better that this should be so in politics as well, it is clear that while there should be continuance of the same persons in power where this is possible, yet where this is not possible by reason of the natural equality of the citizens, and at the same

time it is just that an should share in the government (whether to govern be a good thing or a bad), an approximation to this is that equals should in turn retire from office and should, apart from official position, be treated alike. Thus the one party rule and the others are ruled in turn, as if they were no longer the same persons. In like manner when they hold office there is a variety in the offices held. Hence it is evident that a city is not by nature one in that sense which some persons affirm; and that what is said to be the greatest good of cities is in reality their destruction; but surely the good of things must be that which preserves them. Again, in another point of view, this extreme unification of the state is clearly not good; for a family is more self-sufficing than an individual, and a city than a family, and a city only comes into being when the community is large enough to be self-sufficing. If then self-sufficiency is to be desired, the lesser degree of unity is more desirable than the greater.

PART III
But, even supposing that it were best for the community to have the greatest degree of unity, this unity is by no means proved to follow from the fact 'of all men saying "mine" and "not mine" at the same instant of time,' which, according to Socrates, is the sign of perfect unity in a state. For the word 'all' is ambiguous. If the meaning be that every individual says 'mine' and 'not mine' at the same time, then perhaps the result at which Socrates aims may be in some degree accomplished; each man will call the same person his own son and the same person his wife, and so of his property and of all that falls to his lot. This, however, is not the way in which people would speak who had their had their wives and children in common; they would say 'all' but not 'each.' In like manner their property would be described as belonging to them, not severally but collectively. There is an obvious fallacy in the term 'all': like some other words, 'both,' 'odd,' 'even,' it is ambiguous, and even in abstract argument becomes a source of logical puzzles. That all per-sons call the same thing mine in the sense in which each does so may be a fine thing, but it is impracticable; or if the words are taken in the other sense, such a unity in no way conduces to harmony. And there is another objection to the proposal. For that which is common to the greatest number has the least care bestowed upon it. Everyone thinks chiefly of his own, hardly at all of the common interest; and only when he is him-self concerned as an individual. For besides other

considerations, every-body is more inclined to neglect the duty which he expects another to fulfill; as in families many attendants are often less useful than a few. Each citizen will have a thousand sons who will not be his sons individually but anybody will be equally the son of anybody, and will there-fore be neglected by all alike. Further, upon this principle, every one will use the word 'mine' of one who is prospering or the reverse, however small a fraction he may himself be of the whole number; the same boy will be 'so and so's son,' the son of each of the thousand, or what-ever be the number of the citizens; and even about this he will not be positive; for it is impossible to know who chanced to have a child, or whether, if one came into existence, it has survived. But which is better – for each to say 'mine' in this way, making a man the same relation to two thousand or ten thousand citizens, or to use the word 'mine' in the ordinary and more restricted sense? For usually the same person is called by one man his own son whom another calls his own brother or cousin or kinsman – blood relation or connection by marriage either of himself or of some relation of his, and yet another his clansman or tribesman; and how much better is it to be the real cousin of somebody than to be a son after Plato's fashion! Nor is there any way of preventing brothers and children and fathers and mothers from sometimes recognizing one another; for children are born like their parents, and they will necessarily be finding indications of their relationship to one another. Geographers declare such to be the fact; they say that in part of Upper Libya, where the women are common, nevertheless the children who are born are assigned to their respective fathers on the ground of their likeness. And some women, like the females of other animals – for example, mares and cows – have a strong tendency to produce offspring resembling their parents, as was the case with the Pharsalian mare called Honest.

"SAVING OUR SKINS"

LYNDSEY STONEBRIDGE

Since the attacks of October 7, 2023, and Israel's bloody response, two moments from Hannah Arendt's archive have been helping me get some bearings. This is not the first time in modern history that extreme violence has benumbed our senses, challenging our capacity to make judgments, to think straight, and Arendt is very good at reminding us that in order to grasp what is truly unprecedented about the present, it pays to be attentive to what appears most curious – odd, abrupt, untimely – about the recent past.

The first moment is political. In June 1967, two days into the Six Day War, a letter was published in the *New York Times*. "The crisis in the Middle East is for the United States and the rest of the world a crisis of law and conscience," it began, appealing directly to cosmopolitan sentiments. The letter was signed by many of America's leading intellectuals and writers, including Ralph Ellison, Marianne Moore, Lionel Trilling, Irving Howe and Hannah Arendt who was deeply concerned by events unfolding in the region. A few weeks later, she received a letter asking her to join an organization called 'American Professors for Peace in the Middle East'. She agreed enthusiastically: what better activity for American professors than to commit to peace? Six months later, however, she writes to the APPME demanding that it remove her name from their publicity. She has read their material and it "looks as though" the organization is "a kind of Zionist front," she complains. She has been misled. And then she writes, in a sentence that I think it is fair to say would struggle to be heard today: "I am, and have always been, pro-Israel [...] This does not mean that I have become a Zionist or wish to join the kind of organization you have obviously established." I will always defend Israel's right to exist,

Arendt is saying, but I will have none of your tribal nationalism. As is her habit, she is making distinctions. She is not refusing to take sides, but she is very emphatically refusing to accept the ideological terms upon which the sides are being set.

The second moment is existential and phenomenological. Arendt always wrote from experience, and if there is a consolation in reading her today, it is that her writing reminds us that even in a post-truth world of ideological absolutes the complexity of human experience still exists – we just need to find the words to make it present. This passage from a 1958 letter to Karl Jaspers does just that:

> Alienation and rootlessness, if we only understand them aright, make it easier to live in our time. And we certainly should allow ourselves that little bit of relief. They're like a skin that grows onto us from the outside. And because of that skin, we can afford to remain sensitive and vulnerable (Arendt 1958).

At first glance, this is an odd passage. We are accustomed to assuming that alienation and rootlessness are bad things. Arendt herself had argued just this in *The Origins of Totalitarianism* (1951), not seven years earlier. It was rootlessness and alienation that had made the obscene fictions of Nazi totalitarianism so attractive. Hitler sold a cheap, murderous, but plausible story to the dispossessed that worked precisely because it played into the terror of feeling radically estranged from a common world. Yet here Arendt is saying that the experiences of detachment and uprootedness might work for us – "if we only understand them aright." The alternative to alienation is not fascism but staying with the experience of alienation, however uncomfortable or difficult, so that it becomes part of us, like a skin. And here's the unexpected payoff: once that skin is allowed to grow, keeping us separate from the world, it also works to protect the very things that fascism and totalitarianism, tribalism and nationalism, have no time for: sensitivity and vulnerability.

For Arendt, of course, the two moments – the political and the experiential – are tied together. Accepting the conditions of alienation and rootlessness is the price to be paid for resisting the siren calls of tribal nationalism. It is a lesson worth heeding again today.

Arendt always saw tribal politics for what it was: self-defeating, destructive, and essentially fake. Tribalism was a kind of cheap glue, she argued, binding the fearful and atomized together. But the glue was a fix, not a real foundation which, in the case of Europe resulted in catastrophe. Then, as now, tribal nationalism promised a return to roots, but in reality needed (and needs) rootlessness in order to thrive. In this way, tribalism does the opposite from what it advertises: come home, it says, be safe, grow some roots; but, in truth, it must keep moving, uprooting assumptions and moral standards, in order to keep on generating its own dark ferocity. Far from grounding people to a common earth, tribalism cuts them free from shared reality, gathering passions together in the intensity of its fiction-making. You either belong or you don't, goes the tribalists' fiction.

The tribe is surrounded by enemies. In Arendt's time: Jews, migrants, Ukrainians, leftists, the bourgeoisie, queer people, the disabled, the sick and weak, and enemies within. Now: Jews, Palestinians, Ukrainians, migrants, leftists, global capitalism, LGBTQ+, the disabled, the sick and weak, and enemies within. Against this logic, the scaffolding of political governance begins to weaken. The law is only the law when it works for the tribe. 'Liberalism' is for wimps and shifty elites. Justifications for imperialism, occupation, and finally genocide can, and frequently do, follow. Re-read the passages on tribal nationalism in *The Origins of Totalitarianism*, then take a look at Vladimir Putin's 2021 essay, "On the Historical Unity of Russians and Ukrainians," for a contemporary example of the kind of pseudo-mystical storytelling used to justify tribal violence.

Arendt argued that because it is indifferent to reality, tribalism denies the very possibility of a common humanity in both theory and practice. That denial is what makes tribalism so dangerous: tribalism is a threat not simply to other tribes, but to the possibility of co-existence itself. Here is George Orwell, so often in political lockstep with Arendt, writing in 1945:

> Actions are held to be good or bad, not on their own merits, but according to who does them, and there is almost no kind of outrage – torture, the use of hostages, forced labour, mass deportations, imprisonment without trial, forgery, assassination, the bombing of civilians – which does not change its moral colour when it is committed by 'our' side (Orwell 2018, 36).

Compare Arendt in *The Origins of Totalitarianism*: "Tribalism and racism are the very realistic, if very destructive, ways of escaping the predicament of common responsibility" (Arendt 1951, 236). Both those sentences could have been written at any time over the past two years.

It is not the language of tribalism that sounds anachronistic today, but its putative opposite, and our second term at the Hannah Arendt Conference in 2024: cosmopolitanism.

Arendt was never persuaded that the West's victory over fascism was a victory for humanity ("reckless optimism" she called the premature celebrations of a new humanism after the war), and was sceptical about the promise of a new postwar cosmopolitanism. If we are tempted to look to Arendt for a cosmopolitan alternative to today's tribalism, we are going to be disappointed.

Kant himself had argued that the hypocrisies of colonialism would undo the project of global universal rights, and Arendt agreed. The tragedy which followed, she remarked, was that by the time "Europe in all earnest began to prescribe its 'laws' to all other continents" it had "already lost her belief in them." Europe exported its own political failures, suppressing other forms of political knowledge, particularly those from the global south, in the process.

Many would argue that the West is currently paying the price for those failures. In a lecture given in September 2024, the journalist and writer Pankaj Mishra argued that the victories over totalitarianism and fascism of the twentieth century helped shield Europe and the United States from evidence of their own continuing brutal imperialism. The assault on Gaza, he claimed, has finally shattered the illusion that the West still holds the line for humanism and democracy. With an echo of Arendt's pessimism, Mishra's lecture was entitled "The Last Days of Mankind."

"The solidarity of mankind may well turn out to be an unbearable burden," Arendt concluded in 1958 (just as she was writing that letter about skin to Karl Jaspers) with a bitterness that many might reasonably share today, "and it is not surprising that the common reactions to it are political apathy, isolationist nationalism, or desperate rebellion against all powers that be rather than enthusiasm or a desire for a revival of humanism."

But just as she had no time for reckless optimism, neither would Arendt ever give in to cynicism. The opposition between tribalism and cosmopolitanism was a false opposition. It's not a matter of choosing whether to stay in your tribe or to throw your hopes onto the world's conscience; but of opening up the spaces between. "What begins now, after the end of the history of the world, is the history of mankind. What this will eventually be, we do not know," she wrote in 1958. I support Israel, remember her saying in 1967, *and* I reject Zionism. Those positions do not cancel one another out: you can defend the sovereignty of all nations (including Palestine) necessary to the cosmopolitan rules of global law and reject the ideologies of tribal nationalism.

Keeping her skin intact allowed Arendt to resist tribal thinking in that between moment. It's not perhaps a coincidence that Eugene Ionesco's absurdist allegory about totalitarianism, *Rhinoceros* was first performed just as Arendt was writing her letter to Jaspers. In the play, one by one, the inhabitants of a village grow thick skins to the point that they all become rhinoceroses. What was once a community of people becomes a violent herd. The thick-skinned are proto-fascists, blindly, lethally, indifferent to the world. "I'm not capitulating!" shouts the lone dissenter Bérenger in the last scene, but by then he is entirely alone. Isolated, defenceless, the thin-skinned simply do not survive. Like Arendt, Ionesco had witnessed European totalitarianism at first hand, and knew where tribalism could take history.

Arendt proposes an alternative method of remaining connected to humanity in the face of tribalism's unchecked rampages. We are always touched by politics, stimulated, positively and negatively by the world which we must live in, however much we might wish we did not. But Arendt's skin is not simply defensive - it keeps us in touch with the world to which we belong, to our people, to history, to trauma, but does so without destroying us. As she does often, Arendt is urging us to keep in touch with the world we live in, uprooted and alienated as we are, precisely so that we can protect our vulnerability and sensitivity – the minimal requirements, we might say, for any shared humanity.

Hannah Arendt was not the only woman thinker to reject the terms of both tribalism and a corrupted cosmopolitanism at mid-century. Indeed, if cosmopolitanism now seems politically weak, it is not least because of its failure to protect women. In *Three Guineas* (1938), her controversial long essay on pacifism and one of the last things she published before her suicide in 1941, Virginia Woolf argued against the gendered hypocrisies of liberal internationalism and for a "society of outsiders." "As a woman I have no country. As a woman I want no country. As a woman, my country is the whole world," she wrote. In the last text she wrote before her death two years later in 1943, *The Need for Roots*, the French philosopher and mystic Simone Weil condemned the uprootedness that was both cause and consequence of totalitarian imperialism and made an impassioned plea for a new rootedness based on neighbourliness and love.

These three women had very different visions, but all viewed the failure of the West's political project starkly and unflinchingly, perhaps because, as women, they had both always been on the outside of that project and suffered its consequences. Pankaj Mishra is right to announce the 'end of mankind' in the sense that the West is now losing what moral authority it had. I would end by adding that another unifying characteristic of today's violent tribal nationalisms, from the United States to Afghanistan, Iran to Russia, is a vehement – and scandalously under-remarked – misogyny. Hannah Arendt never wrote as a feminist, but she understood the frailty of political life like few other thinkers. Unlike many of contemporaries, her own politics began not with denying the fragility of our collective existence, but with working out a kind of politics that allows us to touch the world, to remain vulnerable, which is to say, human.

REFERENCES

Arendt, Hannah. "Letter to American Professors for Peace in the Middle East." October 21, 1967, Hannah Arendt Archives, Library of Congress.
Arendt, Hannah. 1992. "Letter to Karl Jaspers (November 16, 1958)." *Hannah Arendt Karl Jaspers Correspondence*, 1926–1968, edited by Lotte Kohler and Hans Saner. New York: Harcourt Brace & Co.
Arendt, Hannah. 2004. *The Origins of Totalitarianism* [1951]. New York: Schocken Books.
Arendt, Hannah. 1968. "Karl Jaspers: Citizen of the World?" In *Men in Dark Times*. Harcourt Brace Jovanovich.
Mishra, Pankaj. "The Last Days of Mankind.: September 28, 2024, *N+1*, https://www.nplusonemag.com/online-only/online-only/the-last-days-of-mankind/.
Orwell, George. 2018. "Notes on Nationalism" [1945]. Penguin.
Putin, Vladimir. 'On the Historical Unity of Russians and Ukrainians,' July 12, 2021, http://en.kremlin.ru/events/president/news/66181.
Weil, Simone. 2023. *The Need for Roots* [1949], trans. Ros Schwartz. London: Penguin, 2023.
Woolf, Virginia. 2015. *A Room of One's Own and Three Guineas*, ed. Anna Snaith. Oxford: Oxford University Press.

"MORE THAN A GAME: THE PSYCHOLOGY BEHIND TRIBALISM IN FOOTBALL CLUBS"

"More Than A Game: The Psychology Behind Tribalism in Football Clubs," is an anonymous essay from a blog associated with the clothing brand *Suave and Debonair.* Published on April 17, 2024, the essay delves into the psychological and social factors that drive intense loyalty and rivalry among British soccer fans. By examining how identity, community, and competition shape fandom, the authors provide insights into the phenomenon of *football hooliganism*. The essay is inspired by the book *The Soccer Tribe* (1982) by Desmond Morris.

If you have ever sat in the stands at a proper football match then you will very likely have experienced something unlike anything else. Sure there is cheering, celebration following a great goal, etc. But I'm talking about something else. Something more disturbing – darker if you like.

Football is tribal. fans are passionate about their team and in many cases hostile to the opposition. There is something about the terraces on a Saturday that can turn even the most mild-mannered middle-aged father of 3 into a yob. That is to say, something happens when perfectly respectable people attend a football match – they can turn into aggressive, unpleasant people with no regard for the normal social rules within which they operate.

I mean, take Jeff for example. Likely a teacher, wears a tweed jacket with those leather patches on the elbows. Spends his week being the epitome of decency, control and politeness but come Saturday at about 3:11pm he is standing up in front of 10,000 people and shouting at a footballer 30 metres away that he is a "useless a***hole" or something similar.

It's not just opposition footballers either – it's his own team, their manager, the opposition fans or worst of all... The referee.

Abuse at matches, individual and group chanting, swearing and mob mentality can make football stadiums intimidating and unpleasant places to be.

So what is it about that arena that seems to bring out the thug in some people. Is it an inevitable consequence of a world obsessed with political correctness that suffocates and cajoles people into behaving in such a restrained way that some outlet is a necessary evil?

Is it the fierce competition of football that makes people think all is fair during the match and so it is the fans responsibility to make their stadium a so-called "difficult place for away teams to go" – do we accept "hostile" behaviour for away teams as part of the competition? Do fans feel they have a responsibility to "get after them" – is pressure on the referee a subconscious strategic attempt at gaining an advantage?

Now don't get me wrong, many many fans go to football games and behave perfectly normally, managing to avoid the use of abusive language or suggesting in no uncertain terms that the referee can't do his job. But it remains the case that in every one of the professional football matches played up and down the UK on a Saturday there will be countless examples of the type of abrasive and aggressive behaviour I am talking about here.

It is said that football fans have a deeper-rooted culture than most other sports. Team allegiance is often passed down through generations creating this enhance sense of belonging and perhaps at least partly responsible for a heightened response to the ebb and flow of a match.

The stakes are high also – winning and losing, promotion and relegation can have a direct impact on the financial landscape around the local club.

Some say that football fans are historically from low social-economic households and as a result will have lower levels of education therefore inevitably leading to lower types of social behaviour and increased levels of aggression – but that seems like too simple an explanation, not to mention outdated for a world where the class system is a really a thing of yesterday.

One particularly extreme type of tribalism is of course football hooliganism, which itself comes in several forms. Pitch invading, player "attacks", significant unrest in the stands and even stadium invasions like we witnessed at the final of Euro 2020 at Wembley.

Interestingly, individual clubs and even countries seem to get labelled as being aggressive. Millwall and Leeds United for instance – both have a big reputation as having disruptive fans and as a result trigger higher levels of police presence wherever they go to an away ground. The Italians are known to be at a higher risk of physical altercations and violence when British clubs pay a visit. It begs the question do some clubs attract and retain a greater level of this "tribalism" than others and if so why?

So let's look at the actual psychology behind all this.

A strong example of group identification, feeling of belongingness and loyalty is the passion for a football team, which may therefore be viewed as sort of tribal love. Desmond Morris described in an impactful book this tribal character of the link between, not only football players, coaches and directors, but between the fans and the teams. Football was described as a tribal phenomenon and the author framed in an evolutionary view how the attachment for a preferred football team and nation has achieved such significance for very large audiences (Morris, 1981). The cognitive neuroscience of fan binding to a team is poorly studied from the neuro-imaging point of view. Nevertheless, its social importance is irrefutable and the phenomenon of team love is worth deeper scientific investigation.

When it comes to the more extreme side, Dr Hutter described a state of deindividuation, where we behave as an anonymous member of a group rather than an individual – likely a contributing factor to why individuals who would not act in a violent manner on their own, can in some cases do so when they feel part of a larger group.

When all is said and done, we love our football teams. "Our team" can form part of our identity. People get the team logo tattooed, buy replica shirts, even name their children after their favourite players. The joy so many people get from watching, following, debating and celebrating their football team is a precious and beautiful thing.

Next time you go to a match look for the individuals that are clearly quiet, polite and respectable people outside of the ground and see how they lean into their natural aggressive tribal instincts when it comes to "their club" – watch them as they berate the match officials and threaten the opposition.

It's nature, modern man in a rarely seen raw and unfiltered moment – one that will quickly pass when the final whistle goes.

"TRIBALISM AND MODERN POLITICS: LESSONS FROM IRELAND"

FINTAN O'TOOLE
(WITH JOSEPH O'NEILL)

Before I begin, I want to clarify a key term. I'll be using the word 'tribalization', but not in the ways it has been discussed by others. I have a particular idea of tribal instinct as the love we feel for those we know. However, that's not the sense in which I'll be using 'tribalization' here.

Instead, I want to talk about political tribalization – a process that can take hold in a democracy when people stop identifying primarily with a larger entity, like the state or the nation, and instead define themselves through two mutually opposed political identities. These identities often revolve around competing claims of victimhood. In such a system, each side perceives the other as inflicting intolerable harm, regardless of the actual facts. It ceases to matter who is oppressing whom – what matters is that the sense of victimhood becomes competitive and universally available.

This ties into the broader question of identity, particularly how political identities become deeply polarized. It's worth noting that, for the vast majority of the time, most people don't think much about their collective political identity. It's not something they actively dwell on – until it becomes problematic. When issues of injustice, oppression, or existential threat come into play, political identity suddenly takes center stage.

George Bernard Shaw put this idea well when he spoke about national identity. He compared it to a tooth; you never think about your teeth unless one is rotten or causing you pain. But when it does, you can think of nothing else. The same is true of political identity: something people rarely consider can come to dominate their thoughts and emotions, and that pain must be addressed.

In my talk today, I want to explore two key dimensions of this process. First, why political tribalization can be so powerful. Second, how – if at all – pluralism can eventually emerge from such conflict, which ties into the theme of this conference.

To illustrate this, I'll focus on Northern Ireland – not for its own sake, but because it serves as a microcosm of these dynamics. This was a small place where something extraordinary happened: two communities, both predominantly white and Christian, with little daily difference between them, sustained a vicious conflict for thirty years – one that few anticipated. A year before the violence began, almost no one believed it would happen. Once it started, almost no one imagined it could last for three decades.

While I won't belabor the parallels with the United States today, I do think they are worth considering. At the time, those of us who lived through the Northern Irish conflict – including myself, from the Republic of Ireland, just sixty miles from the border – viewed it through the lens of anachronism. It felt like a tear in the fabric of time, as if the religious wars of sixteenth- and seventeenth-century Europe had somehow persisted in this remote corner of the world, long after they had been resolved elsewhere.

A common, if not particularly good, joke at the time captured this feeling: when landing in Belfast, the pilot would say, 'Welcome to Belfast. Please set your watch back an hour – and 300 years'. There was a pervasive sense that this conflict belonged to the past, that it was an outdated remnant of history rather than a contemporary political reality.

What's striking now is that this conflict no longer seems like an anachronism. Instead, it might look more like a warning – perhaps even a glimpse of the future rather than a strange return to the past.

With that in mind, I want to explore what lessons we can take from this conflict – both in terms of its causes and, more optimistically, how it was eventually addressed. I realize that some of you may not be familiar with the details, so I'll give a very brief overview. Forgive me if it's necessarily broad and oversimplified, but this should help situate things.

Ireland, of course, is an island located between Britain and America – though much closer to Britain. Its history has been shaped by a long and often fraught relationship with Britain and the British Empire, spanning roughly 700 to 750 years. One of the defining aspects of this history is the way religious and national identities became deeply intertwined. After the religious wars in Europe, the general principle was that people would adopt the religion of their ruler: Protestant if the ruler was Protestant, Catholic if the ruler was Catholic. But Ireland was an exception. For a variety of reasons – particularly a growing sense of national identity – the majority of the Irish population refused to adopt the Protestantism of their British rulers.

The British takeover of Ireland was a long process, but by around 1603–1604, it was largely complete. By that time, the British monarchy had firmly identified itself with Protestantism. Most people in Britain followed suit, but in Ireland, around 80 % of the population remained Catholic. As a result, Catholicism became deeply tied to Irish national identity.

Complicating matters further was the presence of Protestant settlers, who had arrived from Scotland and England over the centuries. This created a significant Protestant minority in Ireland. Over time, religious identity became closely linked to political aspiration: in broad terms – though with many exceptions – Catholics tended to support Irish independence, while Protestants generally wanted Ireland to remain part of the United Kingdom. The eventual compromise that emerged from this tension was the creation of Northern Ireland. The northeast was the most economically developed part of the island and had the highest concentration of Protestants, primarily Presbyterians and Episcopalians. As a result, when Ireland gained independence, this region was carved out to remain part of the United Kingdom, while the rest of the island became the Republic of Ireland.

Northern Ireland was deliberately designed to maintain a permanent Protestant majority. Interestingly, last year, for the first time, Protestants became a minority there – a reminder of how demographics can reshape political realities. But at the time of its creation, around thirty percent of the population was Catholic and nationalist. This minority was seen as disloyal and was systematically marginalized. Discrimination was deeply entrenched, and Catholics faced significant barriers in areas like housing, employment, and political representation.

While the situation wasn't as extreme as racial segregation in the American South under Jim Crow or apartheid in South Africa – comparisons that were sometimes made – it was still profoundly unjust. By the 1960s, inspired by the American Civil Rights Movement, a peaceful campaign for equal rights emerged in Northern Ireland, calling for an end to systemic discrimination against Catholics. The movement took direct inspiration from figures like Martin Luther King Jr. and sought to dismantle majority rule structures that entrenched inequality.

However, Irish nationalism has a long history of violent resistance and underground movements. As the civil rights movement clashed with a reactionary government determined to suppress it, the situation escalated. What began as a peaceful demand for equality soon gave way to violent conflict, with paramilitary groups playing a central role in the decades of bloodshed that followed.

The conflict wasn't just about political arguments over identity, nationality, or the future; it also involved armed terror groups on both sides and a British government that effectively became a participant rather than a neutral authority. Instead of upholding the rule of law and democratic principles, the British government resorted to internment without trial and abandoned many of its own legal and ethical standards. It even deployed the British Army onto the streets of Irish cities, most infamously during the Bloody Sunday massacre, when soldiers opened fire on unarmed protesters. These factors all became defining elements of the conflict, which lasted from 1968 to 1998 – a full thirty years.

What can we learn from this about political tribalization? A common assumption is that conflicts arise from incompatible identities. While there's truth to that, Northern Ireland also demonstrates the opposite: conflict itself creates incompatible identities. Conflict reinforces and even reshapes divisions between people.

In the years leading up to 1968, Northern Irish society was actually becoming more integrated. Many people lived in mixed neighborhoods, interfaith marriages were increasing, and social interactions between Catholics and Protestants were common. Van Morrison, for example, grew up in Protestant East Belfast, playing music in clubs alongside Catholics without thinking twice about it. Young people were focused on the usual things – having fun, listening to music, forming relationships – not on religious or political divides.

But conflict changes that. It imposes physical separation, which in turn leads to mental separation. Neighborhoods become divided, and over time, people retreat into hardened identities.

This connects to a broader issue with identity politics – a term that's often misunderstood. In reality, much of what's called 'identity politics' is actually the politics of denying identity. We all have multiple identities that shift depending on the context. People exist within multiple 'tribes' at once, moving between them throughout their lives. That's why the concept of a fixed, singular identity is misleading.

French historian Ernest Renan argued, in *What Is a Nation?*, that nations are built largely on forgetting. A nation, he suggested, is a group of people bound together by shared misconceptions about their origins. Identity politics often distorts history in a similar way, reducing identity to a simplified, static version of what people are 'supposed' to be. Conflict reinforces these false narratives, pushing people into rigid ideas about who they are – ideas that are neither historically nor culturally accurate.

But the bigger question is: how can a conflict like this sustain itself for thirty years? It's easy enough to understand how it starts – systemic injustices, a government's heavy-handed response to demands for reform, and the eruption of violence. Yet even in 1968, when violence began, few expected it to last more than a couple of years. Most assumed that after a difficult period, things would stabilize. No one, looking at the situation at the time, predicted it would continue for three decades.

So, the key issue – one that remains relevant to today's crises in democracy – is: what makes tribalization so persistent? If it lasts this long, it must provide something useful – some kind of power dynamic or sense of satisfaction that benefits certain groups. And here's the paradox: the vast majority of people don't actually want conflict. They want to live their lives in peace. So why does it continue? Or, to put it another way: why is it so hard to stop?

There are five key factors worth highlighting:

1. INTERNAL SOLIDARITY AND SUPPRESSION OF CRITICISM

Polarization creates a strong sense of internal solidarity. People feel closer to their own community because they perceive an external threat. This can foster a sense of social cohesion and even a certain pleasure in belonging. However, the downside is that it also suppresses internal criticism. A common response to dissent is: 'Yes, we have problems on our side, but now isn't the time to address them: we're under threat'. This creates a form of solidarity built on denial, where self-reflection and accountability are sacrificed for the sake of unity. But despite being based on falsehoods, this dynamic is powerful and effective.

2. SIMPLIFICATION OF IDENTITY

Tribalization makes identity seem straightforward: 'us vs. them'. In reality, defining 'us' is always complicated; groups are fluid, diverse, and full of contradictions. But in a polarized environment, identity becomes defined negatively: We know who we are because we are not them. This is a deeply simplifying force. Samuel Beckett supposedly gave the best definition of Irishness when asked if he was English. His response? *Au contraire.* That sums up the nature of identity in a conflict; it is defined primarily by opposition.

3. ELIMINATING THE NEED TO DELIVER BENEFITS

In a functioning democracy, politicians are expected to improve people's lives. But that's difficult, especially in a time of growing economic inequality, where wealth is concentrated among a shrinking elite. Political tribalization offers a convenient alternative: Leaders no longer need to provide tangible benefits. In Northern Ireland, no Protestant or Catholic politician dramatically improved life for their community during the conflict. Yet the most extreme figures remained dominant because they shifted the narrative. Instead of asking, 'Are we better off?' people were led to ask, 'Are they suffering more than we are?' This goes beyond a zero-sum game – where one side's gain is another's loss – to a negative-sum game, where everyone suffers, but as long as the other side suffers more, that's seen as a victory.

The reality was catastrophic for everyone. Lives were lost, the economy was destroyed, and the trauma persists today, seen in Northern Ireland's high suicide rates. But in a system driven by polarization, that suffering doesn't necessarily translate into political pressure to stop the conflict. As long as people believe they are losing more than we are, the dynamic continues.

4. SELF-PERPETUATING VIOLENCE

One of the most dangerous aspects of deep polarization – especially when it leads to violence – is that it fuels itself. The logic becomes one of retaliation:

They did this to us, so we must do this to them. Each act of violence is seen as a response to the last, and each new atrocity renews the sense of victimhood. This creates a perpetual motion machine of conflict, where even if most people want peace, they don't want to stop fighting until they've 'gotten even' for the last attack. The cycle is endless because suffering is real – people are genuinely being victimized – which constantly regenerates the justification for more violence.

5. AVOIDING THE HARD WORK OF ETHICAL THINKING
Thinking seriously about right and wrong during a conflict is difficult. Most people are appalled by violence and injustice, but in a polarized environment, moral responsibility is easily deflected. Northern Ireland even gave the English language a word for this phenomenon: 'whataboutery'. Whenever someone criticizes their own side – 'That bombing was horrific. I'm ashamed of it.' – the immediate response is: 'But what about what they did to us?'

Whataboutery becomes a self-perpetuating excuse that prevents moral reckoning. Instead of asking, 'What should we do to stop this? What is my responsibility as a citizen?', people fall back on endless justifications based on past grievances. This makes it much harder to break the cycle of violence and polarization.

These five points are relevant to the broader challenges democracy faces today. Now, how can we stop polarization, and how did it stop in Northern Ireland? There are a few important lessons.

First, you can't simply wish polarization away. You can't just say, 'Let's all love each other' or 'Let's be friends'. There needs to be structural engagement with people's sense of identity. Telling people their identity is wrong won't work. Instead, you must acknowledge their identity and find ways to express it peacefully and without conflict. The solution in Northern Ireland, although imperfectly framed, was a concept of 'parity of esteem'. Rather than delegitimizing anyone's identity, you affirm that all views are legitimate, even if you don't agree with them.

Second (and here I disagree with Sebastian Junger's view of the tribe), it's not about asking, 'What are you willing to die for?' which implicitly asks, 'What are you willing to kill for?' People will die for all sorts of misguided causes. What you need to ask is, 'What can you live with?' Most people can live with complexity and ambiguity. When you remove the apocalyptic mindset and focus on what will help people get on with their lives, you open up a very different – and often more effective – dialogue.

Third, you must create a sense that the future is negotiable. Polarization often stems from a view of the future that feels like an existential threat. People think, 'If we don't have this conflict now, we're finished'. To resolve this, you have to demonstrate that the future can be shaped and that it is possible to negotiate a way forward, even with uncertainty.

Lastly, pluralism shouldn't be forced or presented as a moral lecture. It should be offered as a choice – an attractive one. The key element in the Northern Ireland peace process, as enshrined in the international treaty, is the right of everyone in Northern Ireland to identify as Irish, British, or both, depending on their choice. This redefines identity as something flexible and open-ended. The key is that identity can change over time; it's up to the individual.

So, while the situation in Northern Ireland is far from perfect and polarization still exists, there's been extraordinary progress since the Belfast Agreement in 1998. It's a very different society today, and life for ordinary people has vastly improved. The idea of pluralism is possible, and the key is to offer it before the situation escalates too far, as it did in Northern Ireland.

JOSEPH O'NEILL [JO]: Thank you for that insightful reflection on Ireland as an example of conflict resolution. Ireland is often seen as a rare case where communities in deep conflict managed to resolve their differences. In fact, those who were involved in the Good Friday Agreement talks are now sought after to advise others on how to achieve similar outcomes. The Good Friday Agreement was signed in 1998, just before the internet became an essential part of our lives. My question is: how might the process have unfolded differently if the conflict had continued for another decade, entering the era of Facebook, Instagram, and the social media influences we now deal with?

FO: Thank you for your question. The conflict could have gone on for another thirty years. It was generational. I spent a lot of time there, speaking to people who had been involved in violence, and many were getting older and had children. A key part of the resolution was simply the desire for a better future for their kids. This echoes what Niobe mentioned yesterday about boy culture – the appeal of violence at seventeen or eighteen years old. Once people get drawn into that, it can last for decades. So, yes, the conflict could have continued.

As for social media, things might have been much worse. Social media today enables rapid disinformation, especially in communities already in conflict. We see this with rioting and anti-immigrant sentiments across Europe. It allows false narratives and invented outrages to spread quickly. The capacity to incite violence and sustain conflicts through social media would have made things much harder. We were probably lucky to end the conflict before these capabilities truly came into play.

JO: The Good Friday Agreement was an act of moral imagination. I remember being a student in England in the early 1980s when John Hume, a key figure in the Agreement, was already discussing the framework. It was called the New Ireland Forum, and he was advocating for concepts that would later become part of the Good Friday Agreement. One of those concepts was truth and reconciliation, which gained global significance. It seemed like there was a cultural space for this idea at the time. I wonder, is that idea still feasible today? For instance, when we look at the tribalism in society today – groupings defined by competitive victimhood – can we still access that space for truth and reconciliation, as Joe Biden imagined at the start of his presidency when he hoped to bring America together?

FO: That's a great question, and in fact, one of the key failures of the Northern Ireland process was that we didn't have a proper truth and reconciliation process. For such a process to work, it must be universal and based on Enlightenment principles of human rights. If it's not universal, people will only want the truth about what was done to them, not what they did to others. In Northern Ireland, what we ended up with was a selective truth, and that doesn't lead to true reconciliation.

We've had some significant public inquiries, like the Bloody Sunday inquiry, which was crucial for the families of the victims, as it exonerated those who were killed. These inquiries into individual atrocities, especially by the state, are important. But there's been no real truth-telling by the paramilitaries. This leads to a situation where people demand accountability for specific atrocities, but there's no framework to address them all comprehensively.

When thinking about America now and the broader issue of healing, it needs to be based on a genuine attempt at truth-telling. This would involve looking at American history, its role in international conflicts, and domestic issues. But right now, it seems unlikely that there's a common framework or consensus in the U.S. that could facilitate such a process.

JO: There's one aspect of the Irish situation that stands out, and that's Europe. I wanted to ask you about that. By the way, I'm holding We Don't Know Ourselves, which Fintan published a few years ago. It's both a personal history and a political biography of Ireland, because Fintan's life aligns with a crucial period in Irish history. In one of the chapters, you discuss Europe. Of course, Europe has changed the way Ireland views its identity, offering a shared, transnational sense of belonging that crosses borders. Could you say more about that?

FO: Sure. When we talk about identity and identity politics, much of it is wrapped up in anxiety. People often think of identity as something handed down from the past that must be preserved unchanged. But that view leads to anxiety, which in turn fosters tribalization. Why? Because nothing from the past can remain unchanged. The true nature of identity is how groups have adapted to change over time. Everyone faces change in different ways, and that's what makes us unique. We maintain continuity and hold onto things that matter, while adapting to profound shifts.

Take Ireland, for example. The Ireland I was born into in 1958 is completely gone. But is Irish identity gone? Absolutely not. In fact, it's thriving. It's thriving because it's a better place now. People are no longer leaving. When I was growing up, Ireland had a very clear, pure Irish-Catholic nationalist identity. It was a Catholic state, fully embedded in the law – no contraception, no divorce, no abortion, strict gender roles –and it was awful. People didn't rebel against it; they simply left.

Now, Ireland is a much more creative, open, and imaginative place. One important aspect of this new identity is the sense of being European. A pivotal moment in our history was when Britain left the EU and we stayed in. That's when we really asserted our independence. Ireland is no longer an appendage to Britain. Being part of the EU vindicates our identity; it gives us a seat at the table. As a small nation of five million people, we now have the same standing as Germany or France. That's a remarkable achievement for a country with a history of oppression and denial of its nationhood.

And the same applies to Ukraine. The end game for Ukraine isn't about specific territorial disputes like the Donbas. It's about Ukraine having an equal role in Europe, alongside Germany, France, Poland, and Ireland. Becoming part of the EU won't dilute Ukraine's identity – it will reinforce it. It provides a sense of security and legitimacy, allowing countries to participate in the decision-making processes that affect them.

JO: That's a powerful point – you're saying that tribal identity causes chronic anxiety when it's defined by a constant backward gaze. It reminds me of something from Quebec, where the license plate says, Je me souviens ('I remember'). But no one ever explains what they're remembering. They may have forgotten. If your identity is rooted in remembering the past – what you were, where you come from – then you're bound to feel anxious, always trying to preserve something that can't be preserved.

Q1: I really appreciated your talk. It was so informative and sparked a lot of ideas. I'd like to share one with you for consideration. Your example of Ireland, especially Northern Ireland, is exactly what you could apply to the American Civil War and even the civil conflict we're experiencing in the U.S. today. If we think these issues are happening over there, we should realize they're right here too. And this was the same 150 years ago. I think we have something to learn from listening to young people – especially mass shooters. We don't typically want to listen to them, but in this case, it's crucial. You're talking about boy culture, where revenge outweighs reconciliation, and that's exactly it. Boy culture is a hierarchy, where some people are seen as more human than others. No one wants to be at the bottom of the hierarchy. If people who once saw themselves at the top are pushed to the bottom – and they have access to weapons – they may lash out, and that's what we're seeing with mass shooters. These shooters even say as much in their manifestos – they're fighting to avoid being on the bottom of the hierarchy. They feel that it's unfair and that they've been marginalized.

So, how does this dynamic play out in Ireland? Everyone wants to be on top, and no one wants to be on the bottom. But we keep putting people at the bottom and wonder why they're angry and voting for people like Trump. I'd love to hear your thoughts on how we can disrupt this hierarchy in the context of Ireland's reconciliation process. Do you see a parallel there?

FO: I completely agree with everything you've said. One small thing I'd add – something that's difficult to accept – is that the perpetrators of violence in these situations often see themselves as noble. People can commit horrific acts, but in their minds, they're acting on behalf of something greater.

As an Irish person, I know people who built bombs intended for cafes and pubs –designed to kill innocent people. And yet, they're not monsters. They're ordinary people who believed they were fighting for their community. When someone feels they've been pushed to the bottom of the hierarchy, they can channel that frustration into tribalism. Violence becomes a way to assert their identity, a way to feel like they matter. In that mindset, the more extreme the violence, the more powerful the statement.

What has changed in Northern Ireland is the gradual decoupling from extreme polarization. As that happens, a middle ground emerges – people who refuse to be defined by rigid categories. Demographically, Northern Ireland was structured to always have a Protestant majority and a Catholic minority. But today, both groups are minorities. And there's a growing segment – perhaps twenty percent – who don't align with either side, particularly among young people.

If asked in a survey whether they identify as Catholic nationalist or Protestant unionist, they refuse to answer. Those labels don't define them. Instead, they might see themselves in terms of feminism, queer identity, environmentalism, socialism – anything but the old sectarian divides.

This shift changes the political dynamic. For the two traditional groups, winning now depends on persuading those in the middle. They can no longer rely on securing a built-in majority. And that changes everything.

The big existential question remains: Will there be a united Ireland, or will Northern Ireland remain part of the United Kingdom? At some point, there will be a referendum on the issue. But the people who will decide that vote are the ones who currently don't prioritize it. It's not that they don't care – it's just not their primary concern. They are persuadable, but they need to be convinced.

This means the future will be shaped not by rigid divisions, but by dialogue, openness, and persuasion. And that dynamic helps weaken the kind of boy culture that fuels violence – the culture of hard over soft, revenge over reconciliation.

That said, serious challenges remain. Economic exclusion is still a major issue. The conflict took a huge toll, and many communities – especially working-class boys – are still marginalized, poorly educated, and voiceless. The conditions for violence still exist, and we don't know what form it might take next. There can be no complacency.

But there has been a fundamental shift in thinking. Joe mentioned this in the context of the U.S., and we've seen a similar evolution in Ireland. The Irish Constitution used to contain a classic nationalist claim – essentially saying, 'Northern Ireland belongs to us, and we want it back'. That was standard nineteenth-century nationalism; many European countries had similar territorial statements.

In 1998, we changed that language. Now, the Constitution expresses the aspiration to unite "in harmony and friendship all those who share the territory of the island of Ireland, in all the diversity of their identities and traditions."

That's what Irish nationalism means now. I consider myself a proud nationalist in that sense – one that embraces multiple identities and traditions, including new ones. Today, twenty percent of Ireland's population was born elsewhere. After generations of emigration, we've become a destination for immigrants, which is a remarkable transformation.

These changes – intellectual, cultural, and social – create new possibilities. We can't afford to be complacent, especially about economic inequalities. But if these new ideas take hold, we can replace the vicious cycle of the past with a virtuous one.

Q2: How do we combat tribalism without reinforcing it? In today's political climate in America, how can we address MAGA tribalism without simply creating an opposing anti-MAGA or anti-tribal tribe?

FO: Thank you for that question; it's a fantastic one, and probably the most important. What we know is that you don't persuade people by making them feel stupid or inferior. That only pushes them further into their beliefs, especially when those beliefs are rooted in feelings of humiliation, loss, and anxiety. That's the real dilemma.

I'll share what was done in Northern Ireland. In a way, the approach was to accept the reality of tribalism for a time – to acknowledge the existence of two distinct communities and build political structures that represented them. This was always a bit of a fiction because there were never just two communities; many people didn't want to be defined in those terms. But the idea was that by reducing fear and anxiety, you could eventually create space for people to engage in other ways.

I think there are two key points here. First, you have to oppose toxic ideas and emotions without condemning the people who hold them – and that's incredibly difficult. As an outsider, I believe Americans have a duty to fight fascism, racism, and the staggering misogyny that has been evident in the current political climate. You can't be passive in the face of threats like mass deportations or the rounding up of millions of people into camps. Some things simply cannot be reconciled.

But the challenge is in how you fight. The most effective approach isn't to say, 'You people are terrible'. It's to say, 'You are better than this'. You're not the kind of person who wants to see your neighbors taken away. You're not someone who would cheer as children are separated from their families. You wouldn't want to see a woman left to bleed to death in a parking lot because she couldn't access medical care.

One of the things we understand about human nature is that collective pride, when framed positively, can be a force for good. It sets a standard – an aspiration – that people want to live up to. Even if you strongly dislike someone's views, the most effective approach is often to say, 'Your tradition is better than this'.

I've had many conversations with people who hold very conservative Protestant evangelical views. And when you really talk to them, you can say: 'You believe in Christianity. You believe in biblical prophecy, in a universal message, in forgiveness and reconciliation. If that's who you are, then I want you to actually live up to it'.

That's far more powerful than simply telling someone that their beliefs are illegitimate. I think it's the only way forward.

Q3: One of the most interesting points to me was the question of what sustains tribalism. It seems to me that one of the deepest sources of sadness – something many people have likely experienced – is the suppression of identity through negation. An entire generation grew up defining themselves not by who they were, but by what they were not. I'd love to hear your thoughts on how that manifests, especially twenty five or more years after the fact. How do you see that playing out today?

FO: I think you're absolutely right, and this applies to conflicts around the world. When the purest expression of a culture, identity, or history becomes an act of violence – like someone planting a bomb in a pub – it deeply distorts a person's sense of self. That's why I believe culture and the arts are not peripheral but absolutely essential.

People need alternative ways to find meaning, to experience collective belonging, and to test out who they are – without falling into negativity, insularity, or violence. In Northern Ireland, for example – and this might sound surprising – I think poetry played a critical role. Seamus Heaney once spoke about being in a BBC studio in Belfast in 1972, recording poems with other poets, and hearing bombs going off outside. He recalled wondering, 'What are we doing? How futile is this?' But then realizing, 'No, our job is to hold open a space' – an imaginative space where language is not abused.

Conflicts like these thrive on clichés and stereotypes – rigid, simplistic narratives of both oneself and the 'other'. Writers, poets, and playwrights resist that by putting language under pressure, keeping it alive, complex, and supple. That's why something like the Belfast Agreement is so remarkable. It's a masterpiece of structured ambiguity – intentionally open-ended, allowing different people to see different things in it. In that sense, it functions like a novel or a poem, full of layered meanings and possibilities.

Joe, as a novelist, would have a lot to say about this. But I truly believe that if we lose the ability to enter artistic spaces, we are lost – because we will have shut off an essential resource for imagining different ways forward. Art doesn't change the world in a direct or immediate way. Yeats famously asked in one of his poems, 'Did that play of mine send out certain men the English shot?' To which the contemporary Irish poet Paul Muldoon countered, 'Well, if Willy Yeats had saved his pencil lead, would certain men have stayed in bed?'

The truth is, it's not a simple cause-and-effect relationship. But what art does do is maintain a space of integrity, freedom, and resistance to cliché. And as long as we can keep doing that, there is always hope.

Q4: I noticed many parallels between the Northern Ireland conflict and the situation in Gaza – especially in the patterns of whataboutism, competing victimhood, and the existential struggle over the future. Given that, how can we make pluralism an appealing idea in the midst of such active and escalating violence?

FO: One of the terrible lessons of history is that being a victim doesn't necessarily make people better. In fact, it can narrow our ethical horizons, making us feel that anything we do in retaliation is justified. That certainly happened in Northern Ireland, and we see it now – where, for some, Palestinian victimhood seems to justify appalling atrocities against innocent civilians. In turn, for many, that either justifies or shuts down the mental space to imagine the suffering of Palestinians. Once this cycle begins, it's incredibly difficult to stop.

In some ways, what I've been saying is optimistic – after all, the Northern Ireland conflict did eventually end. But in other ways, it's deeply pessimistic, because it lasted thirty years when it never should have. There was no good reason for it to go on that long.

The only thing we can truly hold onto is, strangely enough, the law. Out of the world that Hannah Arendt wrote about, we did manage to build institutions – imperfect, flawed, deeply frustrating institutions – but institutions nonetheless. We created international courts, the United Nations, and a body of international law that demands just one thing: consistency. It tells us that we can't feel outrage only after checking who committed the atrocity and who the victims are. It demands that certain acts be deemed unacceptable simply because they target innocent people.

I know from my own life that confronting this truth is hard. I grew up in the mental world of Irish tribal nationalism. At thirteen or fourteen when the IRA was planting bombs in pubs and killing people, I was delighted. I thought, 'This is great'. And then I had to ask myself: Is it?

I describe this in my book: There was a bombing in Dublin, and my father worked for the bus system. The bomb was placed right outside the canteen where the bus workers ate. This was before mobile phones, and we didn't have a landline at home. For hours, we had no idea if he was alive. We heard reports that some workers had been killed. For five hours, we just didn't know. And then I heard the key in the door – my father was home.

In those five hours, I changed as a person. I realized this is the same for everyone. It doesn't matter if you're British or Irish, Protestant or Catholic, Palestinian or Israeli. The fear, the grief, the suffering – it's the same. And unless we let that knowledge reach the core of our being, we'll never do the hardest thing: stand up to our own side.

It's easy to be outraged by what they are doing. It's much harder to say, 'What we are doing is wrong – and here's why'. It forces us to confront bad ideologies and flawed ways of thinking. And that can make you deeply unpopular. But if we aren't willing to do that, then we lose all sense of moral coherence and consistency. And that's all we have to hold onto.

"THE TOTEM AS NAME AND AS EMBLEM"

EMILE DURKHEIM

EMILE DURKHEIM. Originally published in French in 1912 as *Les Formes élémentaires de la vie religieuse*, the first English translation by Joseph Ward Swain, titled *The Elementary Forms of Religious Life*, was released in 1915. Durkheim, a pioneering sociologist born in France in 1858, examined how religion and social structures influence collective identity. In this work, he explores totemism as a symbolic system that unites communities and reinforces social bonds.

At the basis of nearly all the Australian tribes we find a group which holds a preponderating place in the collective life: this is the clan. Two essential traits characterize it.

In the first place, the individuals who compose it consider themselves united by a bond of kinship, but one which is of a very special nature. This relationship does not come from the fact that they have definite blood connections with one another; they are relatives from the mere fact that they have the same name. They are not fathers and mothers, sons or daughters, uncles or nephews of one another in the sense which we now give these words; yet they think of themselves as forming a single family, which is large or small according to the dimensions of the clan, merely because they are collectively designated by the same word. When we say that they regard themselves as a single family, we do so because they recognize duties towards each other which are identical with those which have always been incumbent upon kindred: such duties as aid, vengeance, mourning, the obligation not to marry among themselves, etc.

Excerpted from: Durkheim, Emile. 2008. *The Elementary Forms of Religious Life* Edited by Mark S. Cladis and translated by Carol Cosman. Oxford University Press, 88–90.

By this first characteristic, the clan does not differ from the Roman gens or the Greek γένος; for this relationship also came merely from the fact that all the members of the gens had the same name, the nomen gentilicium. And in one sense, the gens is a clan; but it is a variety which should not be confounded with the Australian clan. This latter is distinguished by the fact that its name is also the name of a determined species of material things with which it believes that it has very particular relations, the nature of which we shall presently describe; they are especially relations of kinship. The species of things which serves to designate the clan collectively is called its totem. The totem of the clan is also that of each of its members.

Each clan has its totem, which belongs to it alone; two different clans of the same tribe cannot have the same. In fact, one is a member of a clan merely because he has a certain name. All who bear this name are members of it for that very reason; in whatever manner they may be spread over the tribal territory, they all have the same relations of kinship with one another. Consequently, two groups having the same totem can only be two sections of the same clan. Undoubtedly, it frequently happens that all of a clan does not reside in the same locality, but has representatives in several different places. However, this lack of a geographical basis does not cause its unity to be the less keenly felt.

In regard to the word totem, we may say that it is the one employed by the Ojibway, an Algonquin tribe, to designate the sort of thing whose name the clan bears. Although this expression is not at all Australian, and is found only in one single society in America, ethnographers have definitely adopted it, and use it to denote, in a general way, the system which we are describing. Schoolcraft was the first to extend the meaning of the word thus and to speak of a "totemic system." This extension, of which there are examples enough in ethnography, is not without inconveniences. It is not normal for an institution of this importance to bear a chance name, taken from a strictly local dialect, and bringing to mind none of the distinctive characteristics of the thing it designates. But to-day this way of employing the word is so universally accepted that it would be an excess of purism to rise against this usage.

In a very large proportion of the cases, the objects which serve as totems belong either to the animal or the vegetable kingdom, but especially to the former. Inanimate things are much more rarely employed. Out of more than 500 totemic names collected by Howitt among the tribes of south-eastern Australia, there are scarcely forty which are not the names of plants or animals; these are the clouds, rain, hail, frost, the moon, the sun, the wind, the autumn, the summer, the winter, certain stars, thunder, fire, smoke, water or the sea. It is noticeable how small a place is given to celestial bodies and, more generally, to the great cosmic phenomena, which were destined to so great a fortune in later religious development. Among all the clans of which Howitt speaks, there were only two which had the moon as totem, two the sun, three a star, three the thunder, two the lightning. The rain is a single exception; it, on the contrary, is very frequent. These are the totems which can be spoken of as normal. But totemism has its abnormalities as well. It sometimes happens that the totem is not a whole object, but the part of an object. This fact appears rather rarely in Australia; Howitt cites only one example.

However, it may well be that this is found with a certain frequency in the tribes where the totemic groups are excessively subdivided; it might be said that the totems had to break themselves up in order to be able to furnish names to these numerous divisions. This is what seems to have taken place among the Arunta and the Loritja. Strehlow has collected 442 totems in these two societies, of which many are not an animal species, but some particular organ of the animal of the species, such as the tail or stomach of an opossum, the fat of the kangaroo, etc.

We have seen that normally the totem is not an individual, but a species or a variety: it is not such and such a kangaroo or crow, but the kangaroo or crow in general. Sometimes, however, it is a particular object. First of all, this is necessarily the case when the thing serving as totem is unique in its class, as the sun, the moon, such or such a constellation, etc. It also happens that clans take their names from certain geographical irregularities or depressions of the land, from a certain anthill, etc. It is true that we have only a small number of examples of this in Australia; but Strehlow does mention some. But the very causes which have given rise to these abnormal totems show that they are of a relatively recent origin. In fact, what has made certain geographical features of the land become totems is that a mythical ancestor is supposed to have stopped there or to have performed some act of his legendary life there. But at the same time, these ancestors are represented in the myths as themselves belonging to clans which had perfectly regular totems, that is to say, ones taken from the animal or vegetable kingdoms. Therefore, the totemic names thus commemorating the acts and performances of these heroes cannot be primitive; they belong to a form of totemism that is already derived and deviated. It is even permissible to ask if the meteorological totems have not a similar origin; for the sun, the moon and the stars are frequently identified with the ancestors of the mythological epoch.

Sometimes, but no less exceptionally, it is an ancestor or a group of ancestors which serves as totem directly. In this case, the clan takes its name, not from a thing or a species of real things, but from a purely mythical being. Spencer and Gillen had already mentioned two or three totems of this sort. Among the Warramunga and among the Tjingilli there are clans which bear the name of an ancestor named Thaballa who seems to be gaiety incarnate.

Another Warramunga clan bears the name of a huge fabulous serpent named Wollunqua, from which the clan considers itself descended. We owe other similar facts to Strehlow. In any case, it is easy enough to see what probably took place. Under the influence of diverse causes and by the very development of mythological thought, the collective and impersonal totem became effaced before certain mythical personages who advanced to the first rank and became totems themselves.

Howsoever interesting these different irregularities may be, they contain nothing which forces us to modify our definition of a totem. They are not, as has sometimes been believed, different varieties of totems which are more or less irreducible into each other or into the normal totem, such as we have defined it. They are merely secondary and sometimes even aberrant forms of a single notion which is much more general, and there is every ground for believing it the more primitive.

The manner in which the name is acquired is more important for the organization and recruiting of the clan than for religion; it belongs to the sociology of the family rather than to religious sociology. So we shall confine ourselves to indicating summarily the most essential principles which regulate the matter. In the different tribes, three different systems are in use.

In a great number, or it might even be said, in the greater number of the societies, the child takes the totem of its mother, by right of birth: this is what happens among the Dieri and the Urabunna of the centre of Southern Australia; the Wotjobaluk and the Gournditch-Mara of Victoria;

the Kamilaroi, the Wiradjuri, the Wonghibon and the Euahlayi of New South Wales; and the Wakelbura, the Pitta-Pitta and the Kurnandaburi of Queensland, to mention only the most important names. In this case, owing to a law of exogamy, the mother is necessarily of a different totem from her husband, and on the other hand, as she lives in his community, the members of a single totem are necessarily dispersed in different localities according to the chances of their marriages. As a result, the totemic group lacks a territorial base.

Elsewhere the totem is transmitted in the paternal line. In this case, if the child remains with his father, the local group is largely made up of people belonging to a single totem; only the married women there represent foreign totems. In other words, each locality has its particular totem. Up until recent times, this scheme of organization was found in Australia only among the tribes where totemism was in decadence, such as the Narrinyeri, where the totem has almost no religious character at all any more. It was therefore possible to believe that there was a close connection between the totemic system and descent in the uterine line. But Spencer and Gillen have observed, in the northern part of central Australia, a whole group of tribes where the totemic religion is still practised but where the transmission of the totem is in the paternal line: these are the Warramunga, the Quanji, the Umbia, the Binbinga, the Mara and the Anula.

Finally, a third combination is the one observed among the Arunta and Loritja. Here the totem of the child is not necessarily either that of the mother or that of the father; it is that of a mythical ancestor who came, by processes which the observers recount in different ways, and mysteriously fecundated the mother at the moment of conception. A special process makes it possible to learn which ancestor it was and to which totemic group he belonged. But since it was only chance which determined that this ancestor happened to be near the mother, rather than another, the totem of the child is thus found to depend finally upon fortuitous circumstances.

"THE INFANTILE RECURRENCE OF TOTEMISM"

SIGMUND FREUD

SIGMUND FREUD. *Totem and Taboo: Einige Übereinstimmungen im Seelenleben der Wilden und der Neurotiker* was originally published between 1912 and 1913 in the journal *Imago*. Freud, the founder of psychoanalysis, explores the psychological origins of social structures. In this essay, Freud explores the origins of totemic systems in early human societies, arguing that shared symbols and taboos helped shape social bonds and group identity. These systems offer insight into the origins of tribalism and the regulation of behavior within early societies.

The first chapter of this book made us acquainted with the conception of totemism. We heard that totemism is a system which takes the place of religion among certain primitive races in Australia, America, and Africa, and furnishes the basis of social organization. We know that in 1869 the Scotchman MacLennan attracted general interest to the phenomena of totemism, which until then had been considered merely as curiosities, by his conjecture that a large number of customs and usages in various old as well as modern societies were to be taken as remnants of a totemic epoch. Science has since then fully recognized this significance of totemism. I quote a passage from the *Elements of the Psychology of Races* by W. Wundt (1912), as the latest utterance on this question: 'Taking all this together it becomes highly probable that a totemic culture was at one time the preliminary stage of every later evolution as well as a transition stage between the state of primitive man and the age of gods and heroes.'

It is necessary for the purposes of this chapter to go more deeply into the nature of totemism. For reasons that will be evident later I here give

---

Excerpted from: Freud, Sigmund. 2012. *Totem and Taboo*. Translated by A.A. Brill, chapter 4, part 1.

preference to an outline by S. Reinach, who in the year 1900 sketched the following 'Code du Totémisme' in twelve articles, like a catechism of the totemic religion:

1. Certain animals must not be killed or eaten, but men bring up individual animals of these species and take care of them.

2. An animal that dies accidentally is mourned and buried with the same honours as a member of the tribe.

3. The prohibition as to eating sometimes refers only to a certain part of the animal.

4. If pressure of necessity compels the killing of an animal usually spared, it is done with excuses to the animal and the attempt is made to mitigate the violation of the taboo, namely the killing, through various tricks and evasions.

5. If the animal is sacrificed by ritual, it is solemnly mourned.

6. At specified solemn occasions, like religious ceremonies, the skins of certain animals are donned. Where totemism still exists, these are totem animals.

7. Tribes and individuals assume the names of totem animals.

8. Many tribes use pictures of animals as coats of arms and decorate their weapons with them; the men paint animal pictures on their bodies or have them tattooed.

9. If the totem is one of the feared and dangerous animals it is assumed that the animal will spare the members of the tribe named after it.

10. The totem animal protects and warns the members of the tribe.

11. The totem animal foretells the future to those faithful to it and serves as their leader.

12. The members of a totem tribe often believe that they are connected with the totem animal by the bond of common origin.

The value of this catechism of the totem religion can be more appreciated if one bears in mind that Reinach has here also incorporated all the signs and clews which lead to the conclusion that the totemic system had once existed. The peculiar attitude of this author to the problem is shown by the fact that to some extent he neglects the essential traits of totemism, and we shall see that of the two main tenets of the totemistic catechism he has forced one into the background and completely lost sight of the other.

In order to get a more correct picture of the characteristics of totemism we turn to an author who has devoted four volumes to the theme, combining the most complete collection of the observations in question with the most thorough discussion of the problems they raise. We shall remain indebted to J.G. Frazer, the author of *Totemism and Exogamy*, for the pleasure and information he affords, even though psychoanalytic investigation may lead us to results which differ widely from his.

"A totem," wrote Frazer in his first essay, "is a class of material objects which a savage regards with superstitious respect, believing that there exists between him and every member of the class an intimate and altogether special relation. The connexion between a person and his totem is mutually beneficent; the totem protects the man and the man shows his respect for the totem in various ways, by not killing it if it be an animal, and not cutting or gathering it if it be a plant. As distinguished from a fetich, a totem is never an isolated individual but always a class of objects, generally a species of animals or of plants, more rarely a class of inanimate natural objects, very rarely a class of artificial objects."

At least three kinds of totem can be distinguished:

1. The tribal totem which a whole tribe shares and which is hereditary from generation to generation,

2. The sex totem which belongs to all the masculine or feminine members of a tribe to the exclusion of the opposite sex, and

3. The individual totem which belongs to the individual and does not descend to his successors. The last two kinds of totem are comparatively of little importance compared to the tribal totem. Unless we are mistaken they are recent formations and of little importance as far as the nature of the taboo is concerned. The tribal totem (clan totem) is the object of veneration of a group of men and women who take their name from the totem and consider themselves consanguineous offspring of a common ancestor, and who are firmly associated with each other through common obligations towards each other as well as by the belief in their totem.

Totemism is a religious as well as a social system. On its religious side it consists of the relations of mutual respect and consideration between a person and his totem, and on its social side it is composed of obligations of the members of the clan towards each other and towards other tribes. In the later history of totemism these two sides show a tendency to part company; the social system often survives the religious and conversely remnants of totemism remain in the religion of countries in which the social system based upon totemism had disappeared. In the present state of our ignorance about the origin of totemism we cannot say with certainty how these two sides were originally combined. But there is on the whole a strong probability that in the beginning the two sides of totemism were indistinguishable from each other. In other words, the further we go back the clearer it becomes that a member of a tribe looks upon himself as being of the same genus as his totem and makes no distinction between his attitude towards the totem and his attitude towards his tribal companions.

In the special description of totemism as a religious system, Frazer lays stress on the fact that the members of a tribe assume the name of their totem and also as a rule believe that they are descended from it. It is due to this belief that they do not hunt the totem animal or kill or eat it, and that they deny themselves every other use of the totem if it is not an animal. The prohibitions against killing or eating the totem are not the only taboos affecting it; sometimes it is also forbidden to touch it and even to look at it; in a number of cases the totem must not be called by its right name. Violation of the taboo prohibitions which protect the totem is punished automatically by serious disease or death.

Specimens of the totem animals are sometimes raised by the clan and taken care of in captivity. A totem animal found dead is mourned and buried like a member of the clan. If a totem animal had to be killed it was done with a prescribed ritual of excuses and ceremonies of expiation.

The tribe expected protection and forbearance from its totem. If it was a dangerous animal (a beast of prey or a poisonous snake), it was assumed that it would not harm, and where this assumption did not come true the person attacked was expelled from the tribe. Frazer thinks that oaths were originally ordeals, many tests as to descent and genuineness being in this way left to the decision of the totem. The totem helps in case of illness and gives the tribe premonitions and warnings. The appearance of the totem animal near a house was often looked upon as an announcement of death. The totem had come to get its relative.

A member of a clan seeks to emphasize his relationship to the totem in various significant ways; he imitates an exterior similarity by dressing himself in the skin of the totem animal, by having the picture of it tattooed upon himself, and in other ways. On the solemn occasions of birth, initiation into manhood or funeral obsequies this identification with the totem is carried out in deeds and words. Dances in which all the members of the tribe disguise themselves as their totem and act like it, serve various magic and religious purposes. Finally there are the ceremonies at which the totem animal is killed in a solemn manner.

PSALM 22:
'DO NOT BE FAR FROM ME'

KING JAMES BIBLE

In ancient Israel, tribalism was rooted in the strong bonds and identity shared among the twelve tribes. This plea reflects a profound connection to this collective identity, seeking comfort not only as an individual but as part of a covenant community. References to ancestors who trusted in God and were delivered emphasize a shared history and collective memory central to tribal belonging.

My God, my God, why have you forsaken me?
   Why are you so far from saving me,
   so far from my cries of anguish?
My God, I cry out by day, but you do not answer,
   by night, but I find no rest.

Yet you are enthroned as the Holy One;
   you are the one Israel praises.
In you our ancestors put their trust;
   they trusted and you delivered them.
To you they cried out and were saved;
   in you they trusted and were not put to shame.

But I am a worm and not a man,
   scorned by everyone, despised by the people.
All who see me mock me;
   they hurl insults, shaking their heads.
"He trusts in the Lord," they say,
   "let the Lord rescue him.
Let him deliver him,
   since he delights in him."

Yet you brought me out of the womb;
> you made me trust in you, even at my mother's breast.
From birth I was cast on you;
> from my mother's womb you have been my God.
Do not be far from me,
> for trouble is near
> and there is no one to help.

Many bulls surround me;
> strong bulls of Bashan encircle me.
Roaring lions that tear their prey
> open their mouths wide against me.
I am poured out like water,
> and all my bones are out of joint.
My heart has turned to wax;
> it has melted within me.
My mouth is dried up like a potsherd,
> and my tongue sticks to the roof of my mouth;
> you lay me in the dust of death.

Dogs surround me,
> a pack of villains encircles me;
> they pierce my hands and my feet.
All my bones are on display;
> people stare and gloat over me.
They divide my clothes among them
> and cast lots for my garment.

But you, Lord, do not be far from me.
> You are my strength; come quickly to help me.
Deliver me from the sword,
> my precious life from the power of the dogs.
Rescue me from the mouth of the lions;
> save me from the horns of the wild oxen.

I will declare your name to my people;
   in the assembly I will praise you.
You who fear the Lord, praise him!
    All you descendants of Jacob, honor him!
    Revere him, all you descendants of Israel!
For he has not despised or scorned
   the suffering of the afflicted one;
he has not hidden his face from him
   but has listened to his cry for help.

From you comes the theme of my praise in the great assembly;
   before those who fear you I will fulfill my vows.
The poor will eat and be satisfied;
   those who seek the Lord will praise him—
   may your hearts live forever!

All the ends of the earth
   will remember and turn to the Lord,
and all the families of the nations
   will bow down before him,
for dominion belongs to the Lord
   and he rules over the nations.

You are my King and my God,
   who decrees victories for Jacob.
Through you we push back our enemies;
   through your name we trample our foes.
I put no trust in my bow,
   my sword does not bring me victory;
but you give us victory over our enemies,
   you put our adversaries to shame.
In God we make our boast all day long,
   and we will praise your name forever.

But now you have rejected and humbled us;
    you no longer go out with our armies.
You made us retreat before the enemy,
    and our adversaries have plundered us.
You gave us up to be devoured like sheep
    and have scattered us among the nations.
You sold your people for a pittance,
    gaining nothing from their sale.

You have made us a reproach to our neighbors,
    the scorn and derision of those around us.
You have made us a byword among the nations;
    the peoples shake their heads at us.
I live in disgrace all day long,
    and my face is covered with shame
at the taunts of those who reproach and revile me,
    because of the enemy, who is bent on revenge.

All this came upon us,
    though we had not forgotten you;
    we had not been false to your covenant.
Our hearts had not turned back;
    our feet had not strayed from your path.
But you crushed us and made us a haunt for jackals;
    you covered us over with deep darkness.

If we had forgotten the name of our God
    or spread out our hands to a foreign god,
would not God have discovered it,
    since he knows the secrets of the heart?
Yet for your sake we face death all day long;
    we are considered as sheep to be slaughtered.

Awake, Lord! Why do you sleep?
    Rouse yourself! Do not reject us forever.
Why do you hide your face
    and forget our misery and oppression?

We are brought down to the dust;
   our bodies cling to the ground.
Rise up and help us;
   rescue us because of your unfailing love.

"I AM NOT WITH THOSE WHO ABANDONED THEIR LAND"

ANNA AKHMATOVA

ANNA AKHMATOVA'S "I am not with those who abandoned their land" was written in 1922 and published in *Anno Domini* in 1923. Akhmatova's critique of exiles suggests a form of tribalism, emphasizing strong in-group loyalty and a clear distinction between those who remain connected to their homeland and those who do not. She embraces an intrinsic bond between a poet and their native land.

To the lacerations of the enemy.
I am deaf to their coarse flattery,
I won't give them my songs.

But to me the exile is forever pitiful,
Like a prisoner, like someone ill.
Dark is your road, wanderer,
Like wormwood smells the bread of strangers.

But here, in the blinding smoke of the conflagration
Destroying what's left of youth,
We have not deflected from ourselves
One single stroke.

And we know that in the final accounting,
Each hour will be justified…
But there is no people on earth more tearless
More simple and more full of pride.

July 1922

Excerpted from: *The Complete Poems of Anna Akhmatova*. 1992. Translated by Judith Hemschemeyer, 2nd ed. Zephyr Press, 263.

"GROUP FEELING"

IBN KHALDÛN

IBN KHALDÛN, a fourteenth-century Arab historian and philosopher, introduced the concept of 'asabiyyah' or group feeling. In this seminal work, he examines the social cohesion that sustains civilizations, arguing that strong communal bonds are essential for political stability and cultural flourishing. Khaldûn argues that this form of cohesion naturally develops within tribes and small kinship groups, acting as the fundamental bond that drives the rise of civilizations. However, as societies grow more advanced and sedentary, this solidarity weakens, leading to societal decline and eventual conquest by groups possessing stronger 'asabiyyah'.

---

16 THE GOAL TO WHICH GROUP FEELING LEADS IS ROYAL AUTHORITY

This is because group feeling gives protection and makes possible mutual defence, the pressing of claims, and every other kind of social activity. By dint of their nature, human beings need someone to act as a restraining influence and mediator in every social organization, in order to keep its members from (fighting) with each other. That person must, by necessity, have superiority over the others in the matter of group feeling. If not, his power cannot be effective. Such superiority is royal authority. It is more than leadership. Leadership means being a chieftain, and the leader is obeyed, but he has no power to force others to accept his rulings. Royal authority means superiority and the power to rule by force.

When a person sharing in the group feeling has reached the rank of chieftain and commands obedience, and when he then finds the way open toward superiority and the use of force, he follows that way, because it is something desirable. He cannot completely achieve his (goal) except with

---

Excerpted from: Ibn Khaldûn. 2015. *The Muqaddimah: An Introduction to History.* Abridged edition. Princeton University Press, 16–17.

the help of the group feeling, which causes (the others) to obey him. Thus, royal superiority is a goal to which group feeling leads, as one can see.

Even if an individual tribe has different 'houses' and many diverse group feelings, still, there must exist a group feeling that is stronger than all the other group feelings combined, that is superior to them all and makes them subservient, and in which all the diverse group feelings coalesce, as it were, to become one greater group feeling. Otherwise, splits would occur and lead to dissension and strife.

Once group feeling has established superiority over the people who share in it, it will, by its very nature, seek superiority over people who have other group feelings unrelated to the first. If the one (group feeling) is the equal of the other or is able to stave off (its challenge), the (competing people) are even with and equal to each other. Each group feeling maintains its sway over its own domain and people, as is the case with tribes and nations all over the earth. However, if the one group feeling overpowers the other and makes it subservient to itself, the two group feelings enter into close contact, and the (defeated) group feeling gives added power to the (victorious) group feeling, which, as a result, sets its goal of superiority and domination higher than before. In this way, it goes on until the power of that particular group feeling equals the power of the ruling dynasty. Then, when the ruling dynasty grows senile and no defender arises from among its friends who share in its group feeling, the (new group feeling) takes over and deprives the ruling dynasty of its power, and, thus, obtains complete royal authority.

The power of (a given group feeling) may reach its peak when the ruling dynasty has not yet reached senility. (This stage) may coincide with the stage at which (the ruling dynasty) needs to have recourse to the people who represent the various group feelings (in order to master the situation). In such a case, the ruling dynasty includes (the people who enjoy the powerful group feeling) among those of its clients whom it uses for the execution of its various projects. This, then, means (the formation of) another royal authority, inferior to that of the controlling royal authority. This was the case with the Turks under the 'Abbâsids.

It is thus evident that royal authority is the goal of group feeling. When it attains that goal, the tribe (representing that particular group feeling) obtains royal authority, either by seizing actual control or by giving assistance (to the ruling dynasty) according to the circumstances prevailing. If the group feeling encounters obstacles on its way to the goal, it stops where it is, until God decides its fate.

17 OBSTACLES ON THE WAY TOWARD ROYAL AUTHORITY ARE LUXURY AND THE SUBMERGENCE OF THE TRIBE IN A LIFE OF PROSPERITY

This is because, when a tribe has achieved a certain measure of superiority with the help of its group feeling, it gains control over a corresponding amount of wealth and comes to share prosperity and abundance with those who have been in possession of these things. It shares in them to the degree of its power and usefulness to the ruling dynasty. If the ruling dynasty is so strong that no one thinks of depriving it of its power or of sharing with it, the tribe in question submits to its rule and is satisfied with whatever share in the dynasty's wealth and tax revenue it is permitted to enjoy. Hopes would not go so high as to think of royal prerogatives or ways to obtain (royal authority). (Members of the tribe) are merely concerned with prosperity, gain, and a life of abundance. (They are satisfied) to lead an easy, restful life in the shadow of the ruling dynasty, and to adopt royal habits in building and dress, a matter they stress and in which they take more and more pride, the more luxuries and plenty they acquire, as well as all the other things that go with luxury and plenty.

As a result, the toughness of desert life is lost. Group feeling and courage weaken. Members of the tribe revel in the well-being that God has given them. Their children and offspring grow up too proud to look after themselves or to attend to their own needs. They have disdain also for all the other things that are necessary in connection with group feeling. This finally becomes a character trait and natural characteristic of theirs. Their group feeling and courage decrease in the next generations. Eventually, group feeling is altogether destroyed. They thus invite their own destruction. The greater their luxury and the easier the life they enjoy, the closer they are to extinction, not to mention (their lost chance of securing) royal authority. The things that go with luxury and submergence in a life of ease break the vigour of the group feeling, which alone produces superiority. When group feeling is destroyed, the tribe is no longer able to protect itself, let alone press any claims. It will be swallowed up by other nations.

CONVERSATIONS ON TRIBALISM AND COSMOPOLITANISM

"TECHNOLOGY, PLURALISM, AND COSMOPOLITANISM: AMIDST THE RETURN OF TRIBALISM"

ZOË HITZIG AND
ANN LAUTERBACH
(WITH ALLISON STANGER)

ALLISON STANGER [AS]: Roger described this as a closing panel about poetry. But after reading the title he wrote for this session – 'Technology, Pluralism, and Cosmopolitanism Amidst the Return of Tribalism' – you'll notice there's no mention of poetry whatsoever. Given that we have two wonderful poets here, however, I can't help but think that poetry will find its way into the conversation.

Zoë is my co-director at the *Getting Plurality* Research Network at Harvard University. She's also a member of the Harvard Society of Fellows – which, if you don't know, essentially means you have to be one of the smartest people in the world to get in. She holds a PhD in mathematical economics, an undergraduate degree in mathematics, and has already published two volumes of poetry, with work appearing in *The New York Review of Books* and *The New Yorker*. She's an extraordinary thinker and writer, and she may share more about her work with us.

And then, of course, we have Ann Lauterbach. What can I say? She is one of Bard's – and the world's – finest poets. Last night, I heard several people say that Ann always gives the best talk at the Hannah Arendt Conference, even though she's always nervous beforehand. I have no doubt she'll deliver again today. So, without further ado, I'd like to welcome Zoë to the podium.

ZOË HITZIG [ZH]: Thank you, Allison. And thank you to everyone for making this such a great conference so far.

I'll keep my remarks brief, touching on digital technology and pluralism – some of the words in our panel's title – before getting out of the way so we can hear from Ann. It's a real honor to be on a panel with her, as she's someone I've looked up to for a long time.

If there's a central thesis to what I'll say, it's this: Communication – an essential element of any pluralist society – requires the sharing of both content and context. While digital information technologies have dramatically increased the speed and scale at which we share content across vast differences, they have not kept pace in conveying context. Digital technology can play a valuable role in connecting us in a pluralistic society, but its success depends on a healthy balance between content and context – one that, at present, we do not have.

So, I'll begin with a very basic, even naïve, question – one that's more abstract than much of what we've discussed at this conference: How do we communicate with each other?

One simple answer is that communication involves a combination of verbal and nonverbal language that carries content – the 'what' of a message. We interpret that content through context – the 'who', 'when', 'how', 'why', and 'where'. Context is what binds content to meaning.

Think about how communication works in face-to-face settings – what we're all doing here. Consider a specific exchange that took place over the last few days: small talk by the coffee dispenser, a particularly insightful and well-calibrated question during a session, or even an awkward smile as someone emerged from one of the genderless bathroom stalls. Whatever it was, the mere fact that the interaction happened in person likely provided a shared understanding of basic context.

Your answers to certain questions would likely align with the other person's: Where? Olin Hall. When? Mid-October. Who? At the very least, you know it's someone who attends the Arendt Center's annual conference. What's remarkable about in-person interactions – something we shouldn't overlook or take for granted – is how much common contextual understanding they provide. Our interpretations are rich and nuanced, shaped by sensory details and social, biological, and cultural cues honed over millennia.

But face-to-face interaction is also limited in its pluralistic potential. It's constrained by physics – by gravity, by the fact that we can't be in two places at once. Vast oceans separate us. We are bound to a single body, and family, work, and limited resources often keep us tethered to a tight radius around our dwellings. If we could only communicate with those physically near us, our interactions would be few and infrequent. Our possibilities for pluralism would be severely constrained.

Communication technologies changed that. They allow content to travel across distance and time. Think of cuneiform tablets, the printing press, the telegraph, the telephone, the radio. Then email, internet forums, text messages, and social media. Each new technology has expanded communication's reach, but primarily by making it easier to transmit content across distances. This has often come at the cost of context. Every major advance in communication changes not only how we share content, but also how context is conveyed, distorted, flattened, or omitted.

In response, societies have tried to develop norms, expectations, and tools to restore context where it has been lost. Ancient cuneiform tablets were sealed with impressions to authenticate their authorship. Books have long included colophons listing publication details. Since the 13th century, papermakers have embedded watermarks to indicate origin and quality. Telegrams were stamped with the sender's location and date.

As mass media emerged, Hannah Arendt recognized both its potential and its dangers – how it could foster connection but also homogenization, isolation, and propaganda. In other words, mass media accelerated the spread of content, while efforts to preserve context lagged behind. Consider Orson Welles's War of the Worlds radio broadcast, which was formatted as real-time news bulletins. While the number of listeners who genuinely believed in a Martian invasion may have been exaggerated, the event underscored the need to provide clear context when blending fact and fiction. Afterward, radio hosts became more diligent about inserting disclaimers when content was fictional, rebroadcast, or sponsored.

Compare that to today's internet. The idea that we might expect disclaimers to help us interpret online content –an advertisement, a tweet, a suspicious email – now seems almost quaint. Efforts to reassert context are no match for the breakneck speed and scale of online content delivery. Even agreeing on basic facts about a given message has become difficult. Think of fact-checking attempts on Twitter (now X), a chaotic platform with 500 million active users, owned by a billionaire sociopath. It sporadically attaches 'community notes' meant to provide context to tweets, but this is a weak attempt at restoring context to compressed, 280-character messages.

Discussions about the social impact of digital technology often focus on issues like privacy violations, misinformation, disinformation, and deception. But I believe these are all symptoms of a larger issue: the erosion of context. Effective communication – communication essential for a pluralistic society – requires participants to identify and protect the context of their exchanges.

What does it mean to identify context? It means being able to authenticate the 'who', 'why', 'where', 'how', and 'when' of a communication. Who posted this tweet? Who sent this email or text? When was it written? Why? Is it from a person, an organization, an AI? Does the sender have my best interests in mind? Am I seeing this because it's relevant to me, or because I'm being manipulated?

To protect context means ensuring that communication isn't misused outside of its intended purpose. Can I trust that a private email won't end up in a newspaper, a courtroom, or my employer's inbox? Will this message go viral? Will the platform or telecom company use my words to train an AI that will one day replace me – or worse, lead me to buy shoes I don't need, attack someone I don't know, or storm the Capitol?

Many of today's digital communication problems – issues of authenticity, truth, privacy, and data protection – ultimately stem from our failure to preserve context. Without the ability to authenticate context, we can't establish norms for protecting it. And without protections, authentication efforts are futile. In this sense, authenticity and privacy are two sides of the same coin, and treating them as separate problems hinders our ability to address the deeper issue: our growing inability to communicate across differences.

The real problem isn't that we can share vast amounts of content across the globe. It's that this ability has not been accompanied by adequate methods for preserving and asserting context. I don't have easy solutions. The deeper issue – one we must never sugarcoat – is that technological innovation is currently driven by what's profitable, not by what's good for people. And that will remain the case as long as we continue to bow to Big Tech.

Still, thinking about context points us toward some possible ways to build more pluralistic forms of digital communication. I'd break these into two categories: tools for identifying context and tools for protecting it.

For identifying context, cryptographers have developed technologies like zero-knowledge proofs – sometimes called 'anonymous credentials' – that let individuals authenticate aspects of their identity in different contexts without revealing everything about themselves. These could allow users to prove they are human, verify their age, or confirm other relevant traits while maintaining control over their anonymity.

For protecting context, one solution is to use communication channels run by non-profit organizations that prioritize user privacy, like Signal. Another simple but effective strategy is to use disappearing messages – reducing our exposure to surveillance and refusing to be reduced to mere data.

To sum up: In the age of the internet, pluralism depends on our ability to preserve not just what we communicate, but with whom, when, and how. And right now, we are failing to keep up.

ANN LAUTERBACH [AL]: My talk is titled 'Technology, Pluralism, and Cosmopolitanism Amidst the Return of the Tribal: A Poet's Discontinuous Meditation'. Ever since I watched Ray Kurzweil, here at Bard's Fischer Center, sketch two rapidly ascending lines on a huge screen – lines converging at what he called the singularity – I've felt a mix of melancholy, gladness, and anxious fear. Gladness that I will likely not be alive when this event occurs, and fear that it inevitably will, like death. Since then, my darkest thought has been that our species has chosen to will itself extinct – that we've grown tired of the difficulty of living, exhausted by the human condition, squandered our resources, and are now ready to abandon life, propelled forward on a technological arrow shot from Elon Musk's bow. This thought follows me like a shadow, even as I continue to take delight in the shifting sky, the turning leaves, the quizzical expression of a perplexed student.

Of the three of us on this panel, I am the card-carrying Luddite – not that I don't use technology. I do. I'm grateful for its speed, its assistance with my poor spelling and shaky memory, and for the way it eliminates the need for forever stamps in my constant correspondences. But I'm not on social media, I don't have a website, and my technological proficiency is about two percent – like the milk in my coffee. Which is to say, I am about 98 percent Luddite.

The Luddites, you may recall, were 19th-century textile workers in England who opposed machines replacing their craft. This stance might seem fitting for a poet, given the widespread belief that poetry is useless, atavistic, anachronistic – at least the kind of poetry I write, which is drawn from the linguistic archive of my soul, constantly fed by the evolving stream of language in the world. Where this places me on the shifting scale between tribalism and cosmopolitanism is anyone's guess. Perhaps I belong to a tribe of cat-loving poets, raised in 20th-century Manhattan, who prefer hybridity and plurals to dichotomies, binaries, and dualities. I could teach a master class in ambiguity, indecision, uncertainty, and doubt. Can machines doubt?

Hannah Arendt, in *The Human Condition*, describes how the advent of doubt began with Galileo, Copernicus, and the making of the telescope. She writes: "The old opposition of sensual and rational truth, of the inferior truth's capacity of the senses and the superior truth's capacity of reason, pales beside this challenge – that neither truth nor reality is a given, that neither of them appears as it is, and that only interference with appearance, doing away with appearances, can hold out a hope for true knowledge."

How do we "do away with appearances" when almost everything now is an appearance, an apparition? The current crisis in the humanities, I believe, stems from an overvaluation of a certain kind of cognitive intelligence – 'she's so smart!' – and a near-contempt for emotional intelligence, the kind of intelligence shaped by the arts: painting, music, fiction, poetry, the learning of other languages. People from every imaginable background make things. It is our primary human activity, what Arendt calls *homo faber* – the unending variety of things whose sum constitutes the human artifice.

This week's *Hyperallergic* featured a story about Indigenous storytelling through culinary arts, which reminded me of the original meaning of 'tribal': a shared set of customs and beliefs, gatherings and neighborhoods, families and familiars. This was addressed so eloquently in yesterday's panel and again earlier today. Technology, however, has altered the concept of the tribe, even as it manufactures a sense of belonging through silos, branding, slogans, podcasts, and platforms. These often replace or displace the artifacts and activities that once formed the texture of real shared experience.

Allison suggested I watch *Her*, Spike Jonze's 2013 film, to 'get up to speed' on technology. I watched it a few nights ago. It's an overdetermined, attenuated fantasy about a man – last name Twombly – who falls in love with his OS, an artificial intelligence named Samantha. At one point, Samantha sends a real woman to have physical intimacy with Twombly, but he can't bridge the gap between Samantha's disembodied voice and the actual stranger in his bed. The film is about displaced narcissism and misplaced intimacy, symptoms of our technological world.

Among the many losses we are experiencing is the nexus of capacities that depend on speaking to each other in person – as Zoë emphasized in her talk. When we are physically present, our hands, eyes, mouths, tongues, and voices all contribute to comprehension. Our bodies, though fallible, are porous instruments with multiple pathways for perception and response. Dispositions like belief and faith, love and hope, trust and care, doubt and curiosity – these are cultivated through affective gestures and relational vocabularies. Without them, we are left with a world of transactions, where people make love to operating systems and forget how to make artifacts that bring delight, tracing their origins to distant hands.

Speaking of distant hands – if you can, go see the Siena exhibition at the Met. It's astonishing. It offers an intimate connection to hands from centuries ago.

I'm reminded of William James's definition of experience: "My experience is what I agree to attend to. Only those items which I notice shape my mind. Without selective interest, experience is an utter chaos. Interest alone gives accent and emphasis, light and shade, background and foreground, intelligible perspective. It varies in every creature, but without it, the consciousness of every creature would be a gray, chronic indiscriminateness, impossible for us even to conceive."

And yet, we did conceive it. We created this gray, chaotic indiscriminateness, but we disguised it as experience. Attention is inherently selective; it implies that something is not being attended to, that something else is always over there, in the other room, across the street, in another country. Technology has transformed this 'elsewhere' into a mayhem of simultaneous attention – a relentless, cascading stream of entangled narratives and images that leave us bewildered and estranged. This is not cosmopolitanism. It's something else entirely. It arrives on cool, flat, glassy screens – time without space – where our bodies lose their bearings, becoming leftover, inconvenient encumbrances.

Maybe it all comes down to pronouns. What if all the *I*'s – the multitudes of selves – became *they*? What then? The self is plural.

This isn't what Arendt intended by her vision, but perhaps it offers a way out of the hardening carapace that encases our ability to know one another beyond overt identity. We come into the world with few means of communication, but gradually, we expand them. We attach words to objects, to people, to things – and this discovery fills us with wonder. Wonder, Arendt reminds us, was the beginning of philosophy.

That moment of astonishment – when the word 'bird' comes to mean that creature outside, perched on a twig, making its own wordless sound – this is where it begins. And our words come from a multitude of sources, different for each of us. The self is made from a constellation of vocabularies, shaped by myriad experiences, attentions, places, and things.

We cannot be reduced to a single epithet – Gen Z, Black, Jewish.

The self is plural. Hybrid. Mutable.

Let's imagine that our psyches are more like weather than like the tree thrashed by the storm. We are not operating systems. We are not bots. We can change our minds. We can open our hearts.

The tribe we belong to is human.

AS: What's going to happen now is that I'll pose a few brief questions to each of our speakers before turning it over to all of you. I'll keep this short, since I know you're eager to engage with them directly.

First, Zoë, I really loved the driving force of your talk: the idea that today's Internet is turbocharging content delivery while eroding context. I completely agree that context is essential to meaning, and Ann emphasized this as well.

So, I'm wondering: how can we counteract the negative effects of massive digitalization on the human experience? You mentioned some important interventions, and perhaps I could ask you to expand on those. Specifically, when you talked about tools for restoring context, you brought up personhood and zero-knowledge proofs. Maybe you could explain a bit more about what those are? Who here knows what a zero-knowledge proof is? Not many, I presume – so it would be great if you could walk us through that.

I also want to get your take on this proposition: Bots and algorithms don't have rights – humans do. In other words, our laws should prioritize the human tribe, as Ann so beautifully put it. To what extent do you think this perspective could help us uphold and protect the human in a digital age?

And finally, I'd love to hear your thoughts on the various efforts to create a public, non-commercial Internet. There are some fascinating initiatives in this space, and I personally find them quite compelling. What promise do you see in this approach for keeping humans at the center, ensuring that technology augments human intelligence rather than superseding it?

ZH: Those are all such great questions. I don't even know where to start.

I think I'll begin with your first question: What are the hopeful visions for preserving the human in this swirl of mass communication – or, as Ann put it so beautifully, the "elsewhere of simultaneous attention"?

I have two conflicting instincts about this. One comes from what I think of as my more dismal poet side – the part of me that wants to say the answer is to retreat. To go home, disconnect, throw your devices far away, and, in a sense, be forgotten. There's actually a movement around this idea, reflected in some successful laws in the EU and California that enforce a right to be forgotten on digital platforms. This has a technical meaning – allowing people to have certain data erased – but it also remains a kind of fuzzy concept, difficult to fully enforce. Still, I love the idea behind it. What does it mean to walk away, to become illegible? To find parts of your experience that can't be turned into data, can't be captured or quantified? Because once you become knowable in that sense, you risk losing the mystery of being alive, of forming real human connections.

That's one answer – the poet's answer. But maybe it's not dismal. Maybe it's just romantic.

The more pragmatic side of me, though, wants to offer something actionable – something that people can actually believe in. Not just individuals, but those who work in technology, people who want to solve problems. If I stood in front of them and just talked about resisting datafication and embracing the unknowable, they'd probably look at me like I had six heads. They wouldn't know what to do with that.

So, what's the alternative? How can we channel their energy into initiatives that actually address these problems? People working in tech see the issues in society, and they tend to approach them as problems to be solved. And there are, in fact, promising approaches – especially in the world of cryptography.

At the end of my talk, I briefly mentioned anonymous credentials, which I think are really exciting. Right now, when you need to prove who you are online – let's say you're trying to verify your identity on social media – you often have to hand over way too much information. It's overkill. For example, I think Instagram currently requires you to submit a copy of your driver's license to verify your account. That's a huge amount of personal information handed over to a platform that does not have your best interests in mind. But what does Instagram actually need to know? Not your full legal identity – just that you're a real person.

Anonymous credentials allow for this. They let you prove specific things about yourself without exposing unnecessary details. For instance, instead of handing over your ID, you could carry a credential that simply proves, I am a person. That's it. You could use it to verify your presence online without revealing anything else about yourself. It could replace captchas, so instead of solving endless, annoying puzzles, you'd just have this credential that says, 'yes, I'm a human'.

And with that, you maintain both privacy and credibility – something that's becoming increasingly difficult in the digital world. To get that, we need to build a good system. I've written a bit about how such a system could actually work. A few months ago, I published a paper exploring different ways to set it up so that the issuer of the system doesn't end up with too much control or power over it.

That's one promising technology I see as useful. But beyond simply proving that you're a person, you might also need to verify other things – like proving you're over 18. Estonia, for example, has an incredible digital identity program that's both highly privacy-preserving and not Big Brother-level scary. They use it to allow people to vote anonymously online, which I think is an incredible idea. It's hard to imagine something like that happening in the U.S., but if people had a secure way to verify certain claims about themselves privately, it could dramatically expand the possibilities for online democracy.

AS: Ann gave us so much to think about as well. I have two clusters of questions, and I'm trying to crystallize them now. The first has to do with the crisis in the humanities that you mentioned. What do you see as the likely response? This is really an educational question. Should we re-center the humanities? De-ideologize them? Or should we take a more Rousseauian approach, like Rousseau's ideal education for Émile, where there's no exposure to the humanities until after a solid foundation in STEM? The idea being that you need to develop your mind first before turning to the humanities. I was actually thinking that Zoë had the Émile education.

AL: I don't have a clear answer. But the reason I brought it up is that one of my central points is how deeply we undervalue affective intelligence – and the internet has only made this worse. It has turned emotional intelligence into a kind of cartoon.

My concern about the humanities is that their decline aligns with a broader shift in how we define intelligence – what it means to be human, what it means to be smart. We've seen this overemphasis on cognitive intelligence for a long time. Arendt recognized it too. There's that striking passage where she talks about doubt and how, even before Descartes, there was already this idea that the senses were somehow inferior to the mind.

I think that's a huge mistake. It's part of what has divided us from the rest of the animal world and from nature itself. If we were a little less conceited about our brains and a little more attuned to our sensory experience – our sensorium – we might be better equipped to cultivate empathy. Not just self-awareness, but a capacity to feel for others.

So that's why I raised the issue. I don't know the solution, except that we need to rebalance what we consider necessary for becoming a grown-up.

At Bard, I often think about how students arrive as kids. They've just left home, and then four years later, we expect them to step into the world as adults. It's an astonishing expectation – to undergo that transformation on every possible level in just four years.

And one of the most essential ways to prepare students for that transition, I believe, is through the humanities.

AS: I think that's brilliant. And I'm happy to report that, as you're probably aware, recent advances in cognitive science have pretty much blown-up Cartesian dualism.

Our intelligence is embodied. Human intelligence is embodied, and so are our emotions. Ann, you posed that wonderful question: Can machines doubt? And I don't think they can, because doubt is an emotion. It's a kind of withering of meaning, a hesitation that arises from lived experience, and that, too, is embodied.

But I want to throw out a thought experiment – a question that doesn't necessarily have an answer, but I'd love to hear both your thoughts on it. Ann, you mentioned the singularity, and I'm really glad you watched Her. But here's the question: What are computers made of? Chemicals and electricity. Silicon and electricity. And what are humans made of? Well, electricity and carbon. Chemicals.

So, as we look at the rapid advances in artificial intelligence, this raises a provocative question. We often say that human intelligence is embodied, and fundamentally different from machine intelligence. But what if human intelligence could be simulated – not just with software, but by building something new out of chemicals and electricity? What if we could reverse-engineer the human brain? Would that ever truly be possible?

AL: I don't know why we'd want to do that. I don't understand why anyone wants the singularity – the moment when technology surpasses human intelligence. Why is that a goal? I genuinely don't know what problem that's supposed to solve.

And honestly, I think it's a terrible shame. If we ever reach that point, it will only reinforce something that's already deeply ingrained, especially among young people: the idea that your body, your being, is somehow inefficient, negligible, inferior. That it will never be as shiny, as fast, or as smart as the machine you're holding in your hand.

I think that's tragic. It fuels this constant desire to make our faces, our bodies, resemble some bizarre, perfected version of ourselves – one that, unless present company is an exception, is impossible. So why are we doing this? Why do we want this? I honestly don't know. It's confusing to me. And, frankly, it makes me feel ridiculous.

AS: I could suggest one possible motivation to you, which is these boys want to build – and they say this – chatbots that teenage girls will fall in love with. The revenge of the nerds. They forget that teenage girls like bodies too, right?

Q1: Thank you for this panel, and thank you, Ann, for bringing up sense-based intelligence.

This question of technology has been present from the very start of this conference, and I think it complicates the supposed antithesis between cosmopolitanism on one hand and tribalism on the other. It's not clear how that opposition is functioning at all.

Just consider Elon Musk and his obsession with, let's say, self-perpetuation. He's a technologist, yet politically, things are not unfolding the way many assumed they would. Perhaps this is because technology is, in some fundamental way, anti-political. It does not necessarily lend itself to the dynamics of politics as a system of challenge, contest, and negotiation – as McLuhan described it. Technology operates in a different sphere, one where politics doesn't necessarily belong.

At this level, the intentions of the so-called creators – if we can even call them that (I actually reject that term) – are irrelevant. It doesn't matter how well-meaning they are, how determined they are to solve problems. The point is that their inventions take on a life of their own, beyond their control.

This reminds me of Hannah Arendt, who made a crucial distinction between thinking and what she called mere cognition. That distinction is more important than ever. She described thinking as a bootstrap phenomenon – that's her phrase. We don't actually know how humans ever began to think, and there's no guarantee that thinking, in this deep, reflective sense, will continue into the future.

So-called 'thinking machines' need serious critique. The idea itself deserves scrutiny. And if I remember correctly, Lyndsey Stonebridge brought up the prologue to *The Human Condition* earlier. In just a few short pages, Arendt writes about the men who created the atomic bomb. She points out that they failed to grasp something essential: they would be the last people to be consulted on how it was used.

So, yes, this panel raises critical questions. And Arendt was prescient, to put it mildly, about technology, technologists, and the transformation of science into technoscience.

AS: If I may, I'd like to say something about this first. I think you're raising a really important point, and yes, Hannah Arendt was prescient. But it's also crucial that we look closely at what these tools are actually doing –

because some of the advances we're seeing, especially with new chatbots, are truly astonishing. Mind-boggling, even.

Here's something to consider: The recent Nobel Prizes in both physics and chemistry went to computer scientists. A lot of people were upset about this – seeing it as disciplinary trespassing – but what struck me most wasn't the crossover itself. It was the fact that these scientists weren't from universities; they came from industry.

That tells us something about the reality of 21st-century power. Our government – and I've written about this – has effectively outsourced its intellectual capital. The balance of power between the private and public sectors has never in human history looked like this.

And that's part of the reality we're dealing with. These people are moving forward. They're inventing things. And in this era of what Fintan O'Toole has called 'feral capitalism', it may take a coordinated effort to stop them.

AL: I just want to add something to that – especially given my self-proclaimed Luddite position, which also comes with a certain ignorance. But I think it's important not to reject everything happening in technology outright – not that we even could, because we can't.

The real question, I think, is the one Zoë raised: context. Is this technology actually useful and helpful to human beings, or not? That's the distinction we need to be making, but too often, we're not.

Take medicine, for example – there have been astonishing advances because of these technologies. I'm certainly not going to sit here and argue against that.

So what's crucial now is figuring out how to make distinctions – how to separate what serves human well-being from what doesn't. And I think that's exactly what you're trying to get at, right?

ZH: I'll just add quickly that I agree with what Ann and Allison just said. But I also want to say that I'm wary of over-demonizing technology – because, at its core, technology is amazing.

In its essence, technology has always been something that expands what it means to be human. It opens up new possibilities, and that's something we've talked about a lot – the idea that we build ourselves in uncertainty, that the future isn't fixed, that we have the ability to become something different than we are now.

Historically, technology has been part of that – it has allowed us to transcend limitations, to imagine and evolve in ways that make life feel worth living.

But, as Allison pointed out, the real problem isn't technology itself. What's particularly perverse right now is that the people in power – the technologists – talk about technology as if it's deterministic, as if there's a single, inevitable path they are leading us down. And it's theirs. It's not open to real possibility, to alternative futures.

That's what's truly frightening – that technology has become a perversion of its own potential.

Q2: This question is for Zoë. When we talk about digital communication, we're not just talking about user-to-company interactions, but also user-to-user interactions, organizations, and various third parties – each with different motives, ideas, and histories. Given that, and considering privacy in this broader context, does a system that prioritizes complete user anonymity and privacy actually reduce our ability to understand and authenticate context? Does it make accountability more difficult, especially for things like deception and misinformation?

ZH: That's a great question. I think the real challenge, or maybe the opportunity, is to ask: What kind of context is actually needed in a given setting?

There's a philosopher of technology and legal scholar named Helen Nissenbaum – my talk was very much influenced by her – who developed a theory of privacy as contextual integrity. She argues that an information flow is private if it respects the contextual norms of the interaction. It takes a bit of unpacking to see why that's not just tautological – it's actually quite a deep idea.

When I think about the power of tools that shield aspects of identity, I see them as valuable because they allow us to refine what we reveal based on the specific context of an interaction. In some situations, you may want to present your full identity – say, with a digital driver's license, your full likeness, or even thousands of personal photos you share with family. That kind of openness is meaningful in certain contexts. But the power of anonymous credentials lies in their ability to let us tailor what we disclose, depending on the interaction. Instead of all-or-nothing transparency, they offer a way to reveal just enough – balancing privacy with the contextual needs of communication.

Q3: I teach at a small university in Pennsylvania, and I was really struck by your discussion of the right to be forgotten, as well as your references to homo faber – the idea that human beings are fundamentally makers.

Lately, I've been thinking about what I call a crisis of agency, something that Eve Kosofsky Sedgwick also touched on when she talked about the middle ranges of agency. So I'm wondering: how do you see the right to be forgotten in relation to the right to create? How do we balance the right to erase aspects of our digital selves with the right to have agency, to actively shape the world as members of the human tribe?

AL: The right to agency and the right to creativity as a single or as in some way in conflict?

Q3: I think a lot of my students don't understand why they should make anything, or why their making has any meaning when they can simply go to a chat bot that will do it more precisely than they can. The nature of creative agency as being human.

AL: That's a really profound question. Actually, a friend of mine just wrote to me and asked: What would you think if nobody ever read anything you wrote? And then he followed up with, Or, to put it another way: why do you write?

I haven't answered either question. But I could answer the first one immediately, because I never actually think about whether anyone reads what I write. It just doesn't cross my mind. I'm always surprised when someone does.

But the way I'd put this most directly is something like this: For years, I thought Ann was making poems. And then, at a certain point, I realized, no, the poems made Ann. It reversed itself. And I understood that I was the result of this activity – this thing you're calling agency. And that realization was kind of wonderful.

I was lucky. I came from places where there wasn't a lot of hope, where there wasn't a lot of endowed agency. I had to make it up as I went along.

And I chose this peculiar idea of being a poet precisely because I knew it was completely outside the usual markers of success in America – the ones tied to money, or a certain kind of family, or the whole liberal agenda of achievement. I thought, Maybe I can go around all that.

That's very particular to being a poet, or maybe to my time. But I think this idea expands. You can tell kids: Pick up a brush. Make something. See if that doesn't bring you more pleasure, more interest in becoming.

Because really, that's what you were talking about, Zoë – becoming, change. How do we change? That's one of my biggest questions about being human. How does change happen?

And I think one way change happens is by making things. I'm almost certain there's a correlation between being a certain kind of person at one point in your life and feeling different at another – because in between, you made something. And it doesn't even have to be a work of art. I'm biased toward art, of course, because it brings pleasure to others. But I think it could be anything.

Q4: Yesterday, Khaled spoke so beautifully about technology and the idea of the gods leaving while the technology remains. That really stayed with me. I have a question – or really, a nest of questions – so feel free to answer whichever you find most interesting. Could we imagine the singularity as a kind of attempt to summon the gods back? And, following up on Uday's points in the previous discussion, could poetry play a role in some kind of secular or non-tribalistic spirituality? Is there a connection between poetry and technology in that sense? You were touching on this just now, but I'd love to hear more. What is the relationship between poetry and this strange, almost spiritual – even religious – process of technological development? Is there something tribalistic about it? Or is it something else entirely?

AL: Let me put it differently. What I take from this nest of questions is a deeper, fundamental question about spirit – where, if anywhere, it is to be found. Or maybe even, what is it?

Maybe the singularity will lead us to the gods. I think Kurzweil believes that; his diagram certainly seemed to be heading straight for heaven. To me, it looked like it was going directly to hell. But the notion of spirit is complicated. It exists as a kind of third term between the Cartesian mind-body split – something that doesn't have a clear home. And I think that's part of what you're asking: Where is the home for spirit? I can't possibly answer that. But I do think James was right about attention. If there's a way toward spirit – if we want to call it that – it's through a certain kind of attention, through not being distracted.

For me, that attention is often directed toward language. But my love of language isn't some abstract, disembodied love – it's deeply embodied in my love of the world itself. The tactile, physical worldness of the world is connected to the strange, immaterial nature of language. And the relationship between those two things – the materiality of the world and the immateriality of language – has, for me, a kind of spiritual cadence, a rhythm, a ratio. There's something about their mutual attraction, their need for each other, that gives me a feeling of spirit. But I can't give that feeling to you.

That, I think, is the bigger question: Where can spirit be housed? That brings us back to the conversation about tribalism. In a tribe, there's a house for spirit. A structure, a place to belong. But I've never been part of any structured spiritual tribe – except, perhaps, for Bard College.

ZH: One thing worth considering is why people believe that the singularity could lead to some kind of transcendence or higher spiritual plane. Because they do believe that. It's deeply embedded in the discourse around artificial intelligence. In many ways, it's a religious idea.

What I think is valuable is to ask: What's missing that makes people want to believe in that version of transcendence? Why is there such a desire for a narrative that demotes the human in the process?

I don't have a good answer to that. But I want an answer, because if we understood it, maybe we could offer another path.

NIOBE WAY [NW]: I think you've already given us the answer. It's curiosity. You've all touched on it in different ways, but I want to bring it center stage. Let me share a quick story about a three-year-old, because I know we're short on time. I just learned this the other day. A three-year-old asked her uncle: Is what goes on in your brain the same as what goes on in my brain?

And he said, What do you mean?

And she replied: Do the thoughts in my brain – the things I think – are they the same as the ones in your brain?

What I'm getting as is: we're born naturally curious. We're naturally brilliant at figuring out theory of mind, all these sophisticated cognitive processes, all the emotional depth. But we grow up in a culture that doesn't nurture that curiosity.

So, Zoë, you actually did answer your own question. And Ann, so did you.

Zoë, what I learned from you is that context shapes content, and we can capture context through curiosity – by asking who, what, when, how. That's the five-year-old's curiosity.

Ann, how do we bring back the humanities? By nurturing that curiosity – our natural wonder, our desire to understand ourselves through each other. AI does not have that. That's what makes us human.

I want curiosity to be a constant thread in these conversations – about creativity, technology, everything. Because isn't it mind-blowing that a three-year-old could ask that question? What goes on in your brain? Is it the same as what goes on in mine? That level of intelligence, that depth of curiosity; it's astonishing.

AL: And, of course, there's also the issue of doubt. There are two ways to think about doubt. You can see it as something that makes you fearful – a source of uncertainty, even paralysis. Or you can see doubt as a spark. A reason to become curious. And in that case, the cure for doubt is endless curiosity.

NW: Endless curiosity. And I have to remind you, Allison, you told me at lunch that your joy comes from curiosity.

AS: That's absolutely true. Let's restore curiosity – to our classrooms, to our conversations, and to the world. And let's drink to it! Thank you all so much.

"ARE WE A TRIBE?"

THOMAS CHATTERTON WILLIAMS AND
AYISHAT AKANBI
(WITH ROGER BERKOWITZ)

ROGER BERKOWITZ [RB]: This conversation is called 'Are We A Tribe?' Even asking this question to these two speakers may be provocative. Is being Black a tribe? How do we think about that? I mean I think that in certain ways if I asked that question people could say, 'How dare you!'

AYISHAT AKANBI [AA]: It's an interesting question. I don't think I've ever specifically thought of my racial identity as, you know, as putting me in a tribe; but when I think about what a tribe means, at least in the common imagination, and how we use that term today, at least when people use the term 'Blackness'. And there does seem to be some policing around what that means, and how you're meant to show up, and the ways in which you're meant to approach certain conversations. It does feel like there's quite a heavy tribal sense around that. And I would say to some degree I think I am quite tribal in some ways with my racial identity, although I've never generally conceptualized it that way. I think a lot of my impulse to speak on race, even in ways that some people may not always agree with, or may be unpopular, or at least not the most dominant kind of opinion online, I do think it comes from this sort of tribal instinct that I have. If I didn't have that tribal instinct I think maybe I would sit out of these conversations.

But I think tribalism can be positive; at least a tribal instinct can be positive. Tribalism – someone made that distinction earlier – I think that is a little different. But I don't necessarily think having a tribal sense around your racial identity means that you have to romanticize it, means that you have to ignore some of the issues coming from within the community. In fact, I think maybe perhaps the more tribal that you are is the more that you want to put forward ideas and narratives that you think are much more helpful; and the more willing you are, irrespective of the consequences, to say things that may rattle others because it's what you believe and it's your loyalty and your solidarity to that community that makes – *[lost the mike]*

RB: You said that you consider it tribal, and that you feel like there's a tribal aspect. Can you give me an example? What do you mean by that? What does it mean for you to think that there's a tribal identity.

AA: I think of when my mum was a lot younger. When I was a kid I thought my mum was like the most popular woman ever. I thought she knew everybody because whenever we'd bump into anyone Black she would just say hello. And I thought she knew them all. And at one stage I said, 'How do you know so many people? How do you know who this person is?' She was like, 'I don't. They're Black.' I was like, 'what does that mean? Why are you saying hello to these people that you don't know?' She said, 'I may not know them but I see them.' And she recognized, or she imagined, or assumed that because they shared this racial identity that there was some crossover, there was some story between them. Even having locks in the UK – I don't know if it's the same in America, maybe it would be in certain communities – but other people who have locks, they see me, and they often acknowledge me because there's this sense that I have my hair like this for a reason, and they feel some kind of kinship or solidarity with me on that, that we have a shared notion of Blackness that's maybe rooted in some kind of Afrocentric ideal. So that's one form.

When we were speaking in Italy, I think the conversation we had was about something similar to this. It was an ideas mini-festival, but private, with a group of Bard students. I was one of only two Black women there. At lunch, I saw the other Black woman crying. I had an instinct to go over to her and check in. What crossed my mind was, 'I hope she doesn't feel like an outsider. I hope she's not uncomfortable'. My desire to connect with her came from what you might call a tribal place.

I think I'm the kind of person who would check in on anyone who seemed upset, regardless of race, but in this case, I felt less hesitation. I didn't assume she would tell me to mind my business because of our shared identity.

RB: Thomas, you've raised the question of whether one can or should retire from being Black.

THOMAS CHATTERTON WILLIAMS [TCW]: And white.

RB: And white, yes. That we should stop using racial categories altogether. How do you respond to some of what Ayishat said? If you see a young Black person in a group, do you feel an affinity? Is that something we should act on, or should we resist those kinds of identifications?

TCW: I grew up thinking of race as a kind of tribe. I wouldn't have had that vocabulary at the time, but race felt like a collective identity, an alliance of 'us' against 'them'. All through adolescence and high school, I was acutely aware that my friends and I were Black. The white teachers, my white neighbors, Puerto Rican kids, Asian kids – they were not exactly 'us'. We had our own mannerisms, greetings, theme songs, ways of dressing, almost like costumes that we recognized in each other. It felt deeply meaningful.

When I arrived at Georgetown, I still saw myself as a representative of my tribe, sent abroad. I wasn't interested in people outside my group unless they signaled that they were part of it. I spent most of my freshman year living in a self-imposed tribal ghetto at Georgetown.

Then I read philosophy. I read Dostoevsky. It was an encounter with a mind across centuries, geography, and culture – someone who articulated my innermost feelings and contradictions about the world. That moment shattered my ability to see myself as just part of a fixed 'us' tied to my time and place.

It was a gradual process, but after reading Dostoevsky, I started realizing things. My Jewish neighbor in the dorm next to me was actually fascinating to talk to. He knew more about Black music than I did – not necessarily the hip-hop my friends and I were immersed in, but jazz, which most of my Black friends didn't care about at all. That realization made me question what I had assumed was my exclusive cultural domain.

Once that process started, I could no longer believe in tribal identification. Someone asked earlier about what happens when you enter a place – like school – believing you are one kind of person, a tribalist, and leave realizing that your people exist in many different places.

To your point, I found Ayishat online years ago, or maybe she found me. Either way, we immediately connected. She's one of the smartest people I've ever interacted with. And yes, there's something about her Black cultural identity that I recognize and feel an affinity to. But I don't think that has to be tribal. You can expand yourself in a cosmopolitan way while still preserving a sense of familiarity with something specific. It doesn't have to mean dilution. I still feel deeply connected to Black culture – I just no longer see it as the horizon that defines my entire experience of the world.

RB: Shai Lavi and Khaled Furani talk about tradition. One of the things that came up was the idea that traditions are no longer authoritative for us – we can pick and choose. I can decide what kind of Jew I'm going to be, or not be a Jew at all. Thomas, you have a strong sense that identity is a choice. But are there traditions that choose you? Are there traditions you can't opt out of? Or is it all a matter of self-composition, where you curate your life and the traditions you belong to?

TCW: I think identity is always a negotiation – between how you define yourself and how others, including institutions, interact with you. You can't set the terms entirely in a vacuum. That said, you do have a lot of agency. You can reject the categories imposed on you. My father is a Black man, old enough to be my grandfather, from the segregated South. My mother is a white Evangelical Christian from California. I'm what people call mixed-race, though I reject that term because it implies some people are pure.

I grew up in the '80s and '90s in a culture that accepted the idea that one drop of Black blood made you Black. That meant that the white kids I was around in New Jersey – and their parents – often directed racism at me without caring that my mother was white. They weren't interested in the nuances of my 23andMe results.

Hannah Arendt famously said, 'If the world attacks you as a Jew, you respond as a Jew'. But I'm not sure I fully accept that logic. I've experienced racism as a racialized Black person in the United States, but I choose to respond as a humanist.

I've spent the past decade and a half living in Europe. I refuse to let racists define my sense of self. I'd encourage others to adopt a similar stance, rather than doubling down on the identity that their persecutors impose on them.

AA: I agree with a lot of that. When you ask whether there are traditions we have no choice in, I think many people define themselves based on how bigots see them. I reject that entirely. We have a responsibility to give birth to ourselves, to adopt ideas and beliefs that resonate with us, rather than simply accepting those imposed on us.

When I first encountered Thomas, I felt a sense of kinship because he was one of the few people offering a nuanced, complicated perspective on race. It wasn't just about dunking on the left or indulging in predictable online debates. His approach felt deeper, more thoughtful.

So no, I don't feel obligated to adhere to any tradition I was born into. When I spoke earlier about having tribal instincts, I don't think that negates my cosmopolitan side. I don't see the two as being in conflict. For me, tribal instincts don't mean believing my race, culture, or country is better than any other. I still have curiosity about other cultures. I don't view my racial identity as one of innocence.

RB: On the question of tradition: I consider myself a cultural Jew rather than a religious one. A lot of my journey has been about figuring out which traditions matter to me. For instance, I don't eat pork, but I do eat shellfish. Why? I have my reasons. But ultimately, I'm carving out a meaningful version of the tradition I was born into – one that fits my life today.

I get the sense that you two approach this question differently. Ayishat, it seems like you're actively figuring out which traditions, as a Black woman, you want to embrace. Thomas, it feels like you're less interested in that. Maybe I'm wrong? How do you both think about composing a life – choosing traditions to carry forward as a Black man or a Black woman?

AA: That's interesting. When I think about the life I live and want to live – the legacy I want to leave behind – I'm not sure how central being a Black woman is to that. Even the term 'Black woman' – not that I reject it – it feels incredibly loaded today, carrying all kinds of meanings and expectations.

On the question of tradition, there are aspects of my Nigerian culture – certain norms and values – that I'd be reluctant to give up. This may seem surface-level, but for example, I have a deep connection to a particular kind of reggae music. It's like gospel to me. I'm not Jamaican, but it resonates with me profoundly. Maybe that's a tradition.

Similarly, I connect with various Black ethnicities and their cultural expressions, certain values and ways of being. But I don't see any of this as a rigid template. I don't think, 'As a Black woman, I must do X, Y, and Z'. I hope that anyone who has followed my work understands that, while racial experiences shape us, I don't believe they are the most important or exciting things about a person. In fact, I often think that a fixation on race – any race – can actually obstruct real self-discovery.

TCW: When I think about tradition, there are aspects of Black American culture that are profoundly important to me. But I'd also say there are broader American traditions that I consider essential – not just for Black Americans, but for anyone.

Ralph Ellison once described Blackness as a discipline. That resonates deeply when I think about my father. His way of taking the hand he was dealt and playing it with style, charisma, and humor – that's quintessentially a Black American experience. But it's also a universal one. Albert Murray wrote that Hemingway's image of the matador facing the bull is just another version of the jazz musician improvising onstage – both are about making order out of chaos, facing life's hardships and joys, and ultimately confronting our mortality.

That's part of what I take from the Black tradition. But I'm also a contemporary American from the East Coast. The secular Jewish tradition has shaped me profoundly. So has the white Anglo-Saxon Protestant tradition. So have Puerto Rican influences. The place that formed me is a mix of all these traditions.

It's hard to separate identity based purely on ancestry. The Black American identity itself often contains multitudes – ethnic, cultural, and historical influences that go beyond race. So, while you might have a more obvious claim to Jewishness than I do, I actually consider myself, in some ways, a secular Jew as well.

AA: Yeah, and thinking about what you just said – that might be a way to answer the earlier question about identity shifts. The gentleman on the other side mentioned that, when he got to college, his worldview expanded – he became more cosmopolitan, more liberal. I don't know if I'd use the word 'transcend', but I do think that as your understanding of identity expands, you start to recognize just how much other cultures have shaped you. You realize it's not just the people you grew up with or the racial group you were born into. It's film, TV, music, the people in your neighborhood – all of these things shape who you are just as much as, say, my Blackness has shaped me.

TCW: When we saw each other in London a few weeks ago, I remember thinking: 'Whenever I'm in the UK, I feel like aspects of British tradition belong to me, too'. I feel that in many places. Some of this might just come down to personality. Some people are rooted – they feel most at home where they're from and want to stay there. Others – like me – go somewhere new and immediately start imagining living there. I don't think that's something you consciously decide – it's just part of who you are.

RB: That's the joke in my family. Wherever we are, I want to buy a house there.

How do we make cosmopolitanism something deep rather than shallow? That's one of the challenges of this conference, I think. What gives cosmopolitanism a sense of tradition, history, or ritual? If tribalism has covenants and rituals, what are the rituals of cosmopolitanism? Both of you live in major European cities – do you identify as cosmopolitans? And if so, what connects you to a history, to a group, to something meaningful in that identity?

AA: I probably wouldn't have used the term 'cosmopolitan' for myself before today, but since you invited me to this and I've been thinking about it more – yeah, I'd say I am. And I think a fundamental part of cosmopolitanism is curiosity. That's one of its core components: curiosity about how other people live and an openness to recognizing that different cultures have insights and values that can enrich your own life.

At the same time, being cosmopolitan doesn't mean ignoring the flaws within your own culture. You can have tribal instincts, but you shouldn't let them blind you to self-critique. I also think travel – whether international or just exploring different parts of your own country – helps cultivate that perspective. Those are the first things that come to mind, but maybe Thomas will say something that sparks more.

TCW: I really agree with that. I think what makes cosmopolitanism deep rather than superficial is its capacity for self-critique. It's the opposite of saying, 'It just so happens that everyone who looks like me, worships like me, and speaks like me has figured out the truth!' That's a shallow way of seeing the world. Cosmopolitanism is about recognizing value wherever it's found and being willing to accept truth in places you might not expect.

The term 'cosmopolitan' sometimes gets a bad rap because it's associated with money, elitism, or global consumer culture – the idea that if you can get a flat white and hear the same music in any city, you're cosmopolitan. But I don't think cosmopolitanism requires wealth or even travel. My father traveled in his youth, but at some point he stopped. He's still one of the most cosmopolitan people I know because he surrounds himself with books. He continuously engages with different minds, different times, and different places. Cosmopolitanism doesn't require a plane ticket – it just requires curiosity.

It's kind of ironic that the person who first made me feel cosmopolitan was Dostoevsky, because he was the opposite of cosmopolitan. He lived briefly in Germany, but he came back to Russia convinced that the Russian soul was pure and everything else was degenerate. He saw cosmopolitanism as a kind of betrayal. But the power of great literature is that, despite his provincial prejudices, he couldn't help but write something universally human – something that could speak across centuries and cultures. That, to me, is what makes cosmopolitanism meaningful: it's a way of engaging with the world that isn't about shallow consumerism but about tapping into something deeper and more universal.

RB: I love what you both said about travel and books. It reminds me that while cosmopolitanism, as a concept, dates back to the Stoics – Diogenes famously said, 'I am a citizen of the world' – the person who really made the word central to our modern understanding is Immanuel Kant.

Kant never left his hometown of Königsberg, yet he wrote an essay on the "Idea for a Universal History with a Cosmopolitan Purpose." Arendt, in her reading of Kant, argues that for him, thinking itself is a kind of wandering. To think is to put yourself in someone else's perspective. To judge, you have to imagine how your arguments would sound to others, how they might be received by people with different experiences and viewpoints. That might be a model for cosmopolitanism – not just physically wandering, but letting your mind wander into different perspectives.

Q1: I wanted to ask whether you see exploring cosmopolitanism as a wholly individual experience – going around and immersing yourself in different cultures to shape your own beliefs and personal traditions – or whether you think it can be a collective endeavor. Can cosmopolitanism be fostered through institutions like schools by introducing different languages, foods, cultural experiences, holidays, or exchange programs? Or is it something that can only be pursued on a personal level?

AA: That's an interesting question. Some would argue that schools already introduce aspects of other cultures, maybe not extensively, but to some degree. If you live in a major city – or even if you don't – you're probably exposed to different cuisines, for example. But that exposure doesn't necessarily translate into a cosmopolitan attitude.

I imagine there could be ways to cultivate cosmopolitanism collectively, though I don't know exactly what they would look like. That said, I think the experiences that have the deepest, longest-lasting impact tend to be personal. Curiosity, which is at the heart of cosmopolitanism, is difficult to impose. It's something that people tend to develop individually. At least in my experience, and in the experiences of others I know who lean towards cosmopolitanism, that transformation has come from personal encounters. What do you think, Thomas?

TCW: It's a great question. I think there's a distinction between cosmopolitanism and multiculturalism. What you're describing – the idea that institutions can introduce different cultural perspectives – is closer to multiculturalism. Societies can become more multicultural, and institutions can work to expand cultural awareness.

I've seen this shift in my own lifetime. When I was growing up in the 1980s, my parents just called all pasta 'spaghetti' – they didn't distinguish between different kinds of pasta – and no one in my house really knew how to use olive oil. By the 2000s, my mom was making Lebanese food, and grocery stores like Whole Foods were making international ingredients more available. That's an example of increasing multicultural awareness.

But I don't think that's the same thing as the internal, individual process that cosmopolitanism requires. The real shift – the work of truly opening oneself up to different ways of seeing the world – seems to be a more personal journey.

Q2: The discussion so far seems very individualistic – about self-work, travel, and personal exploration. But not everyone has access to those opportunities. Given that racial ideologies, structures, and laws continue to shape the world, how do you think we should engage with those systemic realities while discussing race in such personal, individualistic terms?

TCW: I take that point seriously, but I'd push back a little. When I talk about travel, I don't just mean spending money on plane tickets. Engaging with different perspectives can happen through books, and books are accessible to anyone with a library card. That kind of journey can be just as transformative, if not more so, than physical travel.

I would probably call myself something close to a race abolitionist. I think that these kinds of structures that you're referring to were put in place by very harmful fictions that both create and feed off the kind of abstract color categories that we slot ourselves and each other into. So, you're not going to fix society by making individual choices; but you only have one life, and you have to live your life on your own terms. And so I try to exercise as much freedom as I can while recognizing that doesn't necessarily make everybody free or change the world in its own right. But you can do multiple things at the same time. I'm aware that we don't live in as Utopia yet.

AA: Exactly. And when I mentioned travel earlier, I wasn't just talking about international travel – I was also talking about local travel, even just taking a short train ride to experience a different neighborhood or community. You don't have to get on a plane to appreciate different cultures.

I also don't see any conflict between defining race for yourself on an individual level and still engaging in collective action. Just because you don't define yourself solely in terms of how others perceive you – or in opposition to those who discriminate against you – doesn't mean you're denying the existence of racism or ignoring the struggles of racialized people in society. You can hold both perspectives at once.

Q3: You both mentioned how your parents influenced your sense of tribal instinct. To what extent do we inherit tribes and traditions versus discover them?

TCW: For better or worse, we inherit a lot of our worldview. It's very difficult to unlearn the shortcuts and instincts we pick up from our parents, our community, and our broader cultural environment. No one can build themselves completely from scratch – it would be overwhelming. And honestly, much of what we inherit is worth holding onto. There are traditions that don't necessarily need to be thrown out or reimagined.

At the same time, we inherit biases that can and should be examined. Scrutiny doesn't always mean rejection – sometimes, after thinking critically about what we've inherited, we may decide that it's valuable.

You mentioned our parents. My father was a very cosmopolitan Black man who suffered deeply under American racism. He told me two seemingly contradictory things: first, that race isn't real, and second, that no matter what I did, I would be seen as a Black boy in America. Even though he tried to reject racial tribalism, he still passed on a racialized way of thinking to me. But I had the opportunity to update my experience of Blackness in a way he couldn't. He grew up in a different time, and some of the frameworks that were necessary for him didn't make as much sense for me. For example, I couldn't see the value in continuing to define myself in the same racial terms that enslavers would have used. That logic no longer served me, even if it had once been crucial for survival. So, while we inherit tribal identities, we can also renegotiate them.

AA: Until Thomas started speaking, I hadn't really thought about how much of my tribal instincts came from my parents. But one thing stands out: whenever I hear British people say my country when referring to the UK, or when they say 'we won' or 'we lost' during a football match, I notice that language doesn't feel natural to me. Even though I was born and raised in Britain, I'd probably just say 'back in Britain' rather than 'my country'.

That hesitation likely comes from my upbringing. My mother repeatedly told me, 'You're not British, you're Nigerian'. Even though she wanted me to be born in Britain, she saw British values and customs as somewhat incompatible with how she was trying to raise me. I do think of myself as British, but I'm not entirely comfortable with the language of national belonging.

So yes, I think we inherit a significant part of our family's tribal instincts. But like Thomas said, we have the freedom to wrestle with those inheritances, to question whether they make sense, and to decide which traditions are meaningful and which are just habits passed down without much thought.

Q4: In the earlier session, there was discussion about the extreme right in America, and you brought up the idea of curiosity. My question is: how do we make people more curious? How do we encourage open-mindedness in people who are deeply entrenched in their tribal identities?

AA: I don't know how we make people more curious, but for me, curiosity came from realizing how profoundly ignorant I was about so many things. I think curiosity often starts with acknowledging what you don't know. At the same time, as much as I – like most people – long for belonging, I'm also deeply suspicious of it. Belonging can be comforting, but it can also blind you to flaws within your own community. It can make you resistant to self-critique.

How do we make people more open-minded? That's the million-dollar question. Maybe it starts with making it okay to admit ignorance. Right now, it feels like everyone is expected to have strong opinions about everything. There's a lot of pressure to appear knowledgeable, even on topics we barely understand. But acknowledging ignorance isn't a weakness – it's honesty. And maybe that's where curiosity begins. What do you think, Thomas?

TCW: I'm not sure you can make someone more curious. Now that I'm a parent, I see how much personality is innate. Some people are naturally drawn to exploring new ideas, while others prefer familiarity and comfort.

That's not to say you shouldn't try to expose people to new perspectives – I think engagement is always worthwhile, especially when approached with respect. But I do believe there are limits. Some people will never feel the need to expand their worldview beyond what they already know.

Maybe this is connected to what Sebastian Junger was saying earlier – about how certain tendencies might be biologically encoded in parts of the population. Some people are explorers by nature, while others are more inclined to stay rooted in what they know. And society probably needs both.

At the end of the day, you can encourage curiosity, you can create opportunities for engagement, but not everyone will take them. There will always be individuals – and even entire groups – who simply don't want to engage beyond their tribe. That's a built-in limitation of human nature.

RB: As a professor and someone who invites many speakers to campus – some popular, some less so – I've observed that most young people like breaking the rules. They're naturally curious. They want to hear the person they don't like, to yell, to challenge, to argue. And yet, there's an enormous pressure to only engage with what Sebastian Junger called 'the right opinions'.

I think we've lost the habit of seeing politics as a space for plurality, for debate, for differences of opinion. We've started to think that politics is about truth – about getting the answer right. But politics is also about argument, about pushing and pulling, about shouting and then, hopefully, shaking hands and doing it again next week. And I think that's something we can teach. It's a muscle that can be exercised, and when we're doing our job well at a liberal arts college, that's exactly what we're working to strengthen.

Q5: You used the word 'my' – as in my house, my kids, my country – which implies responsibility. If we ask ourselves daily, 'What belongs to me? Who belongs to me?', we can expand that circle outward, moving from a cosmopolitan mindset to also belonging to multiple tribes.

And for the earlier question – how do you make people curious? – I'd say the ultimate curiosity is about the self. If someone asks, 'Who am I? Am I just my body?', they open the door to the deepest kind of inquiry.

AA: I was a little sad when we moved on from that curiosity question because I kept thinking about it. I believe that a big part of becoming more curious is developing self-knowledge – starting with yourself. Why am I the way I am? Why do I have certain instincts, certain preferences?

When you start asking those questions about yourself, it naturally extends to curiosity about others. You begin to see how other people's experiences might help you understand your own. Conversations become part of a larger puzzle – each person you engage with helps you fit another piece into place. So yes, I think that a deep curiosity about yourself can be the first step toward a deeper curiosity about the world.

TCW: We're back to Socrates: 'Know thyself'. Full circle.

RB: Ayishat, was there a moment when you became curious about yourself? When something made you stop and think, 'Wait, I want to understand this more?' Or did it happen gradually?

AA: Yes, definitely. I think for a lot of people who didn't grow up seeing themselves as particularly intellectual or academic, there's often a turning point. And for many, that turning point comes from tragedy – some kind of loss, trauma, or near-death experience.

For me, it was the loss of a loved one when I was 24. Something about that kind of experience can just pull the ground out from under you. That's what happened to me. I had been going through life on autopilot, but this loss woke me up. It forced me to question everything.

A few months – maybe a year – later, I had what I can only describe as a transcendent experience. It was psychedelic in nature, though I didn't take anything. It was just this shift in perception, this overwhelming sense of clarity. And I realized something so simple but so profound: 'Oh, you're not broken. You just don't like those things.'

That realization – so basic, yet life-changing – completely transformed how I saw myself. It was from that point on that my real journey of self-discovery began.

TCW: Something Ayishat said made me realize I gave an incomplete answer earlier about curiosity. When someone asked, 'How do we make people more curious?', I focused on personality and inherent tendencies. But I think there's another, more optimistic answer: people become curious when they see how learning benefits them – when they realize that greater knowledge, greater experience, can actually improve their lives.

If you can find the right language, the right entry point, to show someone how new knowledge could matter to them – how it could be useful – then I think everyone is potentially accessible in that way. The challenge is figuring out what that key is for each person.

For example, when I first got to college, I had no interest in studying abroad. When people asked if I would, I said, 'Why would I do that?' I couldn't see how it would serve me. It wasn't even a possibility in my mind. But then, something shifted, and I suddenly could see the value in it. And everything changed.

So maybe the answer is that curiosity isn't something you can force on people, but you can create opportunities for them to see its value for themselves.

"CAN WE BE COSMOPOLITAN TRIBALISTS?"

SHAI LAVI AND
KHALED FURANI

KHALED FURANI [KF]: I am a citizen of two countries, both of which are connected to various forms of tribalism, cosmopolitanism, and projects of freedom and enslavement. By that, I mean Israel and the United States, both of which I am a citizen of. However, I'm not a citizen in the sense of my Palestinian nationality or the faith tradition I speak from, which is Islam. I want to think about how to examine and investigate tribalism, cosmopolitanism, and what lies beyond them.

SHAI LAVI [SL]: I come from Tel Aviv. I'm an observant Jew and a committed Israeli, though that doesn't necessarily make me proud these days; perhaps I'm a sad one in this time. I hope we'll have a chance to discuss this, about pride and whether it belongs in our identity or not.

KF: Shai and I both share a certain fondness for the ideas we've learned from Hannah Arendt, despite some of the misguided things we've sometimes heard from her. Hopefully, we can bring that expertise – Shai as a professor of law and I as an anthropologist – into our discussion. To begin, I'd like to pose a question: What are tribalism and cosmopolitanism? Are they timeless phenomena, or are they specifically modern constructions?

SL: To start, I think it's best to think of tribalism and cosmopolitanism together, as a matrix. Part of what we'll try to do is think about this matrix, but also think outside of it. Let me clarify what I mean. Tribalism and cosmopolitanism are just two ways of addressing the real issue at hand. Tribalism refers to our particular belongings, the groups we belong to, while cosmopolitanism talks about our shared humanity. The fact that these ideas are contrasted creates a matrix, one that already assumes a lot about the relationship between them. Our goal will be to think outside of this matrix.

Let me explain a bit about what I see as this matrix, particularly the relationship between tribalism and cosmopolitanism. We can start with cosmopolitanism. Although the idea has ancient roots, it takes on a distinctly contemporary form in relation to tribalism. The idea is that in order to be cosmopolitan, you need to move beyond your particular identity, to transcend your particular belongings. Cosmopolitanism is often seen as a way of thinking beyond these individual identities.

This transition from tribalism to cosmopolitanism is often framed as progress – historical progress, as Sebastian beautifully described in his talk; or evolutionary progress. Humanity starts in clans and tribes and then forms states, eventually scaling up to a cosmopolitan vision. The idea is to move from one to the other.

What's interesting to question, however, is whether this is the only way to think about shared humanity. Do we need to transcend our bounded identities to think about our common humanity, or can we find that shared humanity within our particular commitments?

Tribalism speaks to our bounded identity, to where we come from, but it's not the only way to think about it. When juxtaposed with cosmopolitanism, tribalism often assumes strong exclusion and rivalry. It suggests that our identities are more important than other commitments – "My country, right or wrong." It creates certain expectations about identity.

What we want to explore, Khaled, is how to think about these ideas not just as contrasts – tribalism versus cosmopolitanism – and perhaps not even use these terms so rigidly. Instead, we want to search for new ways to think about our commitments, both to our particular belongings and to our shared humanity.

In this context, Khaled, I want to ask you: Do you think turning to tradition, both as a way of belonging and as a concept or resource, can offer us tools to rethink this tension – or what seems like a tension – between tribalism and cosmopolitanism?

KF: On an anecdotal note, when I received Roger's kind invitation, one of the questions posed to me was: 'How does one navigate the dual loyalties of tribal and cosmopolitan identities?' And I thought, wait a minute – why are they considered dual? Is there an inherent tension, or is it perhaps only an apparent one? What happens if we introduce the concept of tradition into this conversation? Tradition could enter in many ways, and today, we can try to explore some of those. I can think of five or six approaches, though there may be more. It's striking that this concept is largely absent from the conversation. I was pleased to hear you, Roger, speak about tradition today. In the spirit of Hannah Arendt, we might wonder: how would she view the duality of tribalism and cosmopolitanism? Is this tension real or fictitious?

From the perspective of a tradition, it's interesting – let me share two observations, Shai. Some of the leading authors who discuss the "tribalism-cosmopolitanism divide" go to great lengths not to use the word "tradition." Think of figures like Walzer, Nussbaum, or Appiah. Even in their language, the word "tradition" is conspicuously absent, despite how much it could streamline their arguments. But this absence is symptomatic of a deeper neglect of tradition as a concept and category of thought, even philosophically.

What if we live in a tradition that teaches us to belong to a world where both the cosmopolitan and the tribal exist simultaneously, as Arendt might say, Janus-faced? Could we be both at once?

I don't want to be a party pooper, but when we think through the concept of tradition, it helps bracket the conversation and potentially opens it up to a deeper exploration. I'm thinking, perhaps scripturally or theologically – what if there are ways of belonging that go beyond the dichotomy of tribe or cosmopolis? Let me stop here.

SL: For me, returning to tradition as a framework opens up other possibilities. For example, what if we didn't need to transcend tradition but rather dug deeper into it to find our shared humanity?

Take the first book of Genesis, for instance. It speaks of a shared humanity from the very beginning of tradition. We are created in the image of God, but this is not some detached, abstract universalism. It's a language within the tradition. Rather than transcending tradition to reach cosmopolitanism, perhaps we can reach into tradition itself to find a shared humanity. Or, in terms of evolutionary theory, the assumption might be that our primary commitment is to the tribe. But is that what tradition teaches us? Consider the last piece of bread – who do you give it to? Evolutionary theory might suggest giving it to your own, but tribal hospitality could suggest otherwise: that your primary commitment is not to yourself. This is also part of tradition.

So, what possibilities emerge when we don't treat these ideas as mere contrasts?

Let me share an anecdote. I was sitting on a plane next to an ultra-Orthodox Hassidic man, an American who had emigrated to Israel. I asked him, 'Why move to Israel?' He said, 'What do you mean, why? I'm a committed Israeli. I'll fight for a better Israel'. I asked, 'But why you, born in America? Why come here?'

He was surprised by the question. He said, 'All the Israelis I know are so proud to be Israeli'. This made me reflect, and I was able to have this conversation because, in a sense, we share the same tradition. I said to him, 'In our tradition, pride can be problematic. We can say we're blessed to be Jewish or grateful for the opportunities we've had, but pride assumes that you're always on the "good side." You want to be proud of your children, but that's not the primary relationship you have with them. It's a kind of commitment.'

In a tradition, there isn't an external perspective to judge it from if you're fully embedded in it, but it provides tools to think critically and to make the most of that tradition. It's a different relationship altogether. This opens up a space for thinking about all this.

KF: I see two ways in which tradition might expand our conversation about the tribalism-cosmopolitanism duality. The first is by clarifying concepts – making distinctions that help reduce confusion. I've found it helpful, Shai, and I wonder what you think, to distinguish between being part of a tribe and being a tribalist, just as there's a difference between being cosmopolitan and practicing cosmopolitanism. It's important not to confuse these terms.

From my position within the Muslim tradition, it's strange to be a citizen of a tribal state like Israel, while being part of a faith tradition that is very much anti-tribalist – and let me emphasize: not *anti-tribal*. In Islam, the tribe is recognized as a fact of human existence; it's accepted, and one could even argue, honored. But tribalism itself is problematic.

The same could be said about cosmopolitanism. It represents an openness to others or something beyond your immediate collective. But cosmopolitanism, too, has its dangers. Both tribalism and cosmopolitanism can impose violence on the boundaries we draw around ourselves. Tribalism could violate the belonging to a group, while cosmopolitanism could dissolve claims to particularity, leading to a sense of rootlessness.

With these analytical distinctions in mind, I'll offer one more anecdote to illustrate how tradition can help us think through this supposed duality. When I visit Al-Aqsa Mosque in Jerusalem, for example, and meet someone from Jamaica, India, or London, my faith tradition links me to a broader cosmopolitan space. Belonging to a tradition can help you discover your non-belonging as well.

In my Muslim faith, there's an underlying premise that we belong to God – *Inna lillahi wa inna ilayhi raji'un* ("We belong to God, and to God we return"). This understanding transcends the simple belonging to a group; it reminds us of a deeper relationship with the divine. Even if you're a Stoic or follow other traditions, the underlying theme is the same: there is something more fundamental than human belonging.

This complexity should not be abandoned when thinking about how tradition can enrich our conversation. Some traditions push us to think about belonging through the lens of non-belonging, teaching us how we don't belong to this world in some sense. Let me stop here.

SL: I want to return to the topic of Al-Aqsa and sacred spaces, but before we get there, I want to touch on something you said. I like the way you distinguish between being tribal and tribalism, and between cosmopolitanism and being cosmopolitan. But I think the term "tribe" is often overused to describe many different kinds of belonging. We should be cautious about that. People say, "I belong to my family, that's tribal," or "I belong to my religion, that's tribal," or "I belong to my ethnicity, that's tribal," even "I belong to my soccer team, that's tribal." This reminds me of how people often use the term "religion." They call Judaism, Islam, and Buddhism religions, but they also call Marxism or nationalism a religion in some sense. Arendt discusses this in her work on authority, and I think she would say this blurs things rather than clarifies. We need to be careful not to conflate different categories of belonging.

That brings us to the question of scripture. Both the Muslim and Jewish traditions use the word "tribe," but it carries different meanings in each tradition. We should consider those meanings.

I'd also like to share my own anecdote. There's a part of the Wailing Wall in Jerusalem where I like to go. It's a more secluded area, co-ed, where men and women can pray together. It's quieter, and I sit there on Saturday afternoons, listening to the mosque's call to prayer. This setting opens a different understanding of shared humanity. As an observant Jew, I'm sitting as close as I can to the holiest site in Judaism, while hearing the mosque, sharing the same space. This raises the question of what it means to belong to a sacred space that doesn't necessarily divide people but also doesn't transcend their tribal identities. From within these traditions, we can still find commonality.

KF: Yes, yet, with that point, it's shared, though we must also recognize the ways our traditions meet and diverge. I often tell Shai that I think Islam critiques certain aspects of the Jewish tradition, particularly the tribalism within it. In Islam, Muhammad is described as a prophet for all of humanity, which reflects a kind of cosmopolitanism. And the Quran speaks of God's revelation being for all of humanity, as in the phrase al-Nas. Think of the verse/aya in the Quran as sent to Prophet Muhammad for bringing "humans to exit darkness into light." Also, if we look at the story of Abraham – the patriarch who founded a tribe – we see that he also took actions that went beyond the tribe. For instance, in Surah VI, Verse 74, Abraham challenges his father, Azar, asking him why he worships idols. He says, "I see you and your people in great loss," separating himself from his own kin. This suggests that while one can be proud of one's kin, it's crucial not to make that pride absolute. Abraham saw bonds that extended beyond the tribe. It seems to me that even though Abraham is a patriarch, he was willing to recognize connections beyond tribal affiliation.

SL: Khaled has raised an interesting and profound question about the relationship between traditions. I want to hold onto that, but I'm not entirely sure what to make of it, so I'll ask you, Khaled, to clarify.

At face value, it seems like you're suggesting that Islam critiques Judaism for being more tribal, because its revelation was meant for a specific people, not for all of humanity. We've heard this critique from Christianity as well: Judaism is seen as tribal, and the Gospel, particularly from Paul, is seen as universal, meant for the nations.

I want to think about that and ask you about it. But before I do, I think it's worth bringing in the figure of Abraham, because he's important in both the Jewish and Islamic traditions. Abraham is seen as the father of many nations, not just the Israelites or the Jewish people. His name changes from Avram to Abraham, and that extra "h" symbolizes his role as the father of many nations. So, from the very beginning, there's an idea of plurality in his identity.

There are two ways to think about this. One way is to view it through the lens of tribalism vs. cosmopolitanism, suggesting some sort of progression, where the tribal identity eventually gives way to a universal identity. This idea of progression, or supercessionism, is characteristic of Christianity's relationship with Judaism – Christianity initially saw itself as replacing Judaism, with the New Testament offering a universal truth that superseded the particularity of the Jewish tribe.

And sometimes when I hear you speak about Islam, Khaled, I think it follows a similar pattern. Just as Christianity critiques Judaism for its tribalism, Islam seems to critique Judaism for being particular and urges moving beyond the tribal to something more universal. I wonder about that. So, I'll stop here and ask you about that.

KF: Although both critiques may address certain practices of Judaism, I wouldn't rush to conflate them, even though there is a relationship between Christianity and Judaism in terms of one superseding the other. Islam, however, isn't about superseding; it's about returning to the original message. Islam tells the Jews, "You had the good message, but why did you corrupt it?" It doesn't suggest that the message was wrong to begin with. Islam, in this sense, is about returning to Abraham. In the Quran, Abraham is seeking something to believe in, wondering if the moon or the sun is God until he concludes that God cannot be one of these transient things. God, he realizes, is not something you can see with your eyes.

What I'm trying to say, Shai, is that we should avoid conflating Islamic and Christian critiques of Judaism. Each tradition has its own self-understanding and its own way of relating to Judaism. At least in Islam, there is recognition of a shared truth in the belief in one God, and the idea that heaven is potentially open for all. It's not about who you're related to or who's in your heart – it's about what you do.

But before we dive into the eschatological debates, which I don't feel particularly equipped or interested in discussing, let's return to the conversation about tribalism and cosmopolitanism. We've seen how introducing tradition into this conversation can open up various avenues.

I want to invite us, Shai, and perhaps the audience as well, to ask: What kind of duality is this, tribalism versus cosmopolitanism? When did it emerge, and how? Is it a distinctly modern duality? People have always claimed particular identities and universality. Modernity doesn't have a monopoly on this. But could this duality, when viewed through the lens of tradition, be a modern construct, perhaps emerging as a response to a crisis in our existence? Could it be a response to a specific European history of managing difference and plurality? After all, what's the difference that matters most in this formulation? The differences between tribes, peoples, and policies. But as I've alluded to through the Abrahamic narrative, there are deeper differences to consider.

Let me put it this way, and I'll end my point here: Walter Benjamin, a friend of Hannah Arendt, whom she remained loyal to more than Adorno and Horkheimer did, wrote something I think in "The Work of Art in the Age of Mechanical Reproduction" (though it might be in another essay). He talks about how the gods have fled in the modern age, and all that's left for humans is to observe each other. I wonder if this duality is a product of that departure.

SL: I want to hear more from you, Khaled, but let me share some of my thoughts, and maybe you can elaborate on them. I'm struck by how we talk about tribalism today in terms of identity – how we form and shape our identities. I wonder whether this can be contrasted with more traditional ways of thinking about belonging. At what point does belonging become a question of identity? By identity, I mean self-fashioning – deciding who we are and how we present ourselves. This fits well with nationalism and self-determination, where the focus is on determining who we are. It also aligns with identity politics, which centers around how we understand ourselves.

But I wonder whether this sense of belonging as identity contrasts with other forms of belonging – especially those we don't choose, like being born into a particular group. There's also the notion of non-identity, being a stranger rather than being at one with oneself. Specifically, in the context of the Jewish tradition, I think of the commandment not to wrong or oppress the stranger, because you too have been strangers in the land of Egypt. The beginning of the Israelite people, the Jewish people, starts with them as strangers in the land. They receive the Torah outside of the land, and so there's this element of being a stranger rather than feeling at home, embedded in the concept of belonging. I wonder what you think about this.

KF: There are three things I think are worth mentioning: First, as a Palestinian, I find it troubling that Israel represents not just a threat to Palestinian lives, but also to the rich ethical tradition of Judaism. I think both you and I know people who've made this point: that a nation-state itself is a threat to the ethical inheritance of Judaism.

Second, regarding your point about identity – while I don't claim to speak with authority on identity as a concept, I want to raise a question: Why do we frame things as a duality, between foreignness or being a stranger and having an identity? Sometimes I wonder if our obsession with identity is a symptom of a modern crisis – a loss of identity or a lack of anchoring in the world. I'm not offering an answer, but asking: why is identity such a pressing issue today? Does it reflect a deeper sense of dislocation?

Third, you made me think of a prophetic tradition from the Hadith, which has been preoccupying me in the context of this conversation. It might be shocking, but I invite you to think with me about how this tradition can help us reflect on the categories and experiences we're discussing today.

The Prophet Muhammad once said that Islam entered the world as a foreigner and will return as a foreigner. His companions were puzzled – what does it mean that Islam entered and will return as a foreigner? He replied, "Blessed are the strangers." When asked what he meant by "strangers," he said, "Those who command good and forbid evil." Perhaps foreignness isn't just about identity, but also an ethical stance in the world. This idea appears in its secular form in the 20th century, when Adorno wrote in Minima Moralia that part of ethics is being at home nowhere. So when I think of foreignness, I think it's tied to taking an ethical stance – even if it places you on the losing side. It's about defending not just Palestinian lives, but the fundamental idea that all lives matter.

SL: Khaled, I think you've drawn an important distinction – one that applies not only to the Israel-Palestine context but also more broadly, about the tension between the Jewish tradition and the State of Israel, between the people and the state. I want to bring in a quote from Nietzsche's Thus Spoke Zarathustra: "Somewhere there are still people and herds, but not with us, my brethren. Here there are states. A state – what is that? Well, open your ears to me, for now I will say unto you my word concerning the death of peoples. A state is called the coldest of all cold monsters. It coldly lies, and this lie creeps from its mouth: 'I, the state, am the people'."

I think that an historical perspective, grounded in tradition, allows us to conceptualize different kinds of belonging. It helps us critique, think critically, and look beyond identity and pride. We can understand and criticize these constructs.

But I also think, Khaled, that tradition is precisely what we no longer fully possess. This is part of the modern condition. We can't just return to tradition as it once was. Of course, people still maintain their traditions and religions, and I do as well. But I'm not talking about individual commitments here; I'm talking about the world at large. Clearly, traditions – at least in the way we're thinking of them – no longer have the same influence. We live in a modern world of states, with all the negative implications that come with it. But this is the world we inhabit.

I think one of the challenges Arendt posed to Zionism and the broader project was how to engage with the modern moment we're in – how to navigate the process of self-fashioning, identity formation, and national commitment, but in a way that remains critical of the nation-state and the specific constructions of identity and belonging it entails.

KF: One of the major struggles we face in Palestine and elsewhere is disentangling the idea that Jewish people are synonymous with Israel. It's a dangerous and implicit move in modern times to equate the two, which could, in some ways, be a form of anti-Semitism. But beyond this political issue, Shai, I'm not sure I would speak about tradition in the singular. Perhaps the authority of tradition – epistemic, ethical, ontological – has diminished, but I think our conversation would be richer if we allowed for a plurality of notions and understandings of tradition.

Take liberalism, for example. One way to view it is as an opposition to tradition, but as scholars of liberalism would point out, it has itself become a tradition – a tradition of opposing tradition, in some sense. It's not the only way to understand liberalism, but it's one perspective. I'd also like to draw on other sources of thinking about tradition, from Aristotle to thinkers in the Arab world or MacIntyre in the West. This includes not just medieval figures like Thomas Aquinas and Rambam, but also thinkers like Arendt, who see tradition as something we inherit – a transmission, a conversation with beginnings. Tradition, in this sense, is a way to engage with the past in the present while imagining future possibilities. From that perspective, it's hard to see anyone outside of tradition entirely. Even the way we talk about belonging is within a tradition, even though it arose after the collapse of the Roman trinity, as Arendt described it – authority, religion, and… freedom. No, authority, religion, and tradition. So, perhaps we should abandon the idea that we can think or speak from a place completely free of tradition.

SL: I agree with much of what you said. I think even the absence of tradition is itself a certain presence of tradition. The fact that we can't reach back to tradition isn't nothing; it's something we can think about. It's no coincidence that Nietzsche, when he talked about the state, referred to it as the new idol, using religious language to critique the new societal creation. He employed this traditional language to address the challenges of modern society. I think this is in the spirit of what we're trying to explore.

What does it mean to think about tradition – not to revive something dead, but to consider it in the context of contemporary challenges? How do we approach notions like pride, self-fashioning, self-determination, and identity, when what we have in mind isn't the liberal subject – the all-powerful individual determining their own future – but rather a more nuanced understanding of who we are and where we stand?

Q1: Khaled, I want to thank you for your contribution on tradition. But I have a question for clarification – this is not a challenge. I wonder if, in your introduction of tradition, you're in some way introducing another hierarchical binary, between modernity and tradition. It seems to me that, in every modernity, there's tradition, and in every tradition, there's something good from modernity, like gender equality. Is the idea not to flip the hierarchy – put tradition on top and modernity on the bottom, and battle which is having more influence – but to disrupt the binary entirely? To see that the best of tradition is often present in modern belief, and the best of modernity is also found in traditional beliefs. So, we resist flipping the binary, which we constantly do on both the right and the left.

KF: I'm sorry if I came across as suggesting a hierarchy, implying that tradition is above modernity. As a scholar of Arab poetics and Palestinian poetics, I've seen that argument made, and it makes sense to me. I agree with what you're saying – that we need not think of them conceptually as a hierarchy or pit them against each other. However, let me clarify, and I appreciate your question. When I use the term "modernity," I have in mind a very specific political, ethical, and epistemic project, which we are all products of. It's not just intellectual; it's a political project.

Q2: Thanks for making the trip here to talk to us, and for such a rich conversation. I have to start by asking your forgiveness because, every time you said the word 'tradition', I heard Tevye from Fiddler on the Roof singing in the back of my mind.

So, I'm with you on the idea of getting beyond dualism, where we have tribalism and cosmopolitanism. But I'm wondering if what you're talking about isn't very similar to what the Judith Butler has written about when they talk about living as minorities among minorities, or living in exile, or living in diaspora. Exile, in this sense, becomes an act of being critical of those in power. I think something missing from the conversation so far is the question of power. You can care about members of your own tribe, but when you're the hegemon, it becomes problematic for others. There's a rich tradition, especially in Jewish studies; Shaul Magid just wrote a book called Necessity of Exile. It sounds like this has something to do with what you're talking about, and I'd like to hear your thoughts.

Q3: I think you've answered the panel's main question in the affirmative: Tribalism can be cosmopolitan. This is a beautiful example of that. Maybe the next question is: Can enough tribalists be cosmopolitan to make a difference? I'm thinking of the examples you both discussed – praying at the Western Wall, being at Al-Aqsa Mosque, having connections to other traditions or people within your own tradition. But I'm also thinking about how much tension and violence have happened at those very spots. Can the beauty of this conversation be translated more broadly? How could that happen? I think part of the discussion is what kinds of tribes we're talking about. I think, Shai, you were right to mention that there's been some conceptual slippage about the types of entities we're discussing when we talk about tribes.

So far, the discussion has been mostly about religious traditions, with some references to states and nations. There's also been mention of Palestinian nationalism, which includes not just Islam but also Christianity. I think the question of power is relevant here too. Netanyahu probably doesn't care much about these conversations. Hamas probably doesn't either. On October 7, there was no distinction between Jew and Muslim in terms of who was slaughtered. How do we take the beauty of today's conversation and turn it into something that matters politically and socially for the world?

SL: Let me try to answer the last two questions together. I think – at least speaking for myself; Khaled, feel free to share your thoughts – being critical of power is very important. But I think, especially in response to your questions, what's perhaps more important right now is understanding what it means to be powerful in a critical way. That's a different thing. It's one thing to stand outside of power and criticize it. Some of the authors you mentioned are offering a critical position toward power – maybe even the relationship between the prophet and the king if we return to tradition. But for me, and I think for [??], it's a different question.

Now that there is sovereignty, now that we're in the modern moment, and now that we have a state, the question becomes: How do we use power critically, from a powerful but also fragile position? How do we understand that power comes with fragility? How do we understand the formation of modern states, without repeating the European mistakes of the nation-state, which was Hannah Arendt's concern? How do we bring these insights to a moment of power, not just as a critique of it? I think the key question is not how to stand outside and criticize, but how to stand inside and think about how this can happen.

KF: I think I'll have an easier time addressing your question about the repetition of this experience. We are, in some ways, the repetition of something that's been happening for a long time – if you just expand our imagination. When I heard you, I thought of Malcolm X. I thought of his experience on Hajj in Mecca and how that reshaped his relationship to black nationalism. I think of the father of my teacher, Leopold Weiss, also in Mecca, and how that transformed his relationship to his Jewish tradition. I think of Gaza and its churches and mosques that were there until the recent genocidal war on Gaza. So, I don't know what else to say beyond that – that this experience has existed and has been ongoing for a long time.

"BLOODS, CRIPS, AND OVERCOMING TRIBALISM IN LOS ANGELES"

MANDAR APTE, PHILLIP "ROCK" LESTER, AND GILBERT JOHNSON
(WITH NIOBE WAY)

MANDAR APTE [MA]: I spent nearly two decades at a small oil company called Shell. I lived in Houston, and my title was 'Game Changer'. I managed a multi-million-dollar fund and traveled 200 days a year – cosmopolitan by design.

During my first assignment as a petroleum engineer in rural Nigeria, I was attacked by a mob. I had nothing to do with the local conflict – I was just a young engineer – but an entire village came after me with swords, sticks, and stones. I barely escaped. Experiences like that stay with you.

Later, as a Game Changer, I started thinking: 'Can companies like Shell invest in communities affected by violence in a way that goes beyond philanthropy – something that makes business sense?' My experience has been that when your heart is in the right place and your intentions are pure, the universe helps you. I found a business case and invested Shell Game Changer funds into a technology called deliberative polling – deliberative democracy.

That world of violence is where I found my calling, because violence can happen anywhere – whether you live in a gated community or the slums of Mumbai. I believe it operates at three levels: action, speech, and thought. That's where I began applying my meditation practices.

I've studied, practiced, and taught meditation for 21 years – never missing a single day. I started asking myself, 'Where can I integrate this?' The best place? Where divides exist – where people wouldn't normally come together.

That led me to create a film called *From India With Love*. It took me on a journey of rediscovering my roots. India was colonized, but we never truly decolonized our minds. As I explored our ancient traditions and culture, I realized their social relevance today.

That work brought me to South Central LA. I arrived just after Nipsey Hussle was murdered. I met former gang members and community members, and I saw firsthand the deep trauma there. That's where I applied myself – and, in the process, found myself. Everyone I met – whether a six-year-old or an 80-year-old – was carrying trauma. So I brought together people who, on the surface, seemed different, but who shared that common experience.

ROCK: Watching Mandar's work, I saw the breathing exercises and other techniques he introduced to the community – especially for people doing the work on the ground. Some of the individuals are engaged in community-based public safety, gang reduction, and youth development. They deal with heavy situations daily. They're first responders in their own way – showing up at crime scenes, supporting grieving families, calming tensions, and stopping misinformation from spreading.

A lot of times, in communities like ours, rumors spread quickly. If someone gets shot in one place, people assume it was retaliation from another, even when there's no connection. The individuals providing these services – many of whom are former gang members with deep community ties – are trusted. But they often don't have access to healing themselves. They're out there helping others while carrying their own trauma. One person might respond to a single crisis, while another deals with five or six in a day. That's a lot to process, especially when emotions are running high.

Mandar's practices were great – they worked. But South Central LA already had initiatives in place, like the South LA Healing Circle Initiative, which we use to address the seasonal spikes in violence. In the summer, tensions rise – not just from gang activity but also because of heat, frustration, and other stressors. A situation that didn't start as a gang-related issue can escalate into one.

Personally, I don't work much with law enforcement – I stay in my lane, and we all work toward the same goal in different ways. My focus is on youth and people impacted by the system – those re-entering society who need resources to avoid falling into the cycle of mass incarceration. Some of us focus on prevention, while others handle intervention. Prevention is about providing alternatives – things I didn't have growing up. The circumstances I faced pushed me in certain directions, and now we try to offer young people better choices.

We fight for funding to create after-school programs, entrepreneurship opportunities – anything to keep kids engaged in something positive. People make decisions based on the choices in front of them. Our job is to expand those choices.

At the same time, we have to find balance for ourselves. Many of us do this work out of passion, shaped by our own pasts. We've been through it, and we don't want others to go down the same road.

I won't get too deep into this because it's emotional, but when I was 14, I was shot twice. At 15, I was shot again. My mother...

Fast forward to today – we're still here in South Central LA. We come from this. At one time, we wouldn't even be sitting on this stage together because of everything that's happened. There's so much trauma. When we tell our stories, it's not from a third-party perspective – it's firsthand. And that takes a toll.

GILBERT JOHNSON [GJ]: I want to thank the organizers for giving us this space to speak our truth, to share from the heart about what we know and what we've lived since birth. And I want to thank you, Rock, for being vulnerable, for sharing your experiences. It's okay to cry. It's okay to let it out.

Too often, in our communities, we're taught not to cry. We bottle it up, and that bottled-up anger turns into violence. What I've learned in this work is that violence begets violence, poverty begets poverty, and hurt people hurt people – but healed people heal people. That's why we're up here today – because we've taken the time to do the deep healing work, to unlearn the conditioning that so many Black and brown men growing up in South Central have been subjected to.

We come from a place of historical disinvestment. Our communities are overlooked. Our schools have been some of the worst-performing in the country. And let's not ignore the fact that the CIA flooded our neighborhoods with crack cocaine decades ago. Both my mother and father were addicts, which led me into the foster care system. I grew up in a deeply dysfunctional family – every one of my uncles and aunts struggled with alcoholism or drug addiction, all the way down to my grandmother. So, by the time I was 13, I was smoking, drinking, and using drugs, getting involved in activities that were, in many ways, socially engineered.

When we talk about systemic racism, we have to recognize how it was intentionally designed. Tens of thousands of Black families migrated to California to escape the Jim Crow South, only to face new forms of oppression. My grandparents arrived here and couldn't buy land because of restrictive covenants. They were redlined out of homeownership. There were sundown towns – places where Black people couldn't be after dark without risking their lives. And the police enforced this system.

Take the Watts Rebellion. I don't call it a riot because riots are senseless. The people of Watts were fed up. They were ready to tear things down – and they did. Unfortunately, it was their own community because they had no other outlet. There was no space to express their rage at being treated as second-class citizens, subjected to unconstitutional policing, despite paying taxes and working hard. It's part of a long history – going back to slavery, free labor, and the continued barriers placed in front of us when we try to seek opportunity.

There's a huge misconception about gangs. People assume it's always been about Black and brown folks killing each other, robbing, shooting, and stabbing. That's not the full story. The Crips and Bloods originally formed as community groups – tribal in a way, but built to protect their own. Raymond Washington, who started the Crips on the east side of South Central, was influenced by the Black Power movement. He and his brothers came together to say: We're not going to let what happened in Watts happen here again. They were resisting police brutality – the drive-by harassment, the constant intimidation, officers pulling people over for no reason, pointing guns just to instill fear.

Then crack cocaine was introduced, and everything changed. The drug trade created an underground economy, and with that came the rise in violence. But before that? Gangs were fighting with fists, maybe a bat or a bike chain, rarely a knife. It was about proving yourself physically, not killing. The crack epidemic turned everything upside down.

You heard Rock's story. I've lost family members to violence within our own community. It's so common in South Central that we have to take a different approach – like what Mandar was saying, we need non-traditional, non-punitive strategies to address the root causes of crime and violence. That's the work I do now. I lead all re-entry efforts for the City of Los Angeles, helping people transition back into society instead of being caught in the cycle of incarceration. It's powerful work.

NIOBE WAY [NW]: I use the phrase 'hierarchy of humanity' to describe the idea that some people are seen as more human than others. White people, wealthy people, the privileged – they are afforded full personhood, while others, particularly Black and brown communities, are not. This kind of dehumanization has consequences, including violence.

But what I find interesting is the way you framed gangs as a form of resistance to that dehumanization. I want to explore that. Gangs emerge as a response to oppression – but it's a resistance for survival, not for long-term liberation. It's not about glorifying gang culture, obviously. Violence is destructive. But gangs initially formed as a reaction to being treated as less than human. That's a survival mechanism. And yet, that resistance is limited – it doesn't lead to true freedom or systemic change. So, I'd love to hear your thoughts. Take this wherever you want. How do you see the role of gangs as resistance? And what are the limits of that resistance?

ROCK: I'm trying to fully understand the question, but I think Gilbert already laid out a lot of it. When we talk about gangs in LA and how they started, they were really for the community.

My grandmother was part of Neighborhood Watch, and I was always with her because I was the one who made her a grandmother. These weren't older ladies – they were middle-aged women, active in the community. My mom was only 16 when she had me, so I spent a lot of time with my grandmother, attending these meetings. I didn't fully understand it then, but later, I realized how much they were doing to keep our block safe.

Everyone had a role. And what I noticed was that when the police came around, it never felt like safety – it meant something was wrong. The women in Neighborhood Watch would actually go out to meet the police and ask, "Why are you here? What's going on?" They had a structure in place, but sometimes, that structure doesn't get passed down. Someone yesterday mentioned traditions in different cultures – how they aren't always carried forward. That happened in my family. When my grandmother had to go back to work at General Hospital, after 43 years, there wasn't anyone to take the torch.

As a result, things started changing in the community. People started forming groups, and what we now call gangs emerged. But I've always seen the word "gang" as a way to criminalize people who were just part of their community. Not everyone joins a gang – some people are simply raised in a certain neighborhood, and that community becomes like a family. These groups weren't about crime at first. They were about protecting the neighborhood, keeping it safe, and maintaining resources.

They were organizing – just like Neighborhood Watch. They ran voter registration out of one house. Another house was responsible for block parties to bring people together. They were making sure the police stayed out of the community because, again, we didn't see them as a source of safety.

Gilbert mentioned how police in America started as slave catchers. Every time we encountered them, it was negative. So, how do you keep them away? That's where these groups came in. They were meant to protect the community. And a lot of them took inspiration from movements like the Black Panther Party, which was about educating people, teaching them their rights, and taking care of their own.

But then drugs were introduced. And suddenly, the rallying cry changed. It wasn't about Freedom, Justice, and Equality anymore – it became about the drug trade. That's when things really started to shift.

People in certain communities share deep bonds. We all went to the same elementary school, the same junior high, the same high school. We grew up together – in the park, in the projects, wherever. Gangs, at their core, are a reflection of that – of tribes, of a sense of belonging.

But society puts labels on things it doesn't understand, especially when it wants to criminalize or diminish them. People take their opinions, turn them into attitudes, then those attitudes become laws. At one time, Black people were legally considered three-fifths of a person. That was someone's idea – and it became law. The same thing happened with gangs.

Mandar comes into the community and sees people for who they are. They have the same goals as everyone else – to put a roof over their heads, feed their families, take care of their responsibilities. But they're boxed into a system with fewer resources. So, they do what they can to survive. If you don't have the opportunity to do the right thing, and all that's left is the wrong thing, you play the hand you're dealt.

NW: That was so deep and profound. You just disrupted my entire framing of the question. I had assumed that gangs, as they're labeled today, were a form of resistance for survival. That they were just about responding to oppression. But what you just said is that they started off as community building – as resistance for liberation. And then you disrupted the word itself: 'gang'. You pointed out that we slap a label on something, and that label carries a negative connotation. But, in reality, it was a tribe. And when we talk about tribes, we don't automatically assume they're negative. Of course, some tribes do harmful things – but that's not the defining feature. What you just did was remind us of something we should have already known: these groups started from community, which is so important.

GJ: Your question about rebellion made me think of a trip I took to Ghana. Before I went, I had some understanding – through Western education – about my ancestors, their history, and rebellion. But nothing compared to being in Africa, talking to people whose ancestors lived through colonization, land theft, and terror.

One thing I learned was that when African tribes conquered each other, it wasn't about total destruction. They didn't wipe out entire cultures. They allowed the conquered people to keep their traditions, religions, and ways of life.

And that made me reflect on how communal Black people are. In South Central, we don't ostracize people. Black and brown communities actually get along far more than people assume. There's this stigma, this idea that Latinos tell each other, Don't mess with Black folks, they're violent. But the truth is, Black folks are the ones saying, Come to the party, come to the barbecue, come hang out. That openness is in our culture – it transcends generations.

But when we were confronted with systemic racism in America, that rebellion – the natural instinct to protect our community – was twisted into violence.

We used to have that communal, kumbaya energy, but it turned into something else because of external forces – social and economic conditions we didn't create. The jobs that sustained Black families in California were shipped overseas. Reagan defunded mental health institutions, leaving people with untreated illnesses out on the streets. Instead of addressing these crises through a community-driven lens, the government responded with force – militarized police, mass incarceration. And so, rebellion turned into something different. Violence became survival. Crisis became crime. That's how the rebellion that once built communities got redirected. And it's not just history – it's still happening.

MA: Put yourself in my shoes. I had a career at Shell, and then I was welcomed into the South Central community. At my first workshop, 21 people attended – seven former gang members, seven LAPD officers, and seven others, like teachers and nurses. They weren't forced to be there, which means I must have spoken to at least 200 people to get those 21 to take the risk of showing up. As my friend Andre put it, 'He's a crazy guy; he's here to teach meditation.' And these were people from completely different worlds.

Through the workshops I led from 2018 to 2021, I learned something profound. Only two people ever invited me into their homes. Not people of Indian origin, not the privileged, but a leader of a Black gang and a leader of MS-13. They welcomed me with the best hot chocolate I've ever had – an experience I will never forget.

What that taught me is this: Yes, I consider myself cosmopolitan, but above all, I need to be human. That's the middle ground we have to find between cosmopolitanism and tribalism; the balance is humanism. We need to relate to each other as human beings because, at that level, we are the same. We have the same aspirations, the same core values: love, compassion, mutual respect. And just as we brush our teeth every day for hygiene, we need a daily practice to remind ourselves of our shared humanity. That was my greatest lesson.

NW: Yesterday, I mentioned that for nearly 40 years, I've been listening to boys and young men, most of them from working-class communities of color. That's not a coincidence, given my focus on the expression of love and the language of desire for connection. Most of the voices we heard yesterday were young men of color. I've been asked many times: Why them? Why are these particular men the truthtellers of our human need for connection?

So, my question for all of you is this: I want you to channel your 13- or 14-year-old self. Think about how your own desire for connection shaped your life. How did that longing influence who you are, what you've done, what you're doing now? It's a big question, but speak from that place.

GJ: Growing up without a father – really, without a mother or father – there was always a void. I'd see other kids with both parents at home, showing up for school events, for T-ball, for whatever it was. And I felt envy. I hadn't yet learned the term 'abandonment', but I carried this deep anger and resentment.

For the longest time, I told myself, 'If I ever meet my father, we're going to fight first. Then we can talk about reconciliation'. I held onto that hatred for years, but underneath it was pain. That pain fueled a lot of the criminality I got into at a young age.

There's research showing that kids who grow up with a father in the home tend to have better outcomes. I remember gravitating toward other boys without fathers, and we were always in trouble – suspended from school, ditching class, getting kicked out. Meanwhile, the kids with fathers had structure that I didn't. My foster grandmother did her best, but it wasn't the same.

When you grow up in that environment, you become a product of it. The older guys in the neighborhood had money, fresh cars, the nicest clothes, the most beautiful women. That's what I wanted. I grew up in poverty, wearing hand-me-downs, waiting in line at churches for free food. So, the gang lifestyle was magnetic. In the late '80s and '90s, it looked powerful. It looked right.

NW: Where did you find connection during that time?

GJ: With the homies.

NW: And what kind of connection was that?

GJ: It was 'Ride or Die'. 'I got your back, you got mine'. There were a lot of layers to it. I was part of one of the largest Black gangs in Los Angeles – the Rollin' 60s. Within that, there were different factions, different cliques. My clique had a saying: 'You're not a Sixty until you kill a Sixty'. You mentioned my brother Nipsey – rest in peace. I knew him well. He was doing incredible work in the community, but that phrase, 'You're not a Sixty until you kill a Sixty', was real. Even within the same gang, there was tension and friction. But my crew? We were locked in. We got into trouble together, got out of it together. It wasn't healthy, it wasn't pro-social – but it was what we knew. It was all we knew.

NW: I want you to channel your thirteen or fourteen year old self, and think about your desire for connection. Can you share a story of a connection that helped you 'see the light', that shifted you from a more problematic connection – one focused on bad things – to something that helped you love yourself? Do you understand what I mean? I'm interested in a connection that made you realize something important.

ROCK: I don't think there was ever a time when I didn't love myself, even though people from gangs, cliques, or communities might not seem to have that love. But the truth is, they love where they come from. That's where the connection comes from. When I work with gang members or people who are at risk, we've changed the term to 'potential' because it's all about opportunity. If they don't get a chance to do something different, they might go down a different path, but it's because they love where they come from. Gilbert talked about 'ride or die', and when someone is willing to put their life on the line for their community, that's not hate – that's unconditional love.

Where does that love come from? I grew up in [location], where we had a pool in our area, while other communities didn't. When things turned into gang issues, people from other areas couldn't come to the pool anymore. But the park was a place where you could have your first kiss, or meet your first girlfriend – those connections to the community. And there were times when you didn't have food, and your neighbors would give you some. That's how we connected. I grew up on 9th and [Denker]. I loved that block a lot. Even though things were happening in the park, my grandmother bought her house there, and I remember the block parties. We looked forward to those as kids. It wasn't just the kids; the entire community was involved. Everyone knew everyone. That was the connection.

When that connection was threatened – when someone from outside posed a danger – it's natural for the community to stand up for itself. That's how gangs formed. It wasn't about hating others, it was about loving where we came from. But as things progressed, we started to lose a lot of people, and the threats became more real. It got to the point where families weren't just worried about losing a grandmother or a great uncle – they were worried about their 16-year-old son not returning home from school. And that's the reality we're facing, not just in South Central LA, but across the country. Elders are outliving the youth, with kids being gunned down in the streets. That's the biggest concern now. Mothers of Black and Brown sons are asking, 'Is my son going to make it?'

That's what we're working to change. I didn't want to go into the system and experience what it's like to be forced into a racial situation. For example, when I was in the system, there were times when I was on the yard with 60 Crips and only three Bloods. It wasn't the time for gang colors, but you're forced to pick sides because of race. Growing up, it wasn't about race – it was about fighting other groups in our community. But I started to realize that those individuals I thought were my enemies were willing to risk their lives for me, and I for them. That created a bond. The love I had for my community expanded beyond that – it became about all people who look like me, and respecting them.

The connection started to shift from hate to self-love. I learned that what we did to others who looked like us was rooted in self-hate. [Someone] said something that hit home: When you're out there, you're not looking for the person who isn't active – you're looking for someone just like you, someone who poses a threat. That's self-hate. Once I realized that, I began to understand that self-love means extending that love to people who look like me. That's when my journey started. But it's a process, with levels of growth, understanding, and development.

Now, I consider myself a humanitarian. I love people. If I hear about a kid getting hit by a car, I'm not asking if they were Black, Mexican, or white – I'm asking, "Was it a child?" That's the humanity I've embraced. My knowledge has taken me to a place where I'm now focused on finding resources for people and helping them out of situations like violence. We're working to pull people out of poverty and offer opportunities so they don't feel like they're without. There's always room for improvement, and that's the path I'm on now.

MA: When I was thirteen or fourteen, I remember reading The Hardy Boys and watching Superman and Spider-Man. I always wanted to meet Frank and Joe Hardy. My ambition was to solve mysteries and meet people. I was never just part of one group; I was always involved in many. This became a pattern for me. I worked at Shell, but I would spend time with the roughnecks, refinery operators, chefs, janitors and security guards, because I found that's where true humanity exists. When you're in these big structures, you might think the executive vice president or the VP is happy just because of their big paycheck, but actually, it's the roughnecks in the oil industry, the real people, who have authentic happiness.

Another experience I've had is realizing that we don't get to choose our parents or grandparents. They are who they are, and we all carry some kind of childhood trauma, often based on the stories that we were told. As we grow, we need to understand that there are multiple sides to every story. For example, if a father and mother are having a conflict, you might only hear one side of it. But there's always another side, one you might not have been told. As we mature, we need to develop compassion for the decisions others made, or that we ourselves made. Blaming others, or blaming ourselves, doesn't bring us joy or peace. The real question we should ask is, 'Am I happy today?' or 'Am I contented today?' And, 'What can I do to feel contented today?'

IN MEMORIAM

JEROME KOHN
in the exhibition "The Laughter of Hannah Arendt"
by Volker März, Berlin 2006

"REMEMBERING JEROME KOHN"

VOLKER MÄRZ, THOMAS BARTSCHERER, JACK BARTH,
ROGER BERKOWITZ, MATTHIAS BORMUTH, WOUT CORNELISSEN,
ROCHELLE GURSTEIN, ANTONIA GRUNENBERG,
WOLFGANG HEUER, MARIE LUISE KNOTT, STEVE MASLOW,
ELIZABETH MINNICH, THOMAS WILD

VOLKER MÄRZ

We remember and celebrate, with sadness upon his passing on November 8, 2024, at the age of 93, and in admiration and friendship, the life and work of Jerome Kohn. In his role as the trustee of the Hannah Arendt Bluecher Literary Trust since 2001, and through his extensive and highly regarded work as an editor, author, and public speaker, Jerome Kohn has profoundly influenced the reception and understanding of Hannah Arendt's life and work.

Kohn went first to Harvard University to study literature and proceeded to graduate studies in philosophy at Columbia University. He met Hannah Arendt in the late 1960s and continued his studies with her at The New School for Social Research, while also working as her teaching and research assistant. When Arendt died in December 1975, Kohn spoke at her funeral on behalf of Arendt's students. Following her death, Kohn worked with the American writer Mary McCarthy and German literary scholar Lotte Köhler, then trustees of Arendt's literary estate, on transferring her papers and library to the archives of the Library of Congress and of Bard College. McCarthy's posthumous edition of Arendt's *The Life of the Mind* (1978) is based on years of assistance and collaboration with Kohn. He was director of the Master of Arts in Liberal Studies program at The New School from 1980 to 1985 and was the founding director of the Hannah Arendt Center at the New School for Social Research in New York. In 2001, he became trustee of the Hannah Arendt Bluecher Literary Trust. In addition to directing the Center at the New School, Kohn facilitated the formation of Arendt Centers at the University of Oldenburg (Germany) and at Bard College. In 2019, Jerome Kohn was awarded the "Hannah Arendt Prize for Political Thought" (Bremen/Germany).

Kohn edited, published, and wrote introductions to five major books of essays and other writings by Arendt that have played an essential role in disseminating her work and shaping her legacy over the past thirty years. *Essays in Understanding* (1994) and *Thinking Without A Bannister* (2018) assemble over a thousand pages of articles, essays, reviews, and interviews by Arendt on political, philosophical, and literary matters; *Responsibility and Judgment* (2003) and *The Promise of Politics* (2005) collect key unpublished texts from Arendt's papers on the relationship between philosophy and politics; and *The Jewish Writings* (2011), co-edited with Ron Feldman, provide a seminal compendium of Hannah Arendt's public interventions on questions of Jewish history, politics, and culture since the 1940s.

As Arendt's literary executor and trustee, Kohn was instrumental in the development and publication of a vast number of books, essays, anthologies and translations. Kohn's support was essential in the establishment of the new *Critical Edition of the Complete Works of Hannah Arendt* (Wallstein Verlag, 2018–present). He maintained correspondence with a great network of scholars, writers, archivists, and artists throughout the world and was an indispensable resource for information about Arendt's life and work. He was also a cherished interlocutor and a peerless raconteur. [1]

Here, we gather voices from colleagues and friends of many years sharing individual perspectives on this manifold spectrum of Jerome Kohn's life and legacy.

Notes
[1] Jerome Kohn has been remembered by *The New York Times* in this obituary: https://www.nytimes.com/2024/12/13/books/jerome-kohn-dead.html.

THOMAS BARTSCHERER

About ten years ago – early in my acquaintance with Jerry Kohn – we were at a restaurant following an academic event. It was getting late, dessert finished, and a contingent of guests had just departed, leaving behind four: Jerry, a long-time friend of his, someone he'd just met that day, and myself. The four of us drew close, and this new acquaintance remarked, in a conspiratorial tone: 'Finally, the adults are gone!' Jerry laughed, a flash of mischief in his eyes: 'Yes, the adults are gone, and now it's just us kids.'

For a man who was mentor to so many, a man in whom great trust had been placed, whose voice and bearing conveyed such gravitas, it was the mischievous child in Jerry that I loved most.

Jerry was profoundly mischievous. Here was someone who rarely did what he was supposed to do – or so it seemed to me – and yet so often did the right thing. I recall his visits to the annual conferences hosted by the Hannah Arendt Center at Bard College, whether as a speaker or simply as an honored guest. His underlying question – typically more implied than spoken outright – often seemed to be: what has any of this to do with Hannah Arendt? But it was not in the spirit of a reprimand. It was a challenge. He was challenging us – always, he was challenging us – to think what we were doing. He put premises into question, unsettled consensus. He knew his presence at Arendt Center events signaled his blessing, his approval of the Center and its work. When he offered dissent or critique, it was in the service of a higher affirmation. He was the guest whose mischief was the pinnacle of good manners.

Jerry was a mischievous editor, as those of us who have toiled on the Critical Edition of Arendt's work are perpetually rediscovering. If the canons of contemporary scholarly editing are like the dogma of a sect, Jerry was surely a heretic. But to him the work of editing Arendt was never toil. It was a labor of love. As is true for all authors from the past, our understanding of Arendt is shaped by the custodians of her work. For the past quarter century, Jerry was Arendt's chief custodian, and in that role he did her memory and our world a great service. For many of her readers, it is reasonable to say that the Arendt they have come to know so well is Kohn's Arendt. That needs must now change, as a new generation of custodians picks up the work. The example Jerry leaves behind is both daunting and inspiring. However disregarding he was of the predilections of professors, I believe he edited her work confident that he always remained faithful to her wishes, that he rendered Arendt as she would have wanted to have been rendered. And who dare gainsay his judgment on that? Perhaps he learned some of his mischief from her.

Even Jerry's style was mischievous: knotted, elliptical, oblique – to me at times, bafflingly opaque until, after much contemplation, the meaning would emerge in blazing clarity. In conversation, in publications, in lectures, even in emails (those innumerable, inimitable, beautifully rambling emails), Jerry never uttered commonplace things in obvious ways. Once, preparing to be a respondent to a lecture he was giving at Bard in 2016, I found myself getting caught up on every other sentence. "The question 'Who is Socrates?' responds to Plato's disclosure of who Socrates is." Such formulations he tossed out like the playthings of a restless child, already on to the next, and the next.

I say there was a mischievous child in Jerry, but perhaps what I mean is that he was a newcomer. In a lecture by Arendt that Jerry published after her death (in two slightly different versions, under two different titles, neither of which appears on the original typescript!), she maintains that the possibility of human freedom derives from the fact that every human being is a newcomer through birth, a beginner, and as a beginner, endowed with the potential to start something new. Jerry Kohn was a consummate beginner, perpetually starting something new. Returning again and again to old books, he was forever discovering them anew, discovering new things within them and about them. He was instinctively drawn to the new idea, the new project, the new scholar, the new friend. In that lecture he gave at Bard, speaking of Baudelaire's "Le Voyage," Jerry voiced what the poem leaves unsaid: "that the new is the most fleeting thing of all, that it ceases to *be* new as soon as it is recognized as new, and that only death can end the unanchored heart's need to press on." His heart now at rest, may we, in his honor, press on. May we, in his spirit, start anew.

JACK BARTH

Thinking of Jerry, my friend of thirty years, I remember the many long summer afternoons under the pear tree in the garden at his Victorian manor in Greenport, where Jerry conjured many artistic personalities into our circle. For a long time, he was writing a piece – maybe a book? – that he called "the work of art" and he meant "the work" in both senses. I always felt that he was writing that book just for me and I always felt privileged by his deference to me. I think he thought artists were the clearest of beings who could reveal mystical truths, and because of this endearing overestimation, he treated me like an ambassador from a faraway land – at least in some moods and especially when we were in the interrogatory mood. And once in that mood, our exchanges pushed him into new territory as he pushed me in a direction that I didn't know I wanted to end up in until we both got there together. This was sheer fun. We were now two fellows very well met and ready for cocktails and dinner.

ROGER BERKOWITZ

I met Jerry in October, 2006, when he attended a conference I organized celebrating Arendt's 100th birthday. Jerry spoke brilliantly at the conference and after he asked Leon Botstein and myself if we would move the Hannah Arendt Center to Bard. Over the last eighteen years, Jerry has been a confidante and advisor, someone who has helped me think through Arendt's politics as well as the politics of running the Arendt Center. Above all, he has been a friend.

For many members of the Hannah Arendt Center, Jerry was a stalwart at our Virtual Reading Group sessions, always ready with a question or a marvelously revealing anecdote about his friend "Hannah." Every Friday I would look for him. Since his passing, I have religiously marked his absence.

For Arendt Scholars, Jerry was a brilliant interpreter and editor of Arendt's work. But for Jerry's diligence, only the most dedicated specialists would know of "Personal Responsibility Under Dictatorship," "The Tradition of Political Thought," "The Eggs Speak Up," "Understanding and Politics," "The Crisis Character of Modern Society," and her "Letter to Robert M. Hutchins." Jerry's work editing and publishing these texts has been a labor of love and a gift to us all.

For those of us who knew him more personally, Jerry was at once loving and unwaveringly honest, a true friend. I will miss Jerry's long emails, equally thanking me or taking me to task for something I had written in Amor Mundi. I will miss our lunches out on the North Fork near his house. But above all, his smile and his wit.

In 2022, I was honored to be the faculty sponsor when Jerry received an honorary degree from Bard College. The citation I wrote then is an apt way to recall Jerry. It reads as follows:

"How have the citizens of the United States dissipated the power of their Republic?" This question drives Jerome Kohn's lifetime of writing and publishing. Kohn has never shied away from controversy or provocation. As Hannah Arendt's longtime teaching assistant, literary executor, and friend, Kohn has published her work and deepened our understanding of Arendt's thinking. And in his own writing he has emphasized his, and Arendt's, fears around the decline of the American Republic.

The failure of the American Republic is rooted, for Kohn, in the dissipation of political power – the tradition and practice of self-government by which groups of people gather together to act and speak in public in ways that matter. Political freedom requires more than casting a secret ballot. It means to act and speak in ways that make freedom and power palpable. Kohn argues that the original American democratic reality of citizens freely exercising power has been eclipsed by an "encroaching social totalisim" and the dominance of bureaucratic rule.

"Jerry" Kohn's life changed when he read two essays on Bertolt Brecht and "Truth and Politics" by Hannah Arendt in The New Yorker in 1966 and 1977. Unhappy in a doctoral program at Columbia at the time, Kohn sought out Arendt and convinced her to let him audit her courses at the New School for Social Research. Kohn and Arendt became dear friends and he took over as her teaching assistant the following year until her death in 1975. He then served as Arendt's literary executor.

That 1967 meeting also changed the future reception of Arendt's work. Since Arendt's death, Kohn has published five major volumes of Arendt's collected and unpublished writings that have broadened and deepened our understanding of Arendt's work. His many essays on Arendt have brought the insight of a friend and longtime confidante to Arendt scholarship, focusing attention on Arendt's insistence on plurality, freedom, and thinking for oneself.

The depth that Kohn adds to our understanding of Arendt can be gleaned from an anecdote he tells in a forthcoming book of anecdotes and stories about Arendt. He accompanied Arendt to a meeting discussing Hegel's Philosophy of History in 1971. Kohn recounts the meeting with his trademark humility and wit:

"The participants were seated at an oval table in stiff modernist chairs.... After more than two hours of talk, they tentatively concluded that the telos, the end joined to the beginning of Hegel's massive undertaking, is absolute knowledge, the knowledge of Being. Which is to say that History knowing itself as History is Being. The meeting drew to a close with applause for all by all. As we walked back to her office, I asked Arendt, who had been unusually quiet during the meeting, what she thought History with a capital "H" is. "I haven't the slightest idea," she said."

MATTHIAS BORMUTH

Whenever I met Jerry in New York over the last ten years, we always had our conversations over lunch at the same place: Bistro Vendôme, 405 East 58th Street. As a historian of ideas and director of the Karl Jaspers House in Oldenburg, I had plenty of questions about "Hannah," his former teacher, and he was always delighted to answer them. We also exchanged letters by email, and over time we forged something of a philosophical friendship, one founded on our shared interest in Hannah Arendt and her thinking. Once, when we were discussing her essay on Lessing, Jerry wrote to me: "Over the past month, I have thought about writing something with regard to her speech. The title I like would be: Ein Deutscher und ein Jude, und Freunde, a quotation from the essay itself, of course." This was an American who valued the privilege of his friendship with the late Hannah Arendt, and who was always more than willing to share with younger scholars, who sought him out as the editor of her works, the insights associated with this special status.

The last time we met was in September 2023 on Long Island, in Riverhead, near his home, about which he had once written to me: "Here I live a rather solitary life, not at all lonely, with plenty of books and work, but quiet and, as much as possible, just thinking. I share this little house with two friends, one female, one male." Jerry recounted how Hannah had always scoffed at "thinkers by trade," the guild of professional philosophers to which she herself had, at least nominally, belonged in her later years at the New School. He, too, made no complete break with institutional philosophy, as he headed that institution's Arendt Archive without holding a formal faculty position. What mattered most to him was personal reflection and private conversation – allowing for the freer expression of one's opinions beyond the conventions of academia.

As the shy person he was, Jerry had been deeply impressed by his teacher's ability to create, within the sometimes forbidding spaces of the New School, an atmosphere of familiarity, a haven in which individuals tentatively learned to find their own voice and language, thus enabling them to partake in the life of the mind in their own way. This is how the young Jerome Kohn praised Arendt's ability – in the eulogy he was honored to deliver in December 1975 – to open up a space for the drama of thinking. In 2017, I managed to persuade him to search for that text, which he did in fact find about a month later in his "warehouse full of boxes of books and papers."

At the time, he recalled the captivating presence of Hannah Arendt, who, even into his later years, shaped him into a source of inspiring dialogue. While he performed intimate chamber pieces of philosophical conversation with many of those who met him, his teacher offered the grand stage of the seminar for her introductions to thinking – an arena in which, according to Jerry, everyone had the chance to play a part: "Hannah Arendt's presence and the words she spoke lifted us from our accustomed habits and practices into an unfamiliar space, where our learned or traditional reactions were untimely. We now found ourselves in a space of equality, where no one commanded and no one obeyed, a space where one's own opinion counted as much as any other, at least as long as one remained convinced of it, as long as one was not persuaded by a different opinion. In other words, we now saw freedom in a way we had not before, we felt free and equal, which in Hannah Arendt's terminology meant that we were appearing in public, and that we were engaging in politics, of all things, where freedom and equality have rarely if ever co-existed in a state of stability. So far from being worldless, we thought about doing something new by acting into the world, acting together in our newly provided political association, changing what we agreed wanted changing, and even attempting to exert some control over chance – at least while the lecture lasted. While she spoke we ceased being subjects or objects, and each of us became a 'who,' that is, a person who recognized, and was recognized by other persons, other 'who's'; it was in a space filled with light that we discovered each other, a space where our own freedom, joined with that of our peers, gave us the courage to believe that the activities we undertook together might not be futile."

At the time, he reminded me in a letter how deeply meaningful the sentence Arendt wrote in the introduction to *Men in Dark Times* had been to him throughout his life: "The uncertain, flickering and often weak light that some men and women, in their lives and works, will kindle under almost all circumstances." This he wrote, not least, in light of the first period during which a bad actor came to dominate the American political stage, yet he took comfort in the fact that his teacher's critical voice was resonating so widely in such times. "It's a despairing world we live in. To think that such a man as Trump is our president. The Founders must be nervous in their graves. One positive thing that has emerged is that Hannah Arendt's *Origins of Totalitarianism* has become a bestseller. A difficult, 500 page book, written 70 years ago, is now selling six hundred copies a day!"

That her work continued to reach the public through numerous edited volumes of her papers is thanks to Jerry. Sharing her love for the sort of open dialogue that often occurs between friends, he included her lecture on Socrates in The Promise of Politics. Jerry's words about his teacher at her memorial service can, almost half a century later, now be recalled in light of his own passing. "Hannah Arendt's ability to summon up what it means to be a *Mensch*, a human being, to persuade the barely visible to appear in the seeming darkness, places her squarely in the company of Socratic thinkers."

WOUT CORNELISSEN

I first met Jerry Kohn in 2013, when I was introduced to him by Thomas Wild. I had just started a postdoctoral fellowship at Bard College, and Thomas Wild had asked me to become one of the editors of the new, Critical Edition of *The Life of the Mind*. The first few times, Jerry and I met as part of a larger group. Not much later, once I had begun doing the archival research on *The Life of the Mind*, I had the chance to meet with Jerry individually.

Jerry's mind was extraordinarily *alive*. It was hard not to *feel* his words, both in conversation and in correspondence. Usually, he invited me for lunch in a bistro in Manhattan, not far from his apartment, after which we walked on the sidewalks together, crossing avenues and streets, on our way to our respective next destinations. When we spoke, Jerry would always ask for my opinion, when a certain book by someone on Arendt had just come out, or when someone had said something about a certain matter. He would never just "opinionate": he was always interested in what you would think of the matter – thus living out Arendt's insight that meaning isn't coercive and that judgment depends on the willingness to place yourself in the standpoints of others. Gradually, we also started corresponding via email. Almost without exception, Jerry would reply within 24 hours, which would lead to a string of messages between us around a certain topic. Once the thread became too long, he would start a new one.

The Life of the Mind was very dear to him, not only because of its substance – he believed the book was "years ahead of its time" – but also because he had been there from the moment Arendt had begun working on it, after she arrived at the New School, where he served as her teaching assistant until her death in 1975. When he gave "pro-seminars" to her lecture course on "Thinking" and "Willing," she shared a photocopy of each chapter, which he had kept. He generously lent these to me so I could compare them – I remember sitting on a Long Island Railroad commuter train with a box of typescripts, guarding it with my life.

After Arendt's death, he had assisted Mary McCarthy in tracing Arendt's references and answering other questions when she was editing Arendt's text for publication. When he read an essay I had written on Arendt's metaphors of thinking, he agreed with its substance yet added: "you should find yourself a Mary McCarthy!" Around that time, he was working on *Thinking without a Banister*, the last of the five volumes of Arendt's published and unpublished essays he edited. When it came out, he generously gave me a copy, and added that he would now have to "sleep like a bear."

During the Covid-years – Jerry spoke of "the plague" – we couldn't meet in person, but our correspondence continued, now with longer interludes. Sometimes, when I bothered him again with a question about certain materials or facts, he grew impatient with me. I had to play the role of the philologist, mapping materials, meticulously reconstructing the genesis of *The Life of the Mind*. Jerry sometimes mistook this for a lack of interest in content, eager as he was to engage in, and continue, a dialogue about the *matters*, rather than the materials, of thinking. Yet, we had a shared goal: to let Arendt's own words speak to their readers, in order to allow for a better understanding of her work and its meaning in the world we live in.

The volumes of our edition of *The Life of the Mind* came out in April 2024. Upon receiving the news from us, Jerry sent his congratulations and shared his exhilaration. In May, my partner Mirjam and I visited Jerry and his partner Jerry in Cutchogue. It was the first time I saw Jerry in person again in more than three years, and the first time we met each other's partners. It was a most joyful day, filled with lively conversation and lots of good laughs. When I handed the volumes to him, Jerry replied that he would first need to "strengthen my arms to lift them"! I was excited, but also a bit apprehensive: what would Jerry think? A few weeks later, I received an email message from him:

"This only a quick note to say that I have read the first volume of your work. It is like rummaging through a treasure chest! I have a million questions, but now have time only to say how wonderfully enjoyable it is to read *The Life of the Mind* in your edition, and also, and just as much, the array of Hannah's writing you have gathered to supplement it. It is delightful to realize that what is between these blue covers is there to bathe in every day."

When the sad news of Jerry's passing came, I realized how fortunate we had been to see him in May. Compared to many of the "gatekeepers" of the *Nachlass* of other thinkers, Jerry was exceptionally generous. He made it his life's work to let as many people as possible, all over the world, read Arendt's work. He once wrote to me: "The urgency I find as her literary trustee is to keep her works available for those who, possibly, may be willing to care for at least parts of what is now ceasing to be a common world." To this end, it was important to him readers understood not only Arendt's words, but also who she was as a person: "Hannah knew no fear."

ROCHELLE GURSTEIN

It was Dore Ashton, an old friend of Jerry's, who introduced Jerry to my husband and me in the early 1990s. Dore was a new friend of ours and when I told her that I was writing a dissertation about changing ideas of private and public in America and that Hannah Arendt was a towering figure in my intellectual life, she told me that I *must* meet her friend, Jerry Kohn. Soon after, Dore had us all over for dinner at her townhouse in the Village and from that moment on, I was smitten by the man – tall and handsome, dashing in dress and manner, and in command of a brilliance and wit that that made being in his company sheer pleasure.

At first we met occasionally. And then, after a year or so of conversation, where Jerry always expressed curiosity in his far less cultivated, younger acquaintance's ideas and opinions, the two of us began to develop a friendship that would sustain me over the next thirty years. For me, the turning point was an invitation to dinner at his apartment on east 55th Street with his partner Jerry Hoolahan and his close friend, Elisabeth Young-Bruehl. The timing could not have been more fortunate. My mentor, the great historian Christopher Lasch, had recently died and my world felt terribly diminished. To be welcomed into this select Arendtian company felt like I had been granted a new lease on my intellectual and social life.

And that is precisely what I was granted. Anyone who has spoken or corresponded with Jerry or has read his writings has had the experience of being on what he called the "Hannah Arendt thought train" – "the pleasure of knowing where you want to go and simultaneously not knowing where you'll end up," as he put it in an essay on Arendt. These words of Jerry's evoke what made our leisurely, meandering conversations so very distinctive. This was true of serious discussions about the things that mattered most to us, but also of playful banter about the more quotidian stuff of life. Whether we were in a restaurant or cafe, at his and Jerry's chic apartment in the city or their stately Victorian house on the North Fork, from the moment we came together until the moment we said goodbye, the conversation never stopped. The news of the day, the historical moment, reminiscences of friends, gossip, Arendt, how great Jerry Hoolahan's cooking was, Hegel, Klee's *Angelus Novus*, Ruskin, Paris in the 1950s, hurricanes, Barnett Newman, some jokes, Gandhi, taste, beauty, more Arendt, how great Jerry Hoolahan's cooking was, Heidegger, why weren't we all living in Florence together? – that is a partial memory of one of our long Thanksgiving weekends in Greenport.

And then there was the on-going conversation that took place in emails. The miracle of email, as we all know, is that decades of correspondence can be called up in an instant by typing a name into "search," which I just did. There are mountains of them – thankfully! I zeroed in, more or less by random, on our correspondence from 2011 to 2013. By that time, he and Jerry were living mostly in Greenport, so we covered a lot of territory in our emails. What stood out most was Jerry's unflagging generosity as a reader. During those years, I was publishing a regular column in *The New Republic* online about anything that interested me. The day that I would send a column to Jerry, he would immediately respond via the Hannah Arendt thought train. I was surprised to see how many letters between us would spring from his initial thoughts, how adventurous he was in his musings, how inviting he was to my every reply. Reading them now I felt once again the wide range of his learning, the intensity of his insight, the pleasure we both took in the back and forth of conversation. It also reminded me of all the fun we had over the years. Vivid descriptions of the changing seasons from his window in his study were always followed by "isn't that glorious?" Irritated, well-founded complaints about the miserable state of our politics were always followed by a line from Samuel Beckett that we both were fond of, "Christ, what a planet!"

ANTONIA GRUNENBERG

I met my friend Jerome Kohn in 1995 at the New School for Social Research in New York. At that time, Hannah Arendt had already been dead for twenty years. The year before, Kohn had edited a volume of unpublished essays and lecture manuscripts by Hannah Arendt: *Essays in Understanding*.

The four further volumes that he published until his death, the last in 2018, have significantly sharpened the view of the philosopher in the United States as well as in Europe. His forewords to the individual volumes show Hannah Arendt, beyond her great books, as a bridge-builder between academic philosophy and public political thought, as a campaigner for a new political beginning, as a gifted polemicist, as a transnational political writer (a term that does not exist in the classical canon of the humanities). Last but not least, he was the one who repeatedly and emphatically drew attention to the poetic principle in Arendt's political thinking.

With his editorship, which was explicitly aimed at a wider audience, he made Arendt's thinking comprehensible as a work in progress. Now readers could trace the ramifications, ruptures and expansions of her thought from the 1940s to the 1970s.

It is largely thanks to Jerome Kohn that Hannah Arendt became a public figure known far beyond the borders of the universities. Previously unknown texts by her were now read in reading circles and seminars, commented on in journals; doctoral theses were written about them. Since the 1990s, the philosopher has been quoted in European parliaments and honored in speeches; streets and squares have been named after her.

Incidentally, Kohn was one of the few who did not confront Hannah Arendt's relationship with Martin Heidegger with moral condemnations. Instead, he was interested in what these two exceptional thinkers had argued about philosophically and politically in the years after 1950. After all, Arendt's political thinking emerged decisively from its criticism of Heidegger. This is evidenced by her Denktagebuch, her Thinking Journals, which can also be seen as a kind of philosophical X-ray of Heidegger's thinking and personality.

Jerome Kohn has also done a lot for the recognition of Arendt's thought in practical terms: in the 1990s, he founded the Hannah Arendt Center at the New School for Social Research. In 1998, he supported the founding of the Hannah Arendt Center at the Carl von Ossietzky University of Oldenburg, which I established; in 2001, he took over the office of trustee of the Hannah Arendt Blücher Literary Trust, and he became the principle surviving witness to Arendt's life after the death of Lotte Köhler in 2011. He supported the Critical Edition of Arendt's Complete Writings. And so many students he supported with his intellectual and practical advice!

In 2019, he was awarded the Hannah Arendt Prize for Political Thought for his lifetime achievements.

For Kohn, Hannah Arendt was not just the author of texts. Her sometimes provocative theses (see the controversy surrounding the concept of the "banality of evil") and surprising theorems (e.g. her distinction between political and social, between private and intimate spheres; her thesis of the structural similarity of totalitarian systems, her imagination of the political) were part of the re-foundation of a political philosophy as a way of thinking in the Mit-Welt. And Jerry believed in this unfinished business even after Arendt's death.

Jerome Kohn was a republican in the original sense of the word, i.e., an American citizen who saw himself as part of a political community for which he felt genuinely co-responsible. In the introduction to the last volume of his publications from Arendt's estate, tellingly entitled *Thinking without a Banister*, he focused on the decline of American democracy and the rise of totalitarian elements (such as the digital manipulation of reality (and politics). American society had become the object of a social totalism, he wrote, in which a bureaucracy brought with it "the more or less complete suppression of political freedom" and thus also the loss of the political in general.

Jerry loved open conversation, he was curious about what his interlocutors thought; he appreciated the dispute about different perspectives on a text. He was rather concerned about the academic world, knowing full well that freedom of thought is under threat at universities today.

When I wrote to him in the face of Putin's military threats towards Europe and the imminent election of Donald Trump as American president in the summer of 2024, saying, "One has to fight hard against the temptation to drown in fear. However, that would be the end of political thinking," he replied: "Those are wonderful words, Antonina. There is not despair, neither hope, but courage in the newness of your plans for a Hannah Arendt organization." He was alluding to the founding of the *Internationale Hannah Arendt Gesellschaft* in autumn 2024, which I had initiated together with friends and colleagues. He was a founding member

– as was Roger Berkowitz. I had hoped so much that we could build on his alert, unconventional spirit for a while longer. Now he has passed on.

What remains is the image of a friend who loved to think and moved in the world of people (and dogs!) with an insatiable curiosity.

WOLFGANG HEUER

I met Jerry at a conference in Clermont-Ferrand, France, in 1995. He asked me about the newly established Hannah Arendt Center in Oldenburg, a slight skepticism on his face. I reassured him that it was a reputable center. I liked the spectrum of attitudes that I got to know from him over time. His kindness in dealing with colleagues, his generosity towards those who wanted to publish writings from Arendt's estate, the accuracy of his interpretations of Arendt's writings and his modesty. Occasionally, his wordlessly raised eyebrows already indicated that he did not agree. All the more reason for me to regret that he was an outsider at the New School. When we still had the first issues of the HannahArendt.net magazine in print, I brought him a large package to New York and asked him to distribute the issues in the U.S. He looked at me in complete disbelief. How should he do that? He had no one to do it.

Jerry, along with biographer Elisabeth Young-Bruehl and Alexander Bazelow, who spent time in Arendt's apartment transcribing the lectures of Arendt's husband Heinrich Bluecher, formed something like the children of Arendt. Arendt had chosen them.

As the number of conferences on Arendt increased and Jerry and Elisabeth were invited to speak, they one day developed a new type of lecture in which they would speak together and in the form of a conversation. They did this on topics such as "Critique de la souveraineté et de l'État-nation," "What and how we learned from Hannah Arendt," "Hannah Arendt on action and violence with reference to Simone Weil and Rachel Bespaloff on Homer's Iliad," and "On Truth, Lies, and Politics."

The study and varying interpretation of Arendt's work is subject to the course of time. The political situation changes, as does the interest in Arendt and her reception. Jerry was one of the last still-living persons who worked with Arendt. Arendt not only wrote her essays such as "Crises of the Republic," but also expressed her views on political issues in conversations at the university or at her home, occasionally, as contemporaries reported, in heated controversy. Jerry experienced Arendt's involvement in her times. For her, thinking, judging and acting were not intellectually appealing philosophical topics, but quite the opposite: they were the essential phenomena whose failure made the dark times of the 20th century possible. "On Revolution" was therefore not a historical work, the considerations of councils were not political romanticism and the report about

Eichmann in Jerusalem was not journalism. It was always about saving the world from the abyss. Alexander Bazelow wrote to me: "The Hannah Arendt I knew was not the Hannah Arendt everyone writes about. What I admired about her was her tough-mindedness and willingness to face realities that everyone was afraid to acknowledge, even if those realities conflicted with her own writings from the past. I believe she saw the first inklings of the return to neo-liberalism."

Her public criticism of the state of the American republic 200 years after its founding was harsh: the rule of an oligarchy, the penetration of crime into politics, political action with the means of an advertising company and the war economy during the Vietnam War.

Together with Elisabeth, Jerry took part in Arendt's very unusual seminar, "Political Experiences in the Twentieth Century." It was an experiment to use literature to imagine the world of experience of a person in the twentieth century, from the First World War to the atomic bomb. It was an exercise of the imagination as a prerequisite for judgment.

We are left with these memories and with Jerry's words, including his prefaces to Arendt's essays, which he collected and published. I think of him with gratitude.

MARIE LUISE KNOTT

My life closed twice (poem no. 96)
Emily Dickinson

My life closed twice before its close –
It yet remains to see
If Immortality unveil
A third event to me
So huge, so hopeless to conceive
As these that twice befell.
Parting is all we know of heaven,
And all we need of hell.

Dear Jerry,

You know how much I love archives, so you can imagine, how much I appreciate since many years not only your work as the best Nachlassverwalter, but mainly the diligent, persistent and so productive work you did in the field of editing Hannah Arendt's work from the archives. Thanks to you her words matter in your country and in the global intellectual field. That is why through all the years I felt very assured by your friendly backing my work in our common field. I remember us sitting in Sag Harbor together under the tree when I came to the States and to Long Island last time. Unfortunately, that feels like ages ago.

(Quoted from a letter, 7 September 2012)

STEVE MASLOW

In the last of the 276 letters Jerome Kohn and I exchanged over these past dozen years or so, we were discussing…traveling without a schedule ("*I find not knowing where one is almost Kantian!*")…reflecting on Covid past ("*…an occasion for social isolation and personal solidarity*")…and needing to leave NYC for nature ("*This entire country seems on its way to Hell, or at least oblivion, but here at least there are trees and flowers, dogs and human beings.*") These writings coming from Jerome Kohn I should have, of course, recognized my wily mentor lulling me into a false sense of intellectual torpor. <<Would this turn out to be a letter I could read and answer in a day…without the help of my library and several hours of thinking?>> May you please recall now the finale of Tchaikovsky's Fifth Symphony, when the violins shift the mood violently towards euphoria (and the tempo from andante to allegro; the time from 4/4 to 2/2). In mid-paragraph, Jerry modulated and re-addressed me:

Steve, I've had a radical breakthrough after talking to and thinking with Hannah all these years. It's a total change in perspective – something Hannah herself recommends – on political plurality as the conditio sine qua non of human freedom. I'm now seeing plurality from the point of view of the unique individual, the person who joins other unique individual persons to create political plurality. That is not god's creation and at best meets with his approval. Is that not the meaning of Tikkun? It joins Athens and Jerusalem in a new synthesis, at least for me.

Well, at least in this letter, there was no homework assignment: Jerry did not "suggest" I read one of William Kentridge's six Norton Lectures on drawing, nor did I have to understand his untranslated quotations from Aristotle's *Protreptikos* (a favorite work of his and Hannah Arendt's.) Just think and respond. "Light" fare.

Jerry was 92 years old when he wrote that he had undergone this "…*changement de vie totale, or at least in the life of my mind.*" Such was my friendship with Jerry: at once an assurance, that he would share his most important thoughts with you, a fellow-member of a tribe of intellectual inheritors; an inspiration, that the life of the mind knows no age; and an exhortation, to keep reading and writing, preferably without a plan.

But I do not want to discuss these last of Jerry's ideas here, but to try and bring him back as a person, a physical being, who showed himself so elegantly in what Hannah Arendt called the world of appearance, a stage from which he has now withdrawn.

Jerry was a tall man, at the top of which his white, short, neat hair draped like fine Scandinavian knitting. He had a bright forehead into which his brows would dig trenches when he was excited or when he was surprised. Even though Jerry was no actor, his face was an entire theater: he knew how to flash his kingfisher blue eyes to punctuate what he was expressing, or begin to frown and then de-frown, so you knew he disagreed with something you said, but he didn't want to interrupt you. He had a mellifluous voice and would sometimes run out of breath before he finished a sentence. He would then sound raspy, before recovering the basso-tenor quality he had going on. Jerry had impeccable European manners, and the curve of his fork always tined down into his food, after which he would use the knife to cut it. He would not eat while anyone was speaking, and so a lunch could often extend for several hours, and you could forget all about eating while the food was hot. A favorite restaurant of his was Jubilee, on 848 First Avenue, a jewel box of a dining room, with an unusual chef that applied French technique to Italian ingredients, like ravioli filled with *brandade de morue* in an extraordinarily light lobster cream. We ate like we were going to the chair later that evening, and drank like sailors, and towards the end of most of these meals I would observe myself, as if from above, dining with this scholar-prince, just as it was happening. I savored his presence in my life. A famous uncle of mine referred to these peak experiences as self-actualizing moments, but, following Jerry's disdain for jargon, I will just say the feeling that arose was that of getting exactly what you wanted, but didn't know it was coming.

We met late in life; he was 80 and I was 51. I had seen Jerome Kohn lecturing around New York City and at Bard, with Elisabeth Young-Bruehl, who was my professor at university. Jerry was Hannah Arendt's teaching assistant and literary executor, and Elisabeth was her authorized biographer. The two had been friends since they were Arendt's students in the 1970s. Jerry and Elisabeth found ways to talk about Arendt that made her works more accessible and could foreground them with vivid stories from her life. In the interim, at the invitation of Roger Berkowitz, I became the chairman of the Hannah Arendt Center at Bard. Then Elisabeth died suddenly of an aneurysm. It was in writing a eulogy for her, that I reached out to Jerry for advice.

Prior to meeting Jerry, EYB was the only link in my chain to Arendt, and I incorrectly assumed Elisabeth's style would characterize all of Arendt's students. As I became friends with Jerry, the splenetic difference in their temperaments shocked me. When it came to Arendt, he was like a reservoir of knowledge, and she was a fire hose. After sending my remarks about EYB to Jerry, before publishing them in Amor Mundi, he invited me to lunch.

I found myself enchanted by his warm-hearted embraces, his old-world graciousness, his insistence upon understanding Arendt as closer to imagination than to reason, or at least with an awareness of Arendt's ideas about the 'tyranny of logic' in the foreground. Jerry had a genius for friendship, a quality he admired in Arendt and which he practiced religiously. Even at his late stage in life, Jerry made clear he was open to interpersonal connections, and we welcomed each other into a circle of people, mostly around the Hannah Arendt Center.

I thought he embodied the idea of humanism, and had the distinct impression this man would bring you chicken soup if you needed it. But at the same time his scholarship was formidable, polymath and polyglot, and he had zero-tolerance policies towards bad syntax (e.g. I once asked him what his next 'dream destination' was and he replied that he would have to be asleep to tell me.) We shared a love for Italian language and culture (Jerry once wrote, as I was departing for Liguria, that I should "*kiss the ground*" for him) and we were both gay men who were neither closeted nor flamboyant. He was generous with his time, his invitations, his letters, and he was also impatient when you took too long to reply. Only in this respect do I think Jerry was oblivious to how much research and thinking-time it took to answer the proliferation of insights and questions that he posed, branching out in many directions, afire with his insatiable curiosity.

As my work in finance took me increasingly abroad, I corresponded with Jerry more and more. We never did meet up in Italy, as we had promised to do, but I feel like he was there with me, in no small measure because he was in the habit of suddenly calling on the telephone, when he said he was thinking of me. I vividly remember these Kohn-outbreaks: once, in Rome (this story ends with Caravaggio's *Conversione di San Paolo*, and its twin sources of light, being the greatest piece of gay erotica in existence);

another time in Lerici (*Did you try the mussels from the Bay there, known as 'dateri', yet? They were so prized by the Holy Roman Emperor Frederick II (1211–1250) that he accepted two shields-full in lieu of taxes!*); and in Florence, where Jerry had just visited and reported that he had been having a long overdue conversation with Michaelangelo, much as he reported (see second paragraph above) having one with Hannah Arendt in 2023.

We talked about books often, and the only serious disagreement I remember having with Jerry concerned our interpretations of Othello. Writing at the time of the murder of George Floyd, Jerry felt that no satisfactory explanation for Iago's hatred of the Moor had ever been offered. I quoted to him Iago's lines where he indicates he suspected Othello for having been between the sheets with Emilia (Iago's wife). Jerry dismissed Iago's suspicion as insufficient grounds for his blind hatred and the dastardly destruction Iago premeditated against Othello. Of course this talk morphed into the possibility that Arendt may have been mistaken in her assessment of Eichmann, that he simply hated the Jews, a raw hatred. Arendt said she went to cover the trial as a "cura posterior" for herself, but sometimes, as Derrida points out, the remedy is the poison. As I see it, Arendt was, perhaps, having a subjunctive experience of what might have happened to her, dramatized for her and all the world, by the witnesses in that 1961 courtroom in Jerusalem.

I use the word subjunctive here not as a grammatical mood, but as Hannah Arendt and Jerry used it, as a way of thinking in the world. To think in the subjunctive is a manner of seeing the past not as a fixed story, but as one the present is continuously acting upon. It is the subjunctive that gives us the syntax of possibility. The terms "if; could; would; if and when" can express yearning but are also the terms that enact yearning. As in Phaedrus, there is something performative about advancing a series of speculative arguments to explore what could have been. To think in this manner demands both reason and imagination. This was the great gift Hannah gave to Jerry, and he to me.

I loved Jerry Kohn, *mit allem Drum und Dran.* Jerry, I think of you often, *"because,"* as you once wrote to me, *"that is what I like to do."*

ELIZABETH MINNICH

To see who is there, a spectrum?

My friends, how do I write of a man intellectually, morally, politically committed to making present the unique who of a person, the reality of an experience?

Late in life, Jerry and I took up visiting when I came to the city. Between lunches at the unpretentiously elegant "Jubilee" restaurant, we corresponded.

Apologizing (as he always did) for not responding instantly, Jerry wrote, "…I find us so constantly in conversation that I fail to share in writing what we're talking about!" But he did. In his letters are glimpses of my thinking friend writing *in media res*, in the last months of his life.

Jerry wrote of seeking "angles of vision" to illuminate Hannah Arendt. He proposed "four angles – not points of view – which when mentally unified phenomenologically reveal Arendt as a person distinct from any and all of her manifold appearances in the world." To reveal such "angles," he proposed a thought image: a *"Spectrum: light passing through a prism, so we can see non-additively what it is…, the aesthetic."*

He wrote that he told an interviewer, "Her teaching was exemplary." Asked to explain, he did so with interest, and purpose: "An example of itself…When Arendt taught Plato's Socrates, Plato himself, and Aristotle, her students were not so much transported into a past as experiencing a past brought to them in their present….not seen through the mist of time – not as characters leaping about in a film – but as being *there, now, filled with wonder*, as Shakespeare sings of a drowned Duke's eyes having become pearls." And then: "I wanted to continue, but [he] did not." Jerry was puzzled. Perhaps the interviewer (a filmmaker) was too.

Arendt's impatience, however, could wound. After a seminar, Jerry returned to the classroom to find an older woman, recently returned to study, in tears. Jerry spoke kindly to her and strode back to Arendt's office: *Hannah, there is a woman weeping in your classroom. You need to speak with her.* She did.

In those last months, an expanded edition of my book, *The Evil of Banality: On the Life and Death Importance of Thinking*, came out. Jerry wrote, "The whole matter of evil done without intention looms larger every day, with huge consequences for the administration of justice."

Clarifying an earlier note: "regarding the banality of evil, I did not mean that the evil done is thought-defying, but that the person responsible for it is. To me that's what HA saw in Eichmann: nothing. It's nothing that defies thought." My friend concluded, "your book, in its display of the evils of banality, is essential reading today."

"What I've been thinking about lately, and guessing you may feel it still as pressing as when you wrote about it, is Eichmann's evil: that it defies thinking and can be judged. By whom? Might that be the person, an identifiably unique one, who in judging – in that moment – is also an equal member of a community of judges, that is, of a human plurality?"

He had not yet seen the evidently relevant movie "Zone of Interest." His local movie house closed during covid. "It has thrived since," writes Jerry, "as a hatchet throwing instruction center. Literally, it offered lessons in hurling hatchets – as in old 'Chinese' and later James Bond movies!"

As *public life, freedom, equality seemed driven back*, I sent him Mathew Arnold's "Dover Beach." He responded with a cherished story. Growing up near Wallace Stevens, he saw the poet daily walking to work. Offered a ride on a soggy day, Stevens refused. Watching him, Jerry saw that he was pacing the meter, the beat, the flow – – the dance of a new poem to enter the world.

I also sent him music, a brilliant cellist playing Mozart: "My mother [who 'sang at the Met until she married'] was intent on her children being 'musical'....My sister and I were tone-deaf!...I studied – it seems endlessly – piano..[My teacher] finally decided the best thing for me would be to listen to her play....My mother sang the early (whatever that means, Mozart died at 35!) Ruhe Sanft as a lullaby. ...I remember it as ...unbelievable: I could not believe I heard what in fact I was hearing. That did not improve my piano playing... Mozart is a choreographer, as if, after days and nights of dancing with Terpsichore...with great dexterity and renewed energy he *noted* their shapes forever."

"Well," my friend ended, as always far, far too soon, "that went on longer than I intended. Sorry."

THOMAS WILD

Jerome Kohn and I met in late fall of 2001, at a conference celebrating the fiftieth anniversary of Hannah Arendt's *Origins of Totalitarianism*, just weeks after 9/11, at the threshold of a new era no one had yet a name for. Jerry died in early November 2024, just days after the elections, unaware of the results when admitted to the hospital in the morning after the vote, and never learning its eventual outcome. "If Trump wins the U.S. presidency," a handwritten note, left on his desk, reads, "it will be a victory of public opinion over public spirit". The former being favored over the latter by "both sides", the note adds, and leaves us with the question: "What might restore public spirit?"

"The Republic of the United States of America has been in a state of decline for more than fifty years," Jerry opens the introduction to his last edition of essays by Hannah Arendt *Thinking Without a Banister* (2018). The reference evokes the era of the Vietnam war, when executive overreach and incompetence emerged alongside a new species of spin doctors and super donors. Arendt called out this "perversion" endangering all republics, as Jerry reminds us, quoting what Arendt told her students at the time: "Where public spirit is lacking, public opinion comes in its stead."

At that time, in the late 1960s, Jerry had just returned from years in Europe, where he'd become friends with James Baldwin, to embark on graduate studies in philosophy. He'd earlier studied literature at Harvard, performing theater with John Ashbery. Now, reading Arendt's essays on "Truth and Politics" and on "Bertolt Brecht" in the New Yorker changed the course of his life. Then in his mid-thirties, he had convinced Arendt to take him on as a graduate student at The New School. The rest is almost history. This vivid fabric of philosophy, politics, and poetry seems to have formed the weave of their intellectual affinities and eventual friendship. Jerry chose Arendt's eulogy of W.H. Auden as the final piece for *Thinking Without a Banister*, and quoted in his introduction, in correspondence to Arendt's "public spirit", Auden's words: "In the prison of his days / Teach the free man how to praise."

*

A few months after that *Origins* conference, in the spring of 2002, we met for lunch in New York City. There a conversation started that continued until a day before his passing, via letters and emails, calls and visits, discussions in private and on stage, and always shared meals, as an occasion for conversation. We met regularly, at least every other month. En route to La Villetta, Vendôme, or Jubilee, French and Italian restaurants a bit north of the United Nations around First Avenue, where Jerry was welcomed like a special envoy from a distant country, I was filled with anticipation. For there was this world to open up, emerging from conversation. Vivid, mobile, joyful, humorous, caring, thought-provoking. A world of friendship. A way of feeling and being alive.

What do you think of...? this recent book or article on Arendt, that art show, this unnerving move by the government. *Have you heard from...?* this mutual friend or that colleague who recently sent an email. *Oh, and I wanted to talk with you* ... about that particular poem by Ann Lauterbach, and this passage from T.J. Clark's book on Cézanne, *and I meant to ask you...!* Jerry often arrived with a palm sized notepad leaf, filled with reminders to himself for the conversation, not as an agenda, even when it contained business, rather as scribbled traces of a conversation that had started before the actual visit. He who had so many things to say, did never grandstand or lecture, rather genuinely wanted to hear from his interlocutor. I witnessed this humbleness and generosity in various other constellations with him. I'm reminded of Aristoteles' claim about reciprocity as the key component of genuine friendship.

And what a great storyteller he was! This is not contradictory but perfectly complementary to what I just said about his dedicated listening. When asked about Arendt, he'd often respond with a story in the form of an anecdote: poignant and inconclusive, affectionate and funny, not aiming for a moral, but for a momentum to make you think on your own. Once, Jerry had woken in the morning with his building on fire. He just escaped. When he saw Arendt that afternoon, the news had traveled across town, she put her hands on his arms and said with a caring look on her face: "Wasn't it exciting!" He told this story a propos the alacrity of Arendt's mind. Another time: Jerry must have mentioned to Arendt sometime that he was "half-Jewish". Weeks later, on the eve of Rosh Hashanah, Arendt wished him a Happy New Year, "or at least to the Jewish half of you", and they both laughed. We had been talking about the distinction between social identity and human plurality when this anecdote emerged.

*

I believe Jerry was in conversation with Arendt literally every day, with her thoughts, with her words. Partly through his editorial work, the book editions and his thought-provokingly nuanced introductions that shaped our understanding of Arendt's works over the past decades. At the same time, he loved to correspond or talk in person with anyone who was genuinely interested in Arendt, with no difference in 'rank' or familiarity with the work. His emails belong to the world of letters, uniquely refined and generous. How many people I heard saying since his passing: Oh, I still owe Jerry a response to his most recent letter! We will continue to write to him.

As trustee of Hannah Arendt's literary estate, Jerry supported any serious endeavor that would keep Arendt's work in circulation. He never wanted to be the single authority on Arendt, as this would have meant to place a dogma, where thinking, discussion, and meaning are supposed to be alive. He supported the *Critical Edition of Hannah Arendt's Complete Works* from the very first moment on, and thereby its mission to facilitate a future engagement with Arendt's writings whose questions have not yet even been articulated. Jerome Kohn's philosophy as a trustee was unwavering trust in Hannah Arendt's words and thoughts.

Jerry once visited my course on *The Human Condition* at Bard College. He surprised the students, and me, by dwelling for almost the entire class period on a footnote in the chapter on "The Private and the Public Realm" where Arendt discusses a quote from Sophocles' *Antigone*. Beaming with delight, Jerry hovered with us over the unresolvable ambiguous Greek, Hölderlin's translation into German, and Arendt's rendering in English: "But great words, counteracting the great blows of the overproud, teach understanding in old age." What was at stake for him here was the notion of revelatory speech, in distinction from communicative speech. For Jerry, revelatory speech was at the beginning of everything that counts: thinking, friendship, praise of the world – and public spirit. "At the end of a class," Jerry opened the concluding anecdote of his visit, "Arendt was asked by a student to return to the text and explain the meaning of a section they'd discussed but remained perplexing. In response, Arendt picked up the book and, before reciting the entire passage again, said only one word: Listen!"

CONTRIBUTORS

CONTRIBUTORS

AYISHAT AKANBI is a fashion stylist and writer based in London. With over a decade of experience working with clients such as Rod Stewart, Labrinth, and Naomi Campbell, in the last five years she turned her focus to observing cultural trends. Through her talks, interviews, and online posts, Ayishat challenges popular ideas by championing understanding, curiosity, and independent thought. Her belief that self-knowledge and honest reflection can resolve divisions has led her to speak at Google Headquarters, The Sydney Opera House, Tate Modern, and The Victoria & Albert Museum.

MANDAR APTE currently manages Cities4Peace, a nonprofit peacebuilding consultancy of the Art of Living Foundation and the International Association for Human Values (IAHV) that promotes peace in cities and communities across the world. Mandar is also an advisor to the special UN project on "Private Sector Investments for Youth-Led Peacebuilding." As part of this mandate, Mandar is engaging the private sector and educational institutions through his thought leadership. Prior to this, Mandar has produced and directed *From India With Love* – a documentary film that promotes the message of nonviolence in the world. Mandar has a BS (Chemical Engineering) from the University of Mumbai (India) and an MS (Petroleum Engineering) from the University of Tulsa (USA).

JACK BARTH is an artist living in New York City. His work is in the collections of the Museum of Modern Art, the Morgan Library & Museum, the New York Public Library, and other museums in the United States and Europe.

THOMAS BARTSCHERER works in the humanities and the arts and on the study of liberal education and politics. Recent projects include co-editing the new critical edition of Hannah Arendt's *The Life of the Mind* (Wallstein, 2024) and *When the People Rule: Popular Sovereignty in Theory and Practice* (Cambridge, 2023). *Stranger Love*, the six-hour opera he created with composer Dylan Mattingly, was commissioned and presented by the Los Angeles Philharmonic in 2023. His new work with Mattingly, *History of Life*, was commissioned by the Spoleto Festival USA and will premiere in 2026. Since 2017, he has been the Peter Sourian Senior Lecturer in the Humanities at Bard College and a Senior Fellow at Bard's Hannah Arendt Center.

SEYLA BENHABIB is Eugene Meyer Professor of Political Science and Philosophy Emerita at Yale University where she taught from 2001 to 2020. She is currently Senior Research Fellow and Professor of Law Adjunct at Columbia University, and Affiliate Faculty in the Department of Philosophy. She is also a Senior Fellow at Columbia University's Center for Contemporary Critical Thought. She was the President of the Eastern Division of the American Philosophical Association in 2006–2007 and has been a member of the American Academy of Arts and Sciences since 1995, and an Honorary Fellow of the British Academy since 2018. Professor Benhabib is the recipient of the Ernst Bloch Prize (2009), the Leopold Lucas Prize from the Theological Faculty of the University of Tubingen (2012), and the Meister Eckhart Prize (2014; one of Germany's most prestigious philosophical prizes).

ROGER BERKOWITZ is Founder and Academic Director of the Hannah Arendt Center at Bard College. A Professor of Politics, Philosophy, and Human Rights, Berkowitz writes and speaks about how justice is made present in the world. He is author of *The Gift of Science: Leibniz and the Modern Legal Tradition*, co-editor of *Artifacts of Thinking: Reading Hannah Arendt's Denktagebuch* (2017), *Thinking in Dark Times: Hannah Arendt on Ethics and Politics* (2010), *The Intellectual Origins of the Global Financial Crisis* (2012), and editor of the annual journal *HA: The Journal of the Hannah Arendt Center* (now *HA: The Yearbook of the Hannah Arendt Center for Politics and Humanities at Bard College*).

Contributors

MATTHIAS BORMUTH is Professor of Comparative Intellectual History at the University of Oldenburg and Director of the Karl Jaspers-Haus. He has studied medicine and worked as a psychiatrist and psychotherapist for several years. In English he is the author of *Life Conduct in Modern Times: Karl Jaspers and Psychoanalysis* (Dordrecht: Springer, 2006).

LEON BOTSTEIN is president and Leon Levy Professor in the Arts of Bard College. He has published widely in the fields of education, music, history, and culture, and is the author of several books including *Jefferson's Children: Education and the Promise of American Culture*, and editor of *The Compleat Brahms* and *The Musical Quarterly*. He is the music director of the American Symphony Orchestra and The Orchestra Now (TŌN), and conductor laureate and principal guest conductor of the Jerusalem Symphony Orchestra, where he served as music director. He is the founder and artistic co-director of the Bard Music Festival. His work has been acknowledged with awards from the American Academy of Arts and Letters, Harvard University, government of Austria, and Carnegie Foundation.

THOMAS CHATTERTON WILLIAMS is the author of *Losing My Cool and Self-Portrait in Black and White*. He is a staff writer at *The Atlantic*. Prior to that he was a contributing writer at *The New York Times Magazine* and a columnist at *Harper's*. He is a 2022 Guggenheim fellow and a visiting fellow at AEI. His work has appeared in *The New Yorker, The London Review of Books, Le Monde* and many other places, and has been collected in *The Best American Essays* and *The Best American Travel Writing*. He has received support from Yaddo, MacDowell and The American Academy in Berlin, where he is a member of the Board of Trustees. He is a visiting professor of the humanities and a Senior Fellow at the Hannah Arendt Center for Politics and Humanities at Bard College. His next book, *Nothing Was the Same*, will be published by Knopf.

WOUT CORNELISSEN is an Assistant Professor of Philosophy of Law at Radboud University, Nijmegen, the Netherlands. Previously, he held positions at FU Berlin, Vanderbilt University, Utrecht University, Bard College, and VU Amsterdam. He holds a PhD in Philosophy from Leiden University. He is co-editor of the new, critical edition of Arendt's *The Life of the Mind*, which appeared in 2024 as volume 14 of the *Complete Works*.

He published essays on Arendt's conceptions of thinking in *Artifacts of Thinking: Reading Hannah Arendt's* Denktagebuch (Fordham UP, 2017) and The *Bloomsbury Companion to Arendt* (2020), and on her practice of quoting in *The Phenomenology of Testimony* (Brill, 2025).

KHALED FURANI is a professor of anthropology at Tel-Aviv University on the lands of al-Sheikh Muwannis. He researches language and literature, theology, secularism, sovereignty, Palestine, and the history of anthropology. For several years, he taught a seminar on "Reading Hannah Arendt for Anthropology." His books include *Silencing the Sea: Secular Rhythms in Palestinian Poetry* (Stanford University Press 2012) and *Redeeming Anthropology: A Theological Critique of a Modern Science* (Oxford University Press, 2019). He co-edited, with Yara Sa'di-Ibraheem, *Inside the Leviathan: Palestinian Experiences at Israeli Universities* (in Arabic, Van Leer Jerusalem Institute, 2022). His most recent article is "Khalifah and the Modern Sovereign: Revisiting a Qur'anic Ideal from within the Palestinian Condition" (*Journal of Religion*, 2022).

ANTONIA GRUNENBERG is a Professor of Political Science and lives as a political writer in Berlin. She is Co-founder and board member of the Hannah Arendt Prize for Political Thought. She is also DAAD Professor of Political Science and German Studies at the University of Philadelphia and she is professor for Political Science at the Carl von Ossietzky University of Oldenburg where she founded the Hannah Arendt Center. She is a Fellow at the Institut d'Etudes Avancées in Nantes and the co-founder of the Internationale Hannah Arendt Gesellschaft. Her research interests: Political and cultural history of Germany and Europe; political theories of the modern era. Recent books: *Hannah Arendt und Martin Heidegger*, Munich and Zurich 2006; *Walter Benjamin in seiner Zeit*, Berlin 2018; *Das Versprechen der Demokratie*, Munich 2023.

ROCHELLE GURSTEIN is a historian of ideas. She is the author of *Written in Water: The Ephemeral Life of the Classic in Art* (Yale University Press, 2024) and *The Repeal of Reticence: America's Cultural and Legal Struggles over Free Speech, Obscenity, Sexual Liberation, and Modern Art* (Hill & Wang, 1996). Her essays and reviews have appeared in national and "little" magazines.

WOLFGANG HEUER is Privatdozent for political science at Free University Berlin, managing editor of HannahArendt.net, online journal for political thinking, guest professor in Brazil, Chile and Colombia, director at IUC Dubrovnik of the annual course on Europe after the totalitarian regimes, co-curator of the international art exhibition "Hannah Arendt Thinking Space" Berlin 2006. Publications: *Cosmos and Republic: Arendtian Explorations of the Loss and Recovery of Politics*, transcript 2023; *Künstlich intelligent: Dialoge mit ChatGPT*, LIT 2023. *Arendt Handbuch*, 2nd edition Metzler 2022 (with S. Rosenmüller / B. Heiter). *Dichterisch denken. Hannah Arendt und die Künste*, Wallstein 2007 (With I .v.d. Lühe). *Hannah Arendt*, text+kritik Nr. 166/167, 2005 (with T. Wild). Forthcoming: *Anarchy and Violence. The Hidden History of Argentina*.

ZOË HITZIG, an economist and writer, is currently a Junior Fellow at the Harvard Society of Fellows. Her research centers on social tradeoffs in the design of computational and economic systems. She is the author of two books of poetry, *Mezzanine* (2020) and *Not Us Now* (2024), winner of the Changes Prize. She currently serves as poetry editor of *The Drift*, and her work has appeared in *Harper's, The New Yorker, New York Review of Books, Artforum, WIRED* and elsewhere. She holds a PhD in economics from Harvard.

MARIE LUISE KNOTT worked as an editor for ten years. Later she worked as a literary translator from French and English and as a journalist for various publishing houses, newspapers and radio stations. From 1995 to 2006 she was the founder and editor in chief of the German *Le Monde diplomatique*. In 2010 she completed her Ph.D. at Humboldt University: *Denken im Dialog mit der Dichtung: Über Produktionsbedingungen theoretischer Texte im 20. Jahrhundert am Beispiel Hannah Arendts*. Since 2006 she works as curator, editor, translator and author. She has diverse teaching experiences at Universities (FU Berlin, Universität Greifswald) and other german institutions. Her publications include *Unlearning with Hannah Arendt* (2011/2015) and *Exhaustion of Modernity in 1930* (2017). She edited the letters of Hannah Arendt and Gershom Scholem (2010), co-edited a book on John Cage (Empty Mind, 2012) and translated several works by Anne Carson. Her long essay "370 Riverside Drive, 730 Riverside Drive: Hannah Arendt and Ralph Waldo Ellison" (2022), won her the renowned Tractatus Prize for Philisophical Essais at the Philosophicum Lech.

GILBERT JOHNSON is a native of South Central Los Angeles and a dedicated community organizer. He is the CA TimeDone Manager with Californians for Safety and Justice, helping to pass multiple state-level justice reform bills. Gilbert is also a member of the Black Men Maroon Space, a group of formerly incarcerated Black men who engage in somatic transformative practices that unpack and address deep traumatic experiences.

SEBASTIAN JUNGER is the #1 *New York Times* Bestselling author of *The Perfect Storm, Fire, A Death in Belmont, War, Tribe, Freedom,* and *In My Time of Dying*. As an award-winning journalist, a contributing editor to *Vanity Fair*, and a special correspondent at ABC News, he has covered major international news stories around the world, and has received both a National Magazine Award and a Peabody Award. Junger is also a documentary filmmaker whose debut film, *Restrepo*, a feature-length documentary (co-directed with Tim Hetherington), was nominated for an Academy Award and won the Grand Jury Prize at Sundance.

ANN LAUTERBACH is a poet and essayist. Her eleventh collection of poetry, *Door*, was published by Penguin Random House in March 2023 and was short-listed for the Griffin International Poetry Prize. She is the recipient of a New York State Council of the Arts 2025 grant for her forthcoming work, "The Meanwhile." She writes at the intersection of poetics, politics and the visual arts. A recipient of a Guggenheim Fellowship (1986) and a MacArthur Fellowship (1993), she is Ruth and David Schwab Professor of Languages and Literature (Written Arts) at Bard College.

SHAI LAVI is a Professor of Law and heads the Van Leer Jerusalem Institute. He is also the co-director of the Minerva Center for the Interdisciplinary Study of End of Life, and until 2017 was also the founding director of the Edmond J. Safra Center for Ethics – both at Tel Aviv University. He received his Ph.D. from the Jurisprudence and Social Policy Program, University of California Berkeley. His book *The Modern Art of Dying: A History of Euthanasia in the United States* (Princeton University Press) won the 2006 Distinguished Book Award in sociology of law from the American Sociological Association. He is a member of the National Bioethics Council.

PHILLIP "ROCK" LESTER is a community activist, survivor, business owner and formerly incarcerated person. He has been active in multiple civic engagement campaigns, helping to advocate for resources within LA county, notably, Measure J as well as criminal justice reform policies in California. Phillip has an educational background in mathematics, sociology and art. He was honored and awarded in the Fall of 2021 with a Certificate of Appreciation by Arizona State University educators for his role in developing its 'Future ID' program, an on-campus course that demonstrates the impact of system-impacted people having a future vision for success.

VOLKER MÄRZ is a multi-disciplinary artist working as a sculptor, painter, photographer, writer, filmmaker, performer and musician. He realized several Projects and Performances dedicated to European philosophers and thinkers such as Friedrich Nietzsche, Giordano Bruno, Martin Heidegger, Heinrich von Kleist, Franz Kafka, Walter Benjamin, and Hannah Arendt. He lives and works in Berlin and has published more than 10 Artist's books and had multiple solo exhibitions in museums and galleries across Europe, Israel, and South Africa since 1995.

STEVE MASLOW was the first chairman of the board of the Hannah Arendt Center at Bard College, and a former managing director-principal of Bear, Stearns & Co. Inc. He is currently the COO of Hephaestus Analytical, an art authentication firm based in London and New York. As an undergraduate at Wesleyan University, he studied under Elisabeth Young-Bruehl, Hannah Arendt's authorized biographer. Jerome Kohn and Steve met in 2012 and maintained their fierce friendship until the end of Jerry's life.

UDAY SINGH MEHTA is Distinguished Professor of Political Science at the CUNY Graduate Center and the 2022 Yehuda Elkana Fellow (awarded by Central European University and the Hannah Arendt Center at Bard College). Professor Mehta has taught at several universities, including Princeton, Cornell, MIT, University of Chicago, University of Pennsylvania, Hull and Amherst College. He is the author of *The Anxiety of Freedom: Imagination and Individuality in the Political Thought of John Locke* (Cornell University Press, 1992) and *Liberalism and Empire* (University of Chicago Press, 2000) – the latter of which was awarded the J. David Greenstone

Prize for the best book in Political Theory by the American Political Science Association in 2002. In 2003, Mehta was one of ten recipients of the prestigious Carnegie Scholars Prize given to "scholars of exceptional creativity." His forthcoming book is titled *A Different Vision: Gandhi's Critique of Political Rationality.*

ELIZABETH MINNICH is a Distinguished Fellow, American Association of Colleges & Universities. She met fellow graduate student Jerry Kohn when she was Hannah Arendt's Teaching Assistant at The Graduate Faculty of The New School. Her works include the national Ness Award-winning *Transforming Knowledge; The Evil of Banality; The Fox in the Henhouse: How Privatization Threatens Democracy* (Si Kahn, co-author); "Heidegger and Arendt" in *An Unconventional History of Western Philosophy: Conversations Between Men and Women Philosophers*; "Arendt, Heidegger, Eichmann: Thinking in and for the World" in *Soundings*. Positions include: Core Professor, The Union Institute Graduate Faculty; Associate Dean of Faculty, Barnard College; Hartley Burr Alexander Chair, Philosophy and Humanities, Scripps College. She has spoken and consulted widely on transforming exclusive knowledge and education.

FINTAN O'TOOLE is a columnist with *The Irish Times* and advising editor of *The New York Review of Books*. He is the winner of the Robert Silvers Prize for Journalism, the Orwell Prize and the European Press Prize. He is currently working on the official biography of Seamus Heaney. Born in Dublin in 1958, he is a member of the Royal Irish Academy and an honorary international member of the American Academy of Arts and Sciences. He taught at Princeton where was Professor of Irish Letters. His many books include *A Traitor's Kiss: The Life of Richard Brinsley Sheridan*; *White Savage: William Johnson and the Invention of America*; *A History of Ireland in 100 Objects*; and *Heroic Failure: Brexit and the Politics of Pain*. His most recent book, *We Don't Know Ourselves: A Personal History of Ireland Since 1958* was named Book of the Year in the An Post Irish Book Awards and as one of the ten best books of 2022 by the *New York Times*.

LYNDSEY STONEBRIDGE is Professor of Humanities and Human Rights at the University of Birmingham, UK, and a Fellow of the British Academy. Her books include *Placeless People: Writing, Rights, and Refugees*, winner of the Modernist Studies Association Book Prize and a Choice Outstanding Academic Title; *The Judicial Imagination: Writing After Nuremberg*, which won the British Academy Rose Mary Crawshay Prize for English Literature; and the essay collection, *Writing and Righting: Literature in the Age of Human Rights. We Are Free to Change the World: Hannah Arendt's Lessons in Love and Disobedience* was published by Jonathan Cape and the Hogarth Press in 2024, and was shortlisted for the Orwell Prize for Political Writing. She is a regular media commentator and broadcaster, and lives in London and France.

NIOBE WAY is Professor of Developmental Psychology and the founder of the *Project for the Advancement of Our Common Humanity* at New York University (PACH). She is also past President of the Society for Research on Adolescence (SRA) and co-director of the Center for Research on Culture, Development, and Education at NYU.

Her work focuses on the intersections of culture, context, and human development, with a particular focus on social and emotional development and how cultural ideologies influence developmental trajectories. *The Listening Project*, her current project with Joseph Nelson, Hirokazu Yoshikawa, David Kirkland, and Alisha Ali, aims to foster curiosity and connection in and outside of middle school classrooms across New York City.

THOMAS WILD is Professor of German Studies and Literature at Bard College, Research Director at the Hannah Arendt Center. He works on modern German literature and culture, with a particular interest in the intersections of literature and politics, ethics, and multilingualism. Selected books: *Hannah Arendt. Leben, Werk, Wirkung* (2006); *Nach dem Geschichtsbruch. Deutsche Schriftsteller um Hannah Arendt* (2009); editions of *Hannah Arendt's correspondences with Uwe Johnson, Hilde Domin, Joachim Fest; Wolfgang Hildesheimer: 12 Briefwechsel* (2016); *ununterbrochen mit niemandem reden. Lektüren mit Ilse Aichinger* (2021). Thomas Wild is a General Editor of the Critical Edition of Hannah Arendt's *Complete Works*.

www.ingramcontent.com/pod-product-compliance
Lightning Source LLC
Jackson TN
JSHW052309130825
89346JS00001B/1